# WHAT'S THE SECRET?

## To Providing a *World-Class* Customer Experience

### John R. DiJulius III

**WILEY**

John Wiley & Sons, Inc.

Published by John Wiley & Sons, Inc., Hoboken, New Jersey.
Published simultaneously in Canada.

For general information on our other products and services or for technical support,
please contact our Customer Care Department within the United States at
(800) 762-2974, outside the United States at (317) 572-3993 or fax (317) 572-4002.

Wiley also publishes its books in a variety of electronic formats. Some content that
appears in print may not be available in electronic books. For more information about
Wiley products, visit our web site at www.wiley.com.

*Library of Congress Cataloging-in-Publication Data*

DiJulius, John R., 1964–
   What's the secret? : to providing a world-class customer experience /
John R. DiJulius.
      p.   cm.
   Includes bibliographical references and index.
   ISBN 978-0-470-19612-0 (cloth)
   1. Customer services.   2. Consumer satisfaction.   3. Customer
loyalty.   I. Title.
   HF5415.5.D5583     2008
   658.8'12—dc22                                         2008012004

Printed in the United States of America.

10  9  8  7  6  5  4

To what matters most in the world to me—
my family: Stacy my wife and
my three sons (and best buddies),
Johnni IV, Cal, and Bo.

Nothing would have been possible or worthwhile
without your love and support.

Thank you for the honor to be known as
your husband and father.

# Contents

# Preface

## What's the Secret?

- What's the Secret to why good customer service is so hard to find today?
- What's the Secret to why is it so hard to find employees who know how to deliver it?
- What's the Secret to why companies don't train their people better?
- What's the Secret to why companies don't see the value in providing good customer service?

The next time you are with your professional peers and you overhear a conversation about *Secret Service*, do not immediately start sharing your knowledge of the CIA and the department responsible for protecting the president of the United States. Chances are that is not the *Secret Service* they are referring to.

Although sales for my previous book, *Secret Service: Hidden Systems That Deliver Unforgettable Customer Service* (AMACOM, 2003), have been remarkable, and hundreds of businesses across the world have implemented these systems, the term *Secret Service* still can be confusing to some.

Before you read this book, it is imperative you truly understand the meaning of *Secret Service* as it relates to helping your organization become a world-class customer service organization. Since the release of the book in 2003, the term *Secret Service* and what it represents has evolved and today, *Secret Service* is no longer just a book title or a term but a concept, a strategy that thousands of businesses incorporate as their value proposition, to differentiate themselves from their competitors and make superior customer service their point of difference.

Out of curiosity, I looked up the definition of the Secret Service that operates under the government.

> Secret Service: Governmental service of a secret nature charged chiefly with the protection of the president, responsible for the collection, analysis, and appropriate dissemination of intelligence.

Absolutely nothing to do with my version of Secret Service, as it relates to customer service, right? Actually, by substituting just three words, it fits my meaning of *Secret Service* perfectly:

> *Secret Service:* Customer service of a secret nature charged chiefly with the protection of the brand, responsible for the collection, analysis, and appropriate dissemination of customer intelligence.

## What Is *Secret Service* and Why Is It Secret?

*Secret Service* uses hidden systems to deliver unforgettable customer service. These systems obtain customer intelligence and utilize it to personalize the customer's experience, leaving the customer to ask themselves:

"How'd they do that?"
"How'd they know that?"

Secret Service employs behind-the-scenes systems that employees use to anticipate and deliver on the unexpressed needs of the customer, by using a system of *silent cues, visual triggers,* and *visual aids*.

Customer intelligence is customer data (i.e., buying habits, purchasing history, referrals, personal preferences, where they live, or work) that fuels secret service.

Secret Service systems allow the front-line employees, of your organization to consistently create a memorable experience through:

- Engaging the customer.
- Personalizing their experience.

- Remembering their preferences.
- Distinguishing between new, returning, and VIP customers.
- Anticipating and delivering on their unexpressed needs.

As a result of providing *Secret Service*, companies:

- Create stronger relationships with their customers.
- Build emotional capital and brand equity with their customers.
- Turn their customers into brand evangelists.
- Make price less relevant to their customers.

To effectively deliver Secret Service, your employees need to act as detectives by collecting customer intelligence and then using silent cues that alert their coworkers and allow them to personalize the customer's experience.

It should be more obvious now why it is called Secret Service, it has:

- Hidden systems
- Customer intelligence
- Silent cues
- Visual triggers
- Detectives

After seeing a few examples of Secret Service actions, you will quickly realize why it can make your company a world-class (secret) service organization.

Secret Service systems should not add cost or complexity to your organization. Secret Service systems are what we call low-hanging fruit; they must meet the following criteria:

1. Low or no cost;
2. Simple to execute consistently; and
3. Make an immediate impact on the customer.

The following are simple examples of how easy, yet powerful Secret Service systems can allow companies to create memorable experiences:

- *Distinguishing between new and returning customers:* This Secret Service system identifies new from existing customers. For instance at John Robert's Spa, returning customers are draped in black capes for haircuts, and new customers are draped in white capes. Every team member throughout the salon knows this fact and can address our guests accordingly. Thus, the color of the cape is the *silent cue* and *visual trigger.*

- *Anticipating and delivering on customers' unexpressed needs:* A customer purchases a gift card for his spouse for Valentine's Day and the receptionist pulls out several Valentine's Day cards and offers him one to give with the gift card to save him a trip to another store.

- *Personalizing the customer's experience:* In the restaurant industry, by simply asking the question, "What's the occasion?" at the time of reservation, you can trigger a multitude of responses: We are celebrating a promotion, a graduation, an engagement, an anniversary, a reunion. When the customer arrives, the greeter presents him with a special-occasion greeting card and several employees congratulate the customer throughout their experience.

- *Remembering their preferences:* Another one of my favorite Secret Service systems is where a restaurant kept preprinted labels of their top VIP customers. Anytime they came in, their favorite bottle of wine would be waiting for them at their table, with a label on it that read: "From the Private Stock of Tom Smith."

This book is more than a discussion of the problems and warm and fuzzy feel-good customer service stories. It contains the solutions, systems, and answers. It tells how the top customer service companies in the world execute world-class service consistently.

By executing Secret Service consistently, it is possible for your organization to *make price irrelevant:* Based on the experience they receive, customers feel your prices are an incredible value.

Secret Service is a strategy that thousands of businesses incorporate today as their value proposition, differentiating themselves from their competitors and making superior customer service their point of difference.

> Because of the *Secret Service* systems we have put into place, we know our guest better than ever. What's more, there is a greater sense of a "heroic cause" within our team. We are doing more than serving our guest; we are helping them enjoy life more in the company of people they care about.
>
> —*Bob Johnston, President, The Melting Pot Restaurants*

We are all about Secret Service. Our clients think it is amazing what we deliver in our Haircut experience, but it is just a part of being a part of Sport Clips and following our system. Secret Service just validated much of what Gordon Logan and Sport Clips has been doing over the past 13 years and most importantly helped us take it to the next level by engaging our whole organization. John's team was a great facilitator of this improvement process and Sport Clips is positioned to do even more in the years to come.

*—Clete Brewer, President, Sport Clips*

As Partner-in-Charge of client service at our firm, Secret Service is paramount. It is what allows us the opportunity to continue to serve our clients, build new relationships, and generate opportunities to assist new clients.

*—Mike Trabert, Partner, Skoda Minotti*

# Secret Service Terminology

**Above-and-Beyond Opportunities:**   Random acts of heroism providing legendary service to the customer.

**Customer Experience Cycle (CEC):**   The traditional points of contact/interaction a customer will encounter when doing business with you.

**Customer Intelligence:**   Customer data (i.e., buying habits, purchasing history, personal preferences).

**Experiential Actions:**   A personal engaging experience delivered to the customer, by an employee that makes them say "WOW," a delightful surprise that the majority of your competitors do not provide. It could be a standard or random (above and beyond) action. It is the reason why our customers return, refer others and become brand evangelists. Examples of experiential actions include using a customer's name, remembering their preferences, or having their order ready before they placed it.

**Nonnegotiable:**   Standards that team members absolutely must deliver, regardless of the circumstances.

**Operational Actions:**   Actions that team members must execute to assist in the efficiency of the day-to-day transactions with our customers. Examples of operational actions include cleanliness, dress code, inventory, and lighting. They are unnoticeable to customers and are not the reason customers return.

**Secret Service:**   Hidden systems that deliver unforgettable customer service.

**Service Aptitude:**   A person's ability to recognize opportunities to exceed customers' expectations, regardless of the circumstances.

**Service Defects:**   Obstacles and challenges that can occur at any stage of the CEC and that can ruin the customer's experience.

**Service Vision:**   The true underlying value of what your organization brings to your customers, that provides a meaningful purpose for your employees.

**Stages:**   The individual contact/interaction points within the Customer Experience Cycle, such as a phone call, greeting, or checkout.

**Zero Risk:**   A customer has no risk in doing business with your company because you have service recovery protocols. Regardless of any circumstances, in the end the customer knows your company will always make sure they are happy.

# Acknowledgments

Many times, after you give so much toward something—more work, time, and energy than you originally thought—when you are finally done, it can feel a little anticlimatic. Not this time, I can easily say that there have not been too many projects in my life that required the amount of time, commitment, and sacrifice this book has. However, I am finally done, and it feels great. I have given this book everything I had and could not be more proud of the finished product.

*What's the Secret?* has truly been a labor of love that has taken me over five years to complete. It is the culmination of many years of research, exploring, and working with the top world-class customer service companies. Like any great endeavor, I could not have done this alone. I was blessed to be surrounded by an incredible group of people who have inspired me, supported me, and most of all believed in me.

This book would not have been possible without my leadership team in both my organizations, The DiJulius Group and John Robert's Spa. I am so blessed to have so many talented people who have dedicated their professional careers to my vision. People like my wife Stacy DiJulius, Artistic Director; Eric Hammond, Vice President of Operations; my brother Barry DiJulius, COO; my sister Kathy Cheyfitz, Director of Guest Care; and Denise Thompson, Chief Xperience Officer of The DiJulius Group, all lead my companies with so much passion that it has enabled me to focus on this book.

Thanks to all my team members at John Robert's Spa and The DiJulius Group, who daily live up to the heavy burden of being a world-class customer service organization.

I would also like to thank Service Management Group in Kansas City, Missouri, especially Jack Mackey, Vice President of Sales and Marketing and Andy Fromm, President and CEO, for being so generous in sharing all their time, expertise, and research, which provided me with significant data to support my findings. Also, Darlene Campagna and her team at Direct Opinions in Cleveland, Ohio, that also provided me with key customer measurement research, as well as helping The DiJulius Group in the development of the Company Service Aptitude Test (C-SAT).

Thanks to all the great world-class companies that have repeatedly hired me and my team at The DiJulius Group to help them continue to raise the bar for service excellence. I have to admit, I benefited as well by learning their (organizations like The Ritz-Carlton, The Melting Pot Restaurants, Nemacolin Woodlands Resort, Starbucks, Cameron Mitchell Restaurants, The Cheesecake Factory, Panera Bread, Sport Clips, Charming Shoppes, Progressive Insurance, Chick-fil-A, Westfield Insurance, Service Management Group, Lexus, Nordstrom, Hallmark Cards, Breakers Hotel, and Goodyear Tire) best practices, which in turn allowed me to produce this masterpiece.

I want to thank Heather Thitoff, Director of Training at Cameron Mitchell Restaurants and Melissa Gottlieb, Vice President of Sales at Smart Business Network magazine. They both have been a great resource, supporters of Secret Service, and performed the punishing task of reading and critiquing early versions of this book.

A special thank you to my mentors, who have not only been so generous in sharing their brilliance, but are people I proudly call good friends. People like Verne Harnish, founder of Entrepreneur's Organization, CEO of Gazelles, Inc., and author of *Mastering the Rockefeller Habits;* James Gilmore, coauthor of *Authenticity;* Hal Becker, author/speaker; Fredrick Holzberger, CEO of Fredric's Corporation; and Charles Penzone, President of Charles Penzone Salons.

I also have to thank Matt Holt and his team at John Wiley & Sons who believed in this book.

Most of all, thanks to my family: my wife Stacy, and my sons Johnni, Cal, and Bo, who remained patient, supportive, and always believed in me.

# The Customer Service Crisis

# 1

# The Smoking Gun

*Definitive proof of the return on
investment in providing superior service*

---

*You can have a great product, but it takes world-class service
to create brand loyalty.*

Based on extensive research, interviews, and analysis of various businesses, The DiJulius Group has determined the following trends in levels of customer service:

| Level | Description | Companics (%) |
|-------|-------------|---------------|
| 1 | Unacceptable | 12 |
| 2 | Below average | 29 |
| 3 | Average | 38 |
| 4 | Above average | 18 |
| 5 | World class | 3 |

According to this study, 41 percent of companies are operating at unacceptable (1) or below average (2) levels of customer service, while 38 percent of companies are delivering average customer service (3). If you total that up (1, 2, and 3) 79 percent of the companies provide a level of customer service which is average at best. Which leaves us having a good customer experience about one-fifth of the time (level 4) and we only have an exceptional experience with 3 percent of the companies we deal with (level 5).

> You can say what you want about who you (think you) are, but people believe what they experience.
>
> —*Jack Mackey, Vice President, Service Management Group*

## In Denial

Think about your business, what level of customer service does your company deliver? Now, from a customer's perspective, reconsider your answer. The sad truth is that the majority of businesses rank their customer service higher than their customers rank them. The following research reveals how much companies are in the dark about the level of service they are providing.

Bain & Company, a business consulting firm, surveyed customers of 362 companies and found:

- Only 8 percent of customers surveyed described their experience as superior.
- Yet, 80 percent of the companies surveyed believe that the service they provided was indeed superior.[1]

How can 80 percent of the companies think they are providing superior service, but only 8 percent of their customers agree with them? Who's right? The customer!

These findings are very similar to those uncovered by The DiJulius Group. Thousands of companies have taken our Company Service Aptitude Test (C-SAT), which is a detailed, self-assessment survey that managers take to find out what level of customer service they deliver. The C-SAT has proven to be an accurate indicator of the company's customer service level.

Prior to taking the test, participants are asked to rate their company.

---

Before beginning, please select which level you believe best describes your company's customer service:

Level 1   Unacceptable

Level 2   Below Average

Level 3   Average

Level 4   Above Average

Level 5   World Class

---

In this pretest question, approximately 53 percent of participants rate the quality of their service at one to two levels higher than the level determined by the C-SAT. You can take the C-SAT by visiting www.thedijuliusgroup.com/SAT. It is also discussed in detail in Chapter 4, Levels of Customer Service.

## Perception Is Reality

The majority of companies don't realize the level of customer service they are delivering or that their own standards for good customer service are considerably lower than their customer's standards.

## Could *They* Be *Us*?

After I speak about how to improve customer service, several people line up to tell me their personal horror stories, offering me material for my next book. I constantly hear things like, "You wouldn't believe how bad *they* treated me." and "Listen to what *they* did." This begs the question: If all of us agree and nod our heads at how bad they are at customer service, then who are the *they*? The answer is: *They* are *us*! We all can't be the victims. We need to assess our own businesses and accept that there is a good chance we and our companies are contributing to the crisis in some way.

No one will argue that there is a customer service crisis and that the majority of businesses do not make customer service a priority in their hiring, training, or treatment of their customers. Why is that? The answer: Because providing excellent customer service is a lot of work. It means you have to have systems, processes, hiring standards, training, and service recovery protocols in place. It is much easier for an entrepreneur, who is very educated and skilled at his profession, to open a business, hire some people, and start operating. Many assume that providing customer service is common sense: Just take care of the customer. Most organizations make significant investment in customer service a very low priority and it is the first thing that is cut out of the budget when times get tough, not realizing the major impact it has on the bottom line.

# Customer Service and Its Impact on Sales

Is an investment in customer service really worth it? How does the level of customer service a company delivers truly impact key drivers such as customer retention, sales, profit, cash flow, stock prices, employee turnover, and a company's vulnerability to fluctuations in the economy and third-party conditions (i.e., gasoline prices, housing market).

## Customer Satisfaction and Stock Prices

In an article from the *American Management Association's Journal of Marketing*, January 2006, titled "Customer Satisfaction and Stock Prices: High Returns, Low Risk," author Claes Fornell asks the question, "Does an investment in customer satisfaction lead to excess returns?" The empirical evidence presented in the article suggests that the answer is yes![2] Let me repeat that:

> The empirical evidence suggests that an investment in customer satisfaction does lead to high returns at low risk.

Claes Fornell, is the director of the American Customer Satisfaction Index (ACSI) and a professor at the Stephen M. Ross School of Business at the University of Michigan. ACSI is a leading indicator of consumer behavior, measuring the satisfaction of consumers across the U.S. economy. Extensive research proves that an increase or decrease in customer satisfaction, not only greatly impacts each individual organization, but has a significant impact on the future health of the economy.[3]

Equally amazing, the author's findings suggest that satisfied customers are economic assets with high return and low risk. The study also proved that the leading ACSI companies consistently outperformed the market by considerable margins.[4]

It is conclusive that organizations that consistently deliver superior customer service generally enjoy more repeat business, less price elasticity, higher price points, more cross-selling opportunities, greater marketing efficiency, and a host of other factors that usually lead to earnings growth. These companies also enjoy lower expenditures related to warranties, complaints, defective goods, higher employee satisfaction, and market share. In addition, several research studies find that higher customer satisfaction has a positive impact on employee loyalty, cost competitiveness, profitable performance, and long-term growth.[5]

These findings are consistent with previous studies that revealed that companies with higher levels of customer satisfaction are more likely to enjoy higher levels of net cash flow. Similarly, superior customer service companies typically have lower costs of sales and marketing. Remarkably, a one-point improvement in a company's ASCI score can result in as much as a 7 percent increase in cash flow.[6]

If good customer service translates into all the previously mentioned gains, such as repeat business, future revenue, increased market share, productivity, cost competitiveness, long-term growth, less customer defection, and lower employee turnover, it is logical that these factors will eventually affect stock prices and company valuations. And if that is the case, it would be difficult not to take seriously the notion of customer satisfaction as a real, intangible, economic asset.[7]

## Irrefutable Evidence

Several studies compared the top ACSI companies against the market with regards to stock performance over six years, from 1997 to 2003, a period where the stock market had both ups and downs, to show the benefits of good customer service. The results were astonishing. While many businesses know the importance of providing consistent superior customer service, it is unlikely they realize how profound the benefits are. The top customer satisfaction companies (based on their ASCI scores) outperformed the Dow Jones by 93 percent, S&P 500 by 200 percent, and NASDAQ by 335 percent. The results conclusively show that customer satisfaction pays off in up-markets and down-markets. When the stock market dropped in value, the stock prices of companies with highly satisfied customers seemed to have benefited from some degree of insulation. Figures 1.1 through 1.3 show the cumulative returns over time.

A second study from a different time period, comparing the top ASCI companies versus the DJIA, S&P, and NASDAQ markets had similar results. The ASCI companies outperformed the markets each and every year. Figure 1.4 shows the five-year cumulative results.

No one can argue that these results are extraordinary. There are very few actions or strategies a business can implement, if any at all, that can produce comparable financial results. Firms that do better than their competition in terms of satisfying customers (as measured by ACSI) generate superior returns at lower systematic risk.[8]

To demonstrate the significance customer satisfaction has on the financial success of an organization, Figure 1.5 compares the companies

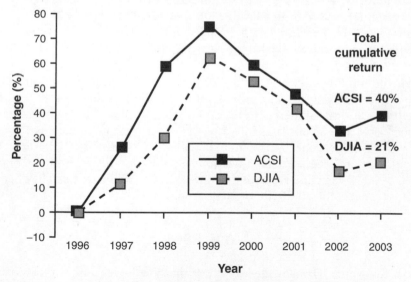

**FIGURE 1.1** Top ACSI Companies versus Dow Jones (February 18, 1997, through May 21, 2003). From "Customer Satisfaction and Stock Prices: High Returns, Low Risk," by Claes Fornell, Sunil Mithas, Forrest V. Morgeson III, and M.S. Krishnan, 2006, *Journal of Marketing,* 70 (January), 3–14. Reprinted with permission from *Journal of Marketing* published by American Marketing Association.

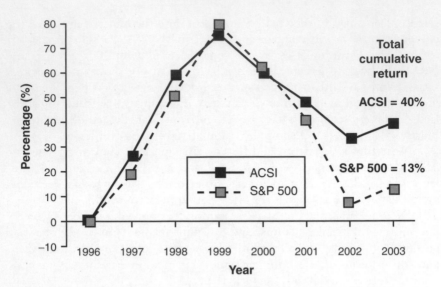

**FIGURE 1.2**  Top ACSI Companies versus S&P 500 (February 18, 1997, through May 21, 2003). From "Customer Satisfaction and Stock Prices: High Returns, Low Risk," by Claes Fornell, Sunil Mithas, Forrest V. Morgeson III, and M.S. Krishnan, 2006, *Journal of Marketing*, 70 (January), 3–14. Reprinted with permission from *Journal of Marketing* published by American Marketing Association.

with the top 50 percent ACSI scores versus the bottom 50 percent. The top 50 percent generated an average of $42 billion in shareholder wealth, while the bottom 50 percent created only $23 billion. One point of customer satisfaction translates into 3 percent of market value increase.[9]

In a study done by the Ken Blanchard Companies, 74 percent of companies declared their organizations were highly focused on customer service improvements. However, only 44 percent indicated that they had a formal process for achieving these desired results.[10]

## Stone Ages

Most companies' financial measurement methodologies for customer satisfaction are extremely misleading and too primitive to be useful. This won't change unless shareholders, corporate boards, and investors put more pressure on companies to account for intangible assets more effectively. Customer satisfaction should be considered an economic asset on the balance sheet and every executive should know the correlation between the level of customer service their company provides and the bottom line.

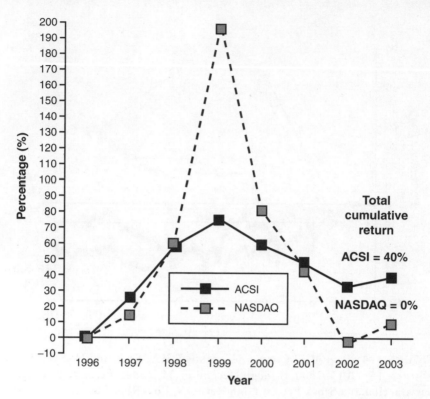

**FIGURE 1.3** Top ACSI Companies versus NASDAQ (February 18, 1997, through May 21, 2003). From "Customer Satisfaction and Stock Prices: High Returns, Low Risk," by Claes Fornell, Sunil Mithas, Forrest V. Morgeson III, and M.S. Krishnan, 2006, *Journal of Marketing*, 70 (January), 3–14. Reprinted with permission from *Journal of Marketing* published by American Marketing Association.

But if customer service is that important, why is it not represented on profit and loss statements or balance sheets? There are line items for advertising, marketing, people development, entertainment, but usually nothing for customer service. Our financial reporting seems to be in the Dark Ages with regards to its omission of factors such as customer service and customer satisfaction. "It is often difficult to translate, accounting doesn't help. Investment in customer service can't be capitalized, nor does it show up as an asset. After all, an intangible, feel-good asset such as customer satisfaction can't be captured on the balance sheet. So spending to improve customer service and customer retention is usually treated as a cost rather than an investment. The result is that those

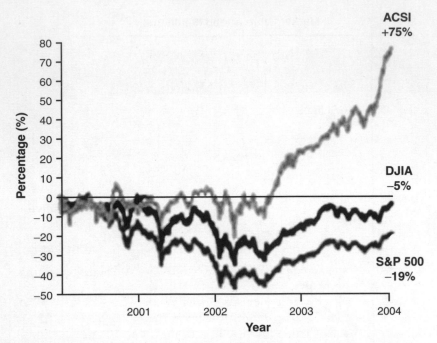

**FIGURE 1.4** Top ACSI Companies versus DJIA, S&P, and NASDAQ Markets (April 11, 2000, through December 31, 2004). From "Customer Satisfaction and Stock Prices: High Returns, Low Risk," by Claes Fornell, Sunil Mithas, Forrest V. Morgeson III, and M.S. Krishnan, 2006, *Journal of Marketing*, 70 (January), 3–14. Reprinted with permission from *Journal of Marketing* published by American Marketing Association.

costs are recorded before the benefits of the investment are realized," says Fornell.[11]

Consider the case of Amazon.com. Their pursuit of a better customer experience has turned out to be exactly right. Amazon estimates they have 72 million active customers, who, in a single quarter, spend an average of $184 a year on the site, up from $150 the year before.

Amazon's return customer business is proof that customer service pays off. With a customer retention rate that consistently hovers around 80 percent, their typical customer is worth about five purchases. By increasing their retention rate to 85 percent, the typical customer will average seven purchases. An increase of only two purchases, right? Well, multiply that additional two purchases by the average purchase price of each order and then by their 72 million users worldwide and it becomes a pretty significant increase. As Fornell points out, "Organizations need to figure a way to apply economic systems that link customer satisfaction to shareholder value."

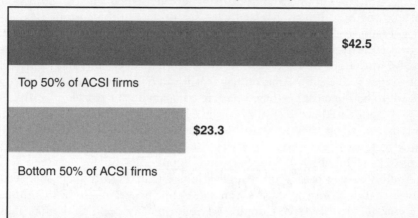

**FIGURE 1.5**  Comparing the Top 50 Percent ACSI Firms versus Bottom 50 Percent in Shareholder Wealth. (From "High-Tech the Old-Fashioned Way: An Interview with Tom Siebel of Siebel Systems," by Tom Siebel and Bronwyn Fryer, 2001, *Harvard Business Review*, March. Copyright 2001 by the Harvard  Business School Publishing Corporation, all rights reserved. Reprinted with permission.)  *Note:* ACSI and MVA data for 1999 base: 73 U.S. companies.

## Service Vision—To Be the Most Customer-Centric Company in the World

In an article that appeared in the January 5, 2008, edition of the *New York Times*, business columnist Joe Nocera noted that Amazon's stock continues to rise, in spite of Wall Street analysts' predictions of the stocks demise due to its focus on such frills as putting customers first. Nocera talks about an incident a few days before Christmas, where he ordered a PlayStation, a $500 gift, through Amazon.com. After it was delivered, signed for by a neighbor, and left in the building's lobby, the package disappeared. To Nocera's surprise and delight, an Amazon customer service representative sent out a replacement unit, which arrived on Christmas Eve. Not only did Amazon not charge him for the replacement, but they didn't even charge him for the shipping.[12]

So why were Wall Street analysts so wrong in predicting the demise of Amazon? Could it be these supposed stock prognosticators put too much emphasis on margins and short-term results and not enough emphasis on the customer service practices that help create a lasting company?[13]

In the article, Nocera went on to recall a recent interview with Jeffrey Bezos, Amazon's founder and CEO, where he explained his "obsession" with customers: "I'm so obsessed with the drivers of the customer experience, I believe that the success we have had over the past 12 years has been driven exclusively by that customer experience. We are not great advertisers. So we start with customers, figure out what they want, and figure out how to get it to them." Amazon has really had only one stated goal since it began: to be the most customer-centric company in the world.

It appears Amazon is succeeding. Millions of people instinctively go to Amazon when they want to buy something online because they have come to trust the company in a way they trust few other online entities. Amazon's technology, its interface, and its one-click buying service are all incredibly easy to use. It offers suggestions for further products that actually appeal to its customers. Its Amazon Prime program—for a $79 annual fee you get two-day free shipping—is enormously popular. Unlike most e-commerce sites, when you have a problem, the customer service telephone number isn't hard to find. Amazon is even willing to correct mistakes that it didn't make.

All of this, however, comes at a price. Customer service isn't cheap. Amazon has invested heavily in improving the customer experience. Take for instance, in just one year, Amazon spent over $600 million in shipping. Wall Street, however, has never placed much value in Mr. Bezos's emphasis on customers. What he has viewed as money well spent toward building customer loyalty, many investors saw as giving away money that should have gone to the bottom line. "What makes their core business so compelling is that they are focused on everything the customer wants," said Scott W. Devitt, who follows Amazon for Stifel Nicolaus & Company. "When you act in that manner, many times Wall Street doesn't appreciate it." What Wall Street wanted from Amazon is what it always wants: short-term results. Precisely what Dell tried to give investors when it scrimped on customer service and what eBay did when it heaped new costs on its most dedicated sellers. Eventually, these short-sighted decisions caught up with both companies.

There is simply no question that Mr. Bezos's investment in his customers, and his focus on the long term, has paid off, even if he had to take some hits to the stock price along the way. Mr. Bezos has said, "If you did something good for one customer, they would tell 100 customers."[14]

## Companies and the Customers Who Hate Them

An article that appeared in the *Harvard Business Review*, June 2007 talks about how companies need to create less company-centric and more customer-centric policies.[15] If customer satisfaction creates loyalty and loyalty produces profit, then why do so many companies infuriate their customers with contracts, hidden fees, fine print, and unnecessary penalties? The article's authors, Gail McGovern and Youngme Moon suggest it is because companies have found that confused and ill-informed customers can be the most profitable.

Perfect examples of these companies are cell-phone carriers, banks, and credit card companies that profit from customers who fail to understand or follow the rules about minutes used, minimum balances, overdrafts, or payment deadlines. It has been estimated that 50 percent of U.S. cell-phone carriers' income is derived from penalizing fees. These strategies may be profitable in the short term, but in today's technology age, public sentiment spreads like wildfire, damaging a company's reputation in blogs and company-specific hate sites.[16]

What many of these companies have in common is that, even though they appear to take their customers for granted, their customers have little choice but to deal with it. Want to change your cell-phone company? Be ready to pay a hefty penalty to break your contract. Want to dump your internet provider? That may be difficult when one provider monopolizes your area.

Standard customer turnover in the cell-phone industry is 25 percent a year, which is shocking, especially considering most have customers sign contracts. This heavy turnover increases the amount of money that needs to be spent to replace these customers through aggressive marketing and advertising. In 2005, the U.S. cell-phone service industry spent more than $6 billion on ads.[17] Which begs the question, how much better would their customer retention and satisfaction be if they took half that $6 billion and put it toward customer service training of their call centers, technical support agents, and retail associates?

Welcome Virgin Mobile USA onto the scene, which entered the industry in 2002 with an unusual customer-focused strategy: a pay-as-you-go pricing plan with no hidden fees, no time of day restrictions, no contracts, and straightforward reasonable rates. With an advertising budget one tenth that of the larger players in the industry, Virgin Mobile USA, in only a few years, already had exceeded 5 million subscribers and a retention rate considerably higher than the industry average, even though its customers can leave at anytime without any penalty. They have a 90 percent customer satisfaction rating, with more than two-thirds of their customers reporting they would recommend Virgin Mobile to friends and family.[18]

The banking industry is not much better. Profits from American banks have increased so dramatically from consumer fees and overdraft penalties that Congress had to reintroduce the Consumer Overdraft

Protection Fair Practices Act. When the customer service bar is low, that means there is a great opportunity for someone to come in and steal the market. And that is exactly what the online bank ING Direct has done, offering savings accounts with no fees, no tiered interest rates, and no minimums. ING Direct is now the fourth-largest thrift bank in the United States, adding 100,000 new customers per month, with total assets of more than $60 million.[19]

The *Harvard Business Review* article offers warning signs to recognize customer unfriendly practices in your company:

- Are your most profitable customers those who have the most reason to be dissatisfied with you?
- Do you have rules you want your customers to break because doing so generates profits?
- Do you make it hard for customers to understand or abide by your rules?
- Do you depend on contracts to prevent customers from defecting?

Deteriorating customer service is not only the customer's issue. Eventually shareholders feel it the worst. For years Home Depot was known for having knowledgeable floor staff available to assist their customers and its stock price reached as high as $70. However, their customer satisfaction fell and their stock price followed by dropping to nearly half.[20]

## Artificial Growth versus True Growth

Growing your business artificially may satisfy shareholders and investors short term, but it is rarely effective over the long term. Examples of artificial growth are mergers, acquisitions, price-cutting, and novelty marketing promotions. But, typically, none of that results in higher customer satisfaction, loyalty, repeat business, referrals, or sustainable growth. There is only one true growth, growth that occurs because customers love doing business with you and sing your praises to their network.[21]

"Mergers and acquisitions often lead to deteriorating customer satisfaction as companies reduce costs," Fornell said. "This was the case for banks in the late 1990s when there was considerable merger activity. It remains to be seen if history will repeat itself, but the data suggest that the recent mergers are not contributing to improved customer satisfaction."[22]

> Price reduction = Resource reduction = Service reduction
> = Value reduction = Customer reduction

If repeat business is created through price discounts or other means that do not cause an upward shift in a company's demand curve, the relationship with the customer will be weaker.[23] Discounting comes with cost-cutting as well, and when lower resources meet an increase in demand that will ultimately reduce the value your customers perceive your company provides. Rarely can you reduce prices without reducing your resources—staffing, amenities, options—which all reduces the service you are able to provide your customers.

When customers experience inferior service, the need for discounting becomes even greater to offset the frustration level of doing business with an organization. Thus, repeat business produced by higher customer satisfaction will be more profitable in general than repeat business generated by price discounts.[24]

A large percentage of organizations today are built not to serve but to sell. The relentless pressure for cheaper product pricing that is applied to organizations today has expedited the globalization of labor, forced the issue of outsourcing, and destroyed otherwise healthy corporate cultures. Once this happens, organizations become vulnerable to any competitor that brings a lower price to the market. No loyalty exists when the nature of the relationship between the buyer and the seller is based on price and nothing more.[25]

In an article titled "The Death of Cost-Cutting" that appeared in *Smart Business* magazine, James Lane and Hersh Chaturvedi point out that CEOs are realizing that there is a different strategy to growing their business other than cutting costs wherever possible. Price drives profits and superior customer service experiences drive price. Their survey found that businesses achieving a premium price are four times likelier to be delivering a superior customer experience.[26] A 5 percent increase in customer retention could yield 25 to 100 percent improvement in profits. Companies with the highest customer loyalty typically grow revenues at more than twice the rate of their competitors.[27]

Sustainable organizations have leaders who model a service-oriented culture that holds human beings in high regard and seeks opportunities to make a positive impact for all stakeholders.[28] Too often when new competition enters the market with a less expensive service or product, many of the other players in the industry rush to cut their prices in fear of losing market share. In many cases when companies focus on creating a relationship and providing superior service, price becomes less relevant to their customers. Instead of dropping prices and hurting margins, organizations should consider increasing the value the customers are getting for their money.

## Making Price Less Relevant

Since opening in 1993, John Robert's Spa, a chain of upscale salons and spas in Cleveland, Ohio, focus has been on legendary customer service. We have won numerous awards for both service and growth, including being named one of the top 20 salons in America multiple times. Cleveland is not a big city like New York, Los Angeles, or Chicago where salons can demand high prices. The average woman's haircut price in Cleveland is $24. John Robert's Spa prices range from $45 to $110, depending on the service provider's experience.

More than 90 percent of our competitors are less expensive, in some cases considerably so, yet we are one of the busiest salons in Ohio while spending virtually nothing on advertising. Even during a sluggish economy (2001–2007), when demand for anything considered discretionary or a luxury, such as spa services (higher priced haircuts, manicures, facials, massages, pedicures, etc.) would be greatly diminished, the spas thrived. John Robert's Spa has enjoyed 15 consecutive years of revenue growth while steadily increasing prices by adding value to the services they provide. Instead of focusing on selling haircuts, John Robert's Spa focuses on creating an experience for guests that provides them with not only the fashion expertise they seek, but more importantly, an escape from daily stress and much needed rejuvenation that our bodies and mind require today (see Chapter 5).

Companies spend millions creating and advertising their brands, yet the customer's experience is what drives customer perception.

## When the Brand's Message Contradicts the Customer's Experience

It is a fact that nearly every market leader across many industries has the highest satisfied customer base, and usually advertises the least. Yet most executives have a difficult time investing revenue in customer service and training. Leaders who rose through customer-facing functions, are more likely to act with reference to customer experience than those who have not. In contrast, executives who rose through finance, engineering, or manufacturing often regard managing customer experience as the responsibility of sales, marketing, or customer service.[29] They will throw millions of dollars at marketing, advertising, and branding campaigns that promote a message that is contradictory to what the customer actually experiences. By investing 50 percent of your marketing budget into dramatically improving the level of your organization's customer service, you will see a significantly greater return on investment (ROI) than you were getting on your marketing and advertising dollars. Your customer base will turn into an unpaid salesforce.

Costco wholesale club, a leader in their industry in customer satisfaction, has grown to over 45 million members despite spending little on advertising or marketing. Between 1994 and 2004 Chick-fil-A grew nearly 15 percent annually, in spite of the fact they had one of the lowest advertising expense percentages to revenue in their industry. Chick-fil-A sets the bar for customer satisfaction companies in the quick service restaurant industry.[30]

In the early 1990s, Enterprise Rent-A-Car was experiencing dramatic growth; "We were seriously compromising our commitment to customer service," says CEO Andy Taylor. Enterprise has taken an aggressive strategy resurrecting their customer service. Enterprise's investment in improving their customer service has certainly paid off. Author, Fred Reichheld cited Enterprise as a model of how to generate customer loyalty.[31] "I have to say that learning to measure and manage customer service was not easy. We only had a vague idea of how difficult it would be. Of course, we didn't anticipate how great the rewards would be for our customers and our people. We were out of balance, with too much emphasis on the financial numbers and not enough on pleasing our customers. We have come a long way toward achieving a more consistent service performance," says Taylor. As a result, Enterprise has gone from $76 million in sales in 1980 to over $7 billion in sales by 2007.

Gary Loveman, COO of Harrah's Entertainment, doubled revenues and earnings by reinvigorating the company and institutionalizing a service culture. Loveman adjusted the compensation program for his general managers so that one-quarter of their bonuses depend on their customer satisfaction results. Every nonmanagement employee of the casino also receives a bonus if his or her property improved its customer service scores by 3 percent over the same period a year earlier. Harrah's has created a service curriculum that every employee had to pass, otherwise they lose their jobs. "Market by market, where our profitability and revenues greatly exceed our relative market position, there's no question but that the results are largely service driven," says Loveman. In four years, during this service makeover, Harrah's revenue grew by over 100 percent and equally as impressive, their employee turnover dropped nearly in half, from 45 percent in 1998 to 24 percent in 2001.[32]

## Customer Satisfaction Is a Fortune Teller

The level of a company's satisfaction can typically be an excellent forecaster of their future success. Author Joe Calloway sums it up best, "If you want to see how a company is doing now, look at their current sales; if you want to know how a company will perform in the future, look at their current customer satisfaction scores."[33] Every company measures performance by "comp sales," or same store sales comparing current year to previous year. Rightfully so, it is one of the most important benchmarks of a company's success in their market. Service Management Group, of Kansas City, who conducts over 28 million customer surveys a year, has discovered that businesses with higher customer satisfaction have higher comp sales growth. Having a loyal customer base drives topline growth. Figure 1.6 illustrates the effect customer satisfaction has on

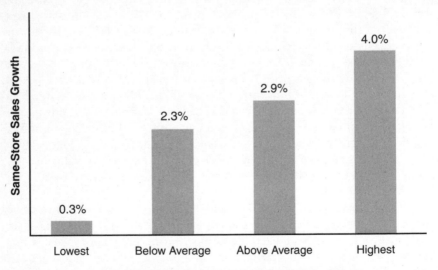

**FIGURE 1.6** Loyalty Impact on Sales Growth (Service Management Client Data). *Note:* Higher intent-to-recommend scores correlate with higher same-store growth.

comp sales. Stores with the lowest "recommend scores" average comp store sales growth of 0.3 percent compared to those at the highest end of the range, which grow at an average of 4.0 percent.

Customer satisfaction also has a huge impact on employee loyalty and turnover. Figure 1.7 shows the higher the employee turnover, the lower the customer service satisfaction levels.

A *Harvard Business Review* article titled *Why Satisfied Customers Defect*, explains that attempts to create a complete customer satisfaction in commodity industry will often raise the product or service out of the commodity category, for example, Starbucks.[34]

As pointed out in *Authenticity* (Harvard Business School Press, 2008):[35]

> *Starbucks earns several dollars for every cup of coffee, over and above the few cents the beans are worth, precisely because it has learned to stage a distinctive coffee drinking experience centered on the ambience of each place and the theatre of making each cup. Perhaps no other company in the world more earnestly and steadfastly seeks to render authenticity—resolutely shaping how consumers perceive it to be.*

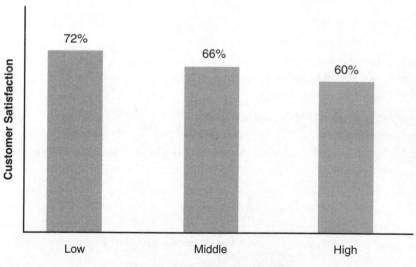

**FIGURE 1.7**  Employee Turnover Impact on Customer Satisfaction (Service Management Group Client Data). *Note:* Higher employee turnover reduces customer satisfaction.

## Conclusion

> Business has never been tougher than it is today . . . the only businesses that are surviving with long term sustainability are fanatical about differentiating themselves through the customer experience they deliver.

### It Is Time to Either Get on, Get off, or Get Run over

There is conclusive proof that with the necessary investment to improve your company's customer service an organization can incur the following benefits:

- Higher customer retention
- Higher customer satisfaction
- Increased sales
- Higher comp sales
- Higher profit
- Increased cash flow
- Higher stock prices
- More shareholder earnings and value
- Lower employee turnover
- Increase in future earnings
- Reduced risk
- Less affected by the fluctuations in the economy and third-party conditions

## Notes

1. Bain & Company. "HBR Understanding Customer Experience" [Bain & Company Survey], February 2007.
2. Claes Fornell, "Customer Satisfaction and Stock Prices: High Returns, Low Risk," *Journal of Marketing*, January 2006.
3. See note 1.
4. See note 1.
5. See note 1.

6. See note 1.

7. See note 1.

8. See note 1.

9. See note 1.

10. Ken Blanchard, "Key to Customer Loyalty," www.kenblanchard.com.

11. See note 2.

12. Joe Nocera, "Put Buyers First? What a Concept," *New York Times*, January 5, 2008.

13. See note 12.

14. See note 12.

15. Gail McGovern and Youngme Moon, "Companies and the Customers Who Hate Them," *Harvard Business Review*, June 2007.

16. See note 15.

17. See note 15.

18. See note 15.

19. See note 15.

20. Christopher Oster, "Customer Service Hall of Shame," *MSN Money*, April 26, 2007 12:01 AM ET, http://articles.moneycentral.msn.com/SavingandDebt /Advice/TheCustomerServiceHallOfShame.aspx.age=2/.

21. Fred Reichheld, *The Ultimate Question* (Boston, MA: Harvard Business School Press, 2006).

22. See note 2.

23. See note 2.

24. University of Michigan News Service. http://www.ns.umich.edu/htdocs /releases/print.php?Releases/2005/Feb05/r021505.

25. Dan J. Sanders, *Built to Serve* (New York: McGraw-Hill, 2007).

26. James Lane and Hersh Chaturvedi, "The Death of Cost-Cutting," *Smart Business*, April 2007.

27. See note 21.

28. See note 25.

29. Christopher Meyer and Andre Schwager, "Understanding Customer Experience," *Harvard Business Review*, February 2007.

30. See note 21.

31. See note 21.

32. David O. Becker, "Gambling on Customers," *McKinsey Quarterly*, no. 3, February 1, 2003.

33. See note 20.

34. Thomas O. Jones and W. Earl Sasser Jr., "Why Customers Defect," *Harvard Business Review*, November 1, 1995.

35. James H. Gilmore and B. Joseph Pine II, *Authenticity* (Boston, MA: Harvard Business School Press, 2007).

# 2

# The State of Service

*Is your company part of the customer service crisis or customer service revolution?*

---

*There's only one boss, the customer, and he can fire everybody in the company from the chairman on down, simply by spending his money somewhere else.*[1]

—Sam Walton

# The Customer Service Crisis

The CEO of a large company, where I had been consulting for a while, told me, "John, you will never starve. You will always be busy with customer service consulting." I was obviously elated, thinking he was happy with my services. Just as I was about to thank him, he continued, "because customer service is just so bad in America today." Well, that was a let-down. But then I saw the bright side. If there is indeed a service crisis, I am confident I have the cure, and I am prepared to change the situation one company at a time.

During the past five years, we have seen more than enough corporate cost-cutting, stock market blues, layoffs, and outsourcing of services to the lowest bidder. As a result, customer service is at such an all-time low that if customer service is not horrible, consumers are relieved!

How bad is customer service today? Well consider this, in December of 2007, the airline industry was fighting a proposed "Flier Bill of Rights," which would punish airlines for stranding passengers on planes without adequate food, water, or sanitation. How unreasonable is that? To expect not to be stuck on a runway for more than three hours, without food, water, and proper waste removal.[2]

> People are realizing the cheaper they go, the more it costs them.

# Return on Hassle

Customers are savvy today, and they realize that poor customer service can be costly when you factor in the return on hassle (ROH)—the additional time it takes to return something—to call customer service three times, to fume on the phone waiting in queue, hoping to get an answer or a resolution, while experiencing added stress related to unnecessary issues. Customers are realizing it is cheaper to pay more for something and have it be done right the first time, rather than patronize businesses with poor customer service. Thus, companies cannot always fall back on, "We are the lowest price, therefore good service should not be expected."

# The Bar Has Been Set

Customer's expectations of service are so low that today businesses have a truly fantastic opportunity to gain a superior competitive advantage. Whatever your business—retail, hospitality, business-to-business—it has never been easier to exceed the customer's expectation by delivering a memorable experience. The few companies that have realized this and make service their value proposition are seeing the return on investment (ROI).

Consumers and businesses will pay a premium when they find companies that put an emphasis on creating relationships. Organizations that deliver world-class service create loyalty and build a bank account of emotional capital with their customers. World-class organizations are less affected by third-party conditions, such as escalating gasoline prices, mass mortgage foreclosures, real estate crashing, a volatile stock market, what the Fed does the with the interest rate, or global events, than companies that do not differentiate themselves by customer service.

# Cracking the Code

*What's the Secret* to why a majority of businesses struggle with a team of 15, 50, or 125 while companies like Disney, Nordstrom, and The Ritz-Carlton get tens of thousands of employees to consistently execute world-class customer service?

Well, here is the million-dollar answer: Look at front-line employees, the ones counted on to deliver service, and time and again you will see two trends:

1. Lack of service aptitude, and
2. Declining people skills.

That's it! You can put down this book. I have cracked the code. A great deal of what is wrong with customer service can be traced back to these two issues. I recommend you keep reading though, so you can find out how to avoid these obstacles and create the necessary world-class systems used by the elite service companies.

## Lack of Service Aptitude

What is superior service? The answer depends on the person you ask because without proper soft skill training, it's relative to one's life experience. If I ask you what is world-class, you may think of a five-star hotel, but if I ask the front-line employee you just hired about his or her best hotel experience, it may be Red Roof Inn.

*Webster's Dictionary* defines common sense as "one's judgment based on their perception of the situation." Essentially, your employees' ideas of superior customer service are based on *their* experiences of customer service. The level of customer service a person is innately capable of giving is relative to his (or her) life experiences up to that point. Where has he traveled and been? What has he experienced? What manners and code of behavior was he taught at home? In all likelihood, there is a huge discrepancy between your vision of customer service and your new employee's vision. He doesn't know how *others*, namely your customers, want to be treated. You need to be prepared to train your front-line employees to recognize how others want to be treated. This book tells you how to do it.

> Don't blame me for giving lousy customer service, how should I know?
>
> —*Your new front-line employee*

Would you hire a banker to perform heart surgery on a family member? Would you hire a biologist to do your tax returns? No! And why not? Because neither has the formal training nor are they certified or licensed. Then why do you expect employees to know how to deliver customer service? None have had any formal training or have been certified. It isn't a class we took in high school. There certainly is no one majoring in customer service in college.

Most businesses conduct interviews with job applicants (hopefully more than just one interview per prospect) where the applicants smile a lot, provide glowing references, and respond properly to questions. So they hire them. Then it is discovered that the new employee has absolutely no concept of how to take care of a customer or how to defuse a simple problem, let alone how to think on his or her feet in a crisis and make things right for the customer. This leads to management being disappointed in the employee's lack of good judgment and then we have turnover and the cycle continues with their replacement.

Front-line employees in nearly every industry make between $7 to $20 per hour. You don't typically see them flying first-class, driving luxury cars, or staying at five-star resorts. Yet, many managers, supervisors, and owners expect these front-line employees to deliver that level of service to customers who are accustomed to those types of experiences.

This doesn't mean that we should pay front-line employees $100,000. Nor do we need to restrict our hiring to people who have certain types of backgrounds. The ability to deliver world-class service has everything to do with a person's service aptitude, and that can be learned and improved. The customer service level of your organization is based on the service aptitude of your employees, starting with your management team down to your front-line employees who have the most contact with your customers.

> Service aptitude is a person's ability to recognize opportunities to exceed a customer's expectations, regardless of the circumstances.

The key to that definition is the last four words, "regardless of the circumstances." High service aptitude is not as critical on your slowest day of the week or on a day when everything is running smoothly. True service aptitude is revealed in a difficult situation, such as when you are short-staffed, or in a crisis, or when service recovery is needed.

Think about it this way: For months you have been promising your spouse a get-away for just the two of you. Finally, you are spending three days in the Bahamas. The two of you are sitting by the pool, ordering piña coladas, and reading magazine tabloids. Life couldn't be better.

Meanwhile, back home, your company just dropped the ball on your platinum-VIP customer. The only person on the scene to handle the situation is your most recently hired front-line employee. Still having fun? Still relaxed? Want another piña colada?

> In most cases, our most recently hired, least-trained, lowest-paid employee deals with our customers the most!

Although most people enter the business world with a very low service aptitude, it can increase dramatically with the proper training in soft skills to start with and with continuous training in customer service. Unfortunately, most companies spend the vast majority of their training on the technical side of the job, usually because they are hiring reactively, filling an empty position with a warm body.

### Employee Service Aptitude Test
One of the best tools for measuring if an employee's service aptitude is high enough to start interacting with a company's customer is the Employee Service Aptitude Test (E-SAT), created by The DiJulius Group

(Figure 2.1). The E-SAT is a customized test that asks 50 to 75 multiple choice questions of the most common situations that may arise between the employee and their customer, ranging from nonnegotiable standards, service recovery, above-and-beyond opportunities, to uncomfortable and difficult situations. We suggest the E-SAT be given before and after the new employee goes through the initial training to monitor how service aptitude has increased. At John Robert's Spa, a new employee cannot start working in his or her department, training

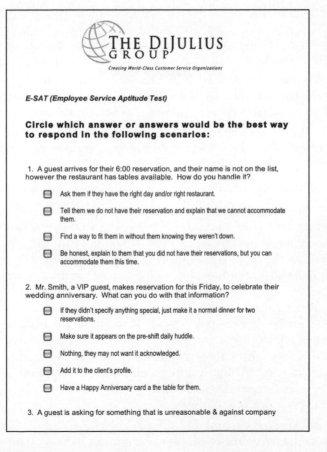

**FIGURE 2.1**  The Employee Service Aptitude Test (E-SAT)

for an actual position, or interact with our guests without passing the E-SAT.

Here is a sample question from an E-SAT we made for a restaurant chain for the hostess position:

---

**Scenario**

A woman waiting for a table approaches (you the hostess) and complains that she has been waiting well over the 20 minutes that she was quoted. You look at her name and the time you checked her in and realize it has only been 18 minutes. How do you handle this?

A. You kindly correct her and inform her that it's only been 18 minutes and if she doesn't believe you, you can show her your check sheet.

B. You say, "Unfortunately, there is still one guest ahead of you, we will do our best."

C. You notice that the couple in front of her are having a great time in the bar and you say, "I apologize, I was just about to call your name, your table is being prepared as we speak."

D. You say, "I apologize, you are second on our list to be seated, however, if you like, I would be happy to get you an appetizer or drinks while you wait."

---

Now granted this is a really easy one, and while most new employees would choose answers C or D, very few would have thought to do C or D prior to taking the test. Not all answers are that obvious. We also create a different, more advanced E-SAT for experienced employees, which instead of having 3 wrong answers and 1 right, may have 2 wrong answers and 4 correct. We ask them to tell us the order in which we want them to try to solve the situation. For example, answer D might be the best, however D is not always possible, if it is not, then A would be the next best resolution, then E, and so on. There are several more E-SAT examples in Chapter 9 or you can visit www.thedijuliusgroup.com/E-SAT for more information about Employee Service Aptitude Tests.

*Professional Service Aptitude*
It is not just the front-line employees who need to increase their service aptitude and more soft/people skill training. I have worked with hundreds of

organizations and professionals such as accountants, financial advisors, consultants, lawyers, programmers, and doctors, who are extremely skilled and trained technically but are not strong at customer/client services or knowing how to build relationships. Every employee needs customer experience training—front line, administrative, professionals, and management.

## Rapid Decline in People Skills

Another reason why we are in the midst of a customer service crisis is the fact that the younger generation has underdeveloped people skills. Today, we have one-twentieth the human interactions that we had back in 1988. We can thank technology for this situation. Here are just a few examples of the eroding people skills in our society:

| We Once Had | Now We Have |
|---|---|
| Bookstores | Amazon.com |
| Movie theaters | Netflix |
| Corporate offices | Home offices |
| Public schools | Home schools |
| Seminars | Webinars |
| Bank tellers | ATMs, direct deposit, online transfer |
| Full-service gas stations | Pay at the pump |
| Youth sports and activities | Playstation and computer games |
| Phone calls | E-mails and text messaging |
| Neighborhoods with front porches | Three-acre lots with decks out back |
| Check-out clerks | Self-checkouts |
| Dine-in restaurants | Drive-throughs |
| Families interacting | Cell phones, iPods, game boys, instant messaging |

Think about this: If today's younger generation lacks the skills gained from human interactions, who is responsible for improving their people skills and increasing their service aptitude? The businesses that hire them! We can't skip this generation and hope the next will be any better at people skills.

We need to have better training programs, not just training on product knowledge and the technical side of the job, but also training on the soft skills. The companies that deliver world-class customer service are the companies that understand this fact and provide training in customer service skills.

## The Customer Service Revolution

> Secret Service is not something you do, it is something that is in you, it is something you are in all areas of your life; to your customers, employees, family, and neighbors.
>
> —*Brian Shelton, Director of Operations,*
> *Melting Pot Restaurants, Kansas City*

I met Brian Shelton in Memphis, Tennessee, where I was the keynote speaker for the Melting Pot Restaurant's annual franchisee conference. He approached me prior to my presentation and said he had just read my book *Secret Service* and he felt *Secret Service* was not something you deliver as much as it was something that you are. He is 100 percent correct; customer service is not an event, it is a cultural evolution, and a journey. One that many companies, especially world-class companies feel they never complete.

> Standing still is not an option. Either you take calculated risks to grow or you slowly wither and die.[3]
>
> —*Michael Eisner, Former CEO, Walt Disney Company*

Many organizations in corporate America are starting to realize that one of the few ways to create long-term brand security is by differentiating themselves through service. Customers are tired of tolerating inferior customer service. If it is true that the better the service, the less price becomes an issue, then it is equally true that the worse the service, the less price becomes an issue. This means that if you constantly drop the ball and do nothing to make things right for the customer, they will not want to do business with you even if you have the lowest price.

Customers are becoming less tolerant of mediocre customer service. Companies will benefit if they make customer service a major focus, and make a commitment to providing consistently excellent customer service, not just a periodic focus as flavor of the month. World-class companies dominate their markets and do not have to compete on price and disappearing margins. Competitors can copy your design, layout, architecture, marketing, colors, signage, pricing, pay structure, hourly rate, products, but it is next to impossible to copy a service culture and the people who share in that service vision. Here comes the customer service revolution.

> Entrepreneurs who deliver the human touch are stealing sales from big impersonal sites and stores.
>
> —*Fortune Small Business, "Extreme Customer Service"*

*Fortune Small Business*'s cover story in their October 2007 issue is titled "Extreme Customer Service." It opens with how overall customer satisfaction is getting worse and customer rage is rising. They estimate: "15 percent of ticked-off customers entertain fantasies of revenge." The article cites several examples of outstanding customer service by companies who are "stealing sales from the bigger impersonal stores."

## Customer Service Is Making a Comeback

This is great news, because for the past 15 years, customer service has gotten lost and the focus for businesses has been artificial growth (acquisitions, first to launch novelty products, and marketing gimmicks). All of this has resulted in customer service once again becoming a critical benchmark in business, as if the concept was just invented.

### The Best Customer Service Companies Are Also the Most Paranoid

One common characteristic of the world-class service organizations I have worked with is that they are never content with the level of service they provide. They are constantly trying to raise the bar a little higher and are never satisfied or content with their current level of service.

I recently had the pleasure of working with The Ritz-Carlton in Sarasota. General Manager Jim McManemon is an 18-year veteran of The Ritz-Carlton and has a passion for customer service that can rival anyone's. He eats, sleeps, and breathes service and is an incredibly motivating leader.

In the weeks leading up to working with Jim and his property, I did my typical due diligence, having him and his leadership team fill out a thorough questionnaire to help me customize my presentation for their group and then having a conference call the week before. On the call with Jim, I asked about his top three objectives for this presentation—what did he want his team to take away. His answer was, "How do we go from good to great, how do we move our guests from satisfied to extremely satisfied, and how do we move our employees from engaged to fully engaged?" He felt that his staff had much more potential. He said, "It is not that we are not capable or not doing great things already, but we want to be doing them 100 percent of the time. We want to go from good to great. We want each employee to be totally engaged with every guest at our resort."

What manager wouldn't want that? But here's the kicker: Just before I had this conversation with McManemon, The Ritz-Carlton Sarasota had just been named a Five-Diamond hotel, *again*. It had the third highest guest satisfaction rating of any Ritz-Carlton. And what was McManemon's response to such a high ranking? "I want to know what we aren't doing that is keeping us from being the highest ranked property."

I have been a guest there twice, and each time I have been blown away by the service and hospitality I received from every employee. And trust me, as a customer service consultant, I may be the hardest person to please.

Think about it: If Jim McManemon, whose property is Five-Diamond, is not satisfied with his rating, what does that say about the rest of us? It may not surprise you that the following year, the Sarasota property ranked #1 in guest satisfaction of all The Ritz-Carlton properties.

## How Many People Work in Your Company's Customer Service Department?

I love asking that question because I always get a few attendees who raise their hands. But the correct answer is, everyone. Every employee in your organization works in customer service and should act and think as if he does.

When Dan Cathy, the CEO of Chick-fil-A, visits any Chick-fil-A store, he goes right up to the customers and introduces himself saying, "Hello, I am Dan Cathy and I work in customer service. I would love to know how your experience with us has been." With a leader like that setting the pace, you can see why Chick-fil-A sales have grown by 40 percent to $1.53 billion, and their number of locations has grown from 958 to 1,160 in the past four years. And because of their commitment to service, Chick-fil-A is notoriously choosy, it typically only awards franchises to only 5 percent of the applicants, while the selection process can take up to a year.[4]

## Who's Your Customer?

This is another great question to ask your managers and employees. Odds are they will list the typical individuals or businesses buying from you. However, there are many other kinds of customers that need to be distinguished. One practice of all world-class service companies is that they view their employees as their primary customer. They also train each internal department, such as human resources, marketing, administration, and accounting to recognize that their actual customers are the other departments within the company.

It is everyone's responsibility to please the customer. When your corporate resource people say, "We don't come into contact with the customer," stop them and make them think about who their customer is. It is probably their operations, your locations, or different departments. We all have customers, and the best customer service companies train all their employees to realize they are all working in the customer service department of the company.

## Who Is Your Competition?

Finally, do your employees know who your real competition is? Is it your nearest competitor? There are several answers to this question: (1) It is anyone that your customers can compare their experiences to. If your customer has just gotten back from a trip to Disney or a weekend at The Ritz-Carlton and, as a result, has heightened their service senses, how will their experience compare when they come in contact with your employees? (2) Your competition is anyone that your customer can spend their discretionary money with. Today, consumers are more discriminating than ever and will spend their time and money where they get the best value and experience. And finally, (3) your main competition is your own reputation. Very few businesses lose customers to their competition that they wouldn't have lost anyway. You are either giving customers a reason to "shop" you or they are so happy with the value and experience they receive that there is no way a competitor can penetrate the relationship you have with your customer.

# The Experience Formula

There are many definitions and measures of customer experience, but at the end of the day, what is customer experience, really? While sophisticated customer satisfaction measurement is extremely valuable, I have a quick and easy experience formula that can be used in any organization and in any situation. You won't even need a computer or calculator. Here it is:

$$R - E = CE$$
*Reality – Expectations = Customer Experience*

This formula is a good tool to measure a customer's experience. This formula is also a training tool that helps employees gain a better understanding of how customers evaluate your company. For instance, a new customer uses your business and has never been extremely satisfied with any of your competitors; his expectations might be a 5 on a scale of 1–10 (10 being the best). Your company, who truly delivers a superior experience, gives him an 8, making your customer service a +3. Any positive number is very good.

You can also use this formula to help front-line employees understand how critical it is to handle customer challenges immediately, to not only correct a situation, but also possibly to exceed their low expectation. What are customers' typical expectations of how well companies handle problems? Maybe a 4 at best. However, your organization is zero risk to deal with and trains and empowers your front-line employees to provide great service recovery. The customer's reality might be a 9, giving your company a customer service score of +5. Obviously there are various scenarios you can apply to this formula, such as the customer who has extremely high expectations based on your company's reputation.

> The better the experience the less price becomes an issue.

Each of us deals with businesses that provide such great service and have fostered such a great relationship with us that we don't have a clue as to how much their competition charges, nor do we care. When companies provide a consistent, world-class experience, price becomes less of an issue. However, many times, when a customer complains about the price, it isn't because they are cheap or not willing to pay it, it is because the experience didn't warrant it.

World-class customer experience organizations, over time, make price irrelevant. Based on the experience they receive, customers feel your prices are an incredible value.

## When the Predator Becomes the Prey

There is an endless list of companies—previous market leaders that eventually lost focus in making service their value proposition—that are gone, have been acquired, or are just not the titans of industry they once were. It is common knowledge that the best way to steal market share from the big boys is through providing superior service and offsetting economies of scale.

## Do You Compete on Price or on Service?

According to *USA Today*, some restaurant chains were forced to slash the prices on their menu due to poor sales as a result of rising gasoline prices. "In the face of a national slump in casual dining, some of the biggest players in the industry have taken to cutting prices to salvage 2006." Outback Steakhouse, Applebee's, Bennigan's, Ruby Tuesday, and T.G.I. Friday's were mentioned as trying to combat declining same-store sales and guest counts.[5]

These are well-known brands, companies that have worked hard for 15, 20, 30 years to get their prices up to where they are, with much deeper pockets than many other companies. Now these companies have decided to reduce prices to counteract declining sales, when they could have instead focused on the experience they provide their customers.

## People Want Either the Best or the Least Expensive

No matter what product or service you provide, you have two options: compete on price or compete on experience. When you compete on price, you attract customers who are opportunistic and looking for the best deal. Margins are too thin today to compete on price. On the other hand, if you choose to compete on experience, you eliminate over 80 percent of your competition, who are cutting costs and service trying to be the cheapest.

Today, customers are pickier and more demanding than ever. Your company's goal should be to create a world-class culture that delivers a world-class experience. Do that, and customers will become more loyal regardless of the economy and more forgiving when you inconvenience them.

Unfortunately, businesses cannot promise they won't make mistakes, but the goal should be, "While you may complain about the service defect, you are going to rave about how well we handled it."

# Get over It!

Management's mentality is sometimes the leading cause why a company cannot deliver superior service. So many people think their situation is unique and use this as the reason why they cannot provide better service. Don't have tunnel vision and think, "some of the examples don't apply to my business," "we are business to business," or "my industry is totally different." A great example is a great example, whatever your business and whoever your customer. I have found that the exact same principles apply in any industry for providing world-class customer service and creating a world-class culture internally. The application may slightly vary, but the formula is always the same.

In my seminars and workshops with leaders from different organizations, I do an exercise that illustrates how similar all business situations are when it comes to dealing with customer service. When people from different businesses/industries share with each other their unique obstacles, it is remarkable how everyone realizes that they all share the exact same barriers. I have yet to come across a company that isn't trying to do the following:

- Differentiate itself from the competition.
- Make price irrelevant.
- Find talented service-minded people in a limited talent pool.
- Get their employees to buy in, be enrolled, and do the right thing.
- Create consistency in the service delivered by front-line employees.
- Have protocol in place to recover when someone drops the ball.
- Create an above-and-beyond culture.

If you look at some of the best customer service organizations, they went outside their industry to break old paradigms. For example, Southwest Airlines was looking for a way to improve the turnaround time of its aircraft, arrival to the gate to push back for the next flight. Reducing this time would help the company stay on time and save a great deal of money. Did they study the airline who had the leading turnaround time in their industry? No! They studied Indianapolis 500 pit crews, who complete a similar process in only 15 seconds. As a result of adapting such techniques, Southwest Airlines reduced its turnaround time by 50 percent and became a leader in their industry.[6]

## Air Mickey

What serves millions of people every year and their customers must stand in line before they can get on a ride? Besides Disney? How about airports. The similarities do not stop there. Airports and Disney parks operate or coordinate parking and transportation services, restaurants, and shops. Both employ teams of security, maintenance, and custodial personnel. That is why more and more airports are looking at Disney's model to see how they can improve their passenger experience. "While not everything that goes wrong at the airport is our fault, it is our problem," says Dickie Davis, Miami airport's Customer Service Division Director. "So it's important to make a personal connection. If someone has lost their baggage, or can't find their gate or the parking garage and encounters an employee who's sympathetic and tries to help, it can take the edge off. It's all about manners and niceness and courtesy."[7]

They are even dressing more like cast members (Disney's term for employees). Airport spokesman Greg Chin says travelers will be able to easily identify all those nice employees by their festive Florida-themed shirts with the airport's large palm tree logo on the back. "We're not a theme park," he says, "but we can take some of the Disney magic and put that here at the airport."[8]

My good friend Verne Harnish, a leading expert and consultant to fast-growth companies, had this to say about business to business (B to B) versus business to consumers (B to C):

> Instead of tuning out, if the example doesn't fit your situation (too big, not my industry, etc.), realize that in fact, there's only one distinction—P to P—people to people. You don't sell to companies, you sell to people! And in the end, people are people. B to B vs. B to C is another artificial distinction.

Well said!

## Customer Rage

Management guru Tom Peters states that it is our patriotic duty to rant and rave. "Name names," he says. "Demand that companies treat us better. Don't accept shoddy service. Our companies can't compete globally if we don't beat on them locally."

Why do we continue to allow this kind of abuse? Customer service is at an all-time low because we as consumers and businesspeople allow it to be. It's time we start holding companies accountable for how they treat their customers. It is time we stand up and say something and not only say it with where we spend our money, but also by telling the manager. Sure, many companies may not care, but some do care and want to know.

When our customers tell us what we are doing wrong, they are giving us the opportunity to make it right with them and hopefully to correct the internal problem so it's less likely to happen to another customer.

## Customer Service Is Not Just about People

Every business also needs to do a technology audit and see if you are creating barriers for your customers. Are you treating them like transactions, or are you creating relationships? Try calling your own company as if you were a customer, and assess its functionality.

Here is a great personal example of how technology is eroding our relationships and preventing companies from providing good service. I received a letter from a national bank saying my car payment was late. They were right. We had moved offices and I had forgotten to contact them. It was my fault, so I called them to pay the car payment over the phone and to change the billing address. Easy remedy, right? Wrong!

I called the number in the letter, which said, "Please call us to discuss." However, when I called, I could not get a human being. *It was not an option!* Normally I have no time for this; however, now it became a contest between their phone system and me. I wasn't backing down.

Finally, after 35 minutes of non-stop aggravation, I cracked the code. I hit the * button and got a human being. The customer service representative I reached couldn't have been nicer, but the bank has a functionality issue, which is the "ease of doing business." The bank is choosing productivity over service. The craziest thing was that I couldn't reach the company to pay them.

# It's All about Service

People ask me all the time, "Isn't teaching companies customer service like fighting an uphill battle—one that can never be won?" Absolutely not! I love customer service because it is so rewarding. It has great altruistic value to our society. When done well, it makes everyone feel great. It helps people, customers love it, and it gets their mind off their daily stress and allows them to escape. Employees love to deliver customer service because it allows them to be part of a bigger purpose instead of just coming to work every day. Businesses love it because of the benefits derived from providing world-class service.

## Flavor of the Month

Many businesses talk about making a commitment to improve their customer service, however, very few actually do. Elevating an organization's customer service is not an event or an inspirational presentation at the annual company meeting. It is a process that needs a commitment from top down. Numerous internal components have to be examined and addressed, from creating the service vision, hiring standards, and training, to measurements and execution. To truly improve a corporation's customer service, it has to be a long-term commitment that builds each year.

Providing a world-class customer experience is certainly not easy nor for everyone. Thank goodness, because those who strive to be world-class would not be reaping all the rewards.

# Notes

1. "Sam Walton Biography," *Fresh Thinking Business*, http://www.freshthinkingbusiness.com/sam-walton.html.
2. Marilyn Adams, "Airlines Hope to Block Flier Bill of Rights," *USA Today*, December 10, 2007, http://www.usatoday.com/travel/flights/2007-12-10-stranding-law_n.htm.
3. The Disney Institute and Michael D. Eisner, "Be Our Guest" (Disney Institute Leadership Series), *Disney Editions*, May 1, 2001.
4. Chuck Salter, "Customer-Centered Leader: Chick-fil-A," *Fast Company*, 87 (October 2004), http://www.fastcompany.com/magazine/87/customer-chickfila.html.
5. Bruce Horovitz, "Restaurants Shave Prices, Plump Menus," *USA Today*, August 24, 2006.
6. Gary J. Naples, *Beyond the Numbers: Managing the Assets of an Automobile Parts Business* (Washington, DC: SAE International, 2000).
7. See note 3.
8. Christopher Meyer and Andre Schwager, "Understanding Customer Experience," *Harvard Business Review*, February 2007.

# 3

# World-Class Service Sins

*What prevents companies from being world class?*

---

*If you are not serving the customer, you better be serving someone who is.*

—Tom Strauss, President/CEO
Summa Health Systems

I f you ask 100 managers, entrepreneurs, and business leaders why delivering superior customer service is so difficult, you will hear the same answers over and over again. Answers like:

"Our business is unique."

"In our industry it is so hard to find employees, let alone ones that care about service."

"We can't afford to pay enough to get quality people."

"The younger generation doesn't care."

"We have a totally different customer, it is much more difficult."

"Employees just take the easy way out."

"Employees just don't care."

"Employees don't get it."

"We are understaffed."

None of these answers are the reason why the vast majority of companies struggle with inconsistent customer service, they are the *results* of the reasons.

Before you can take the necessary steps toward creating a world-class customer service organization, you must first be fully aware of what prevents companies from consistently executing at a high level. In my experience researching and working with hundreds of companies across various industries, what companies need to do and what gets in their way are identical. Just knowing the end result doesn't tell you the real "why." For instance, you may know you have front-line employees who are not engaged and always seem to take the easiest way out versus handling a situation properly. That isn't the why. In most cases, it isn't that they just don't care. Truly understanding the underlying causes of inconsistent or poor customer service is more than half the battle.

The following are the 10 principal sins (obstacles) that prevent companies from delivering excellent customer service:

1. Lack of service aptitude.
2. Decline in people skills.
3. Inability in connecting employees' jobs and their importance to success of the company.
4. Poor hiring standards.
5. Lack of experiential training.

6. Not letting employees have input on systems.
7. Failure to implement and execute consistently.
8. Lack of a strong employee culture.
9. Lack of measurements and accountability.
10. Focus on artificial growth.

## Lack of Service Aptitude

What is superior service? You cannot leave it to the individual employee to define superior service because the answer you get will depend on the experience of the person you ask. Without proper soft-skill training, the answer is relative to that person's life experience and personal interpretation of world-class. What's world-class to one person is not world-class to someone else.

Lack of service aptitude is the leading reason why most companies fail. Those companies are assuming that all of their employees will use their best judgment. Although many front-line employees have not experienced world-class service, they still expect them to know intuitively how to deliver that type of experience to their customers. Totally unrealistic.

Think back to when you were 22. Would you have known how to deliver world-class service then? Most people that age would not. Your training needs to remove the gray area and to create exact protocol for virtually every service scenario. (See Chapter 9.)

## Decline in People Skills

To win brand loyalty companies need to establish strong emotional bonds with their guests, one transaction at a time, involving face-to-face contacts. A brand has a face.[1]

—*John Fleming, Gallup Organization*

The accelerating advances in technology have eliminated so much of our face-to-face interactions with people, that today we have far fewer human interactions than we had 20 years ago. As a result, we have a new generation of people in the workforce who do not have the inherent people skills needed. Get this; it has been reported that one of the most common ways, for young adults 18 to 24, to break up with each other is through text messaging. Think about that, your front-line associate has no problem ending a serious relationship with someone they know well, and you expect them to be personable with a total stranger, your customer?

Companies rely so heavily on automation today that customers are merely a transaction and have very little human contact, thus customers have fewer relationships with employees at companies, are more frustrated and ultimately less loyal.

It is a spiral effect that is hard to slow down or correct. E-commerce exploded partly because consumers were getting tired of lousy customer service from retailers, sales reps, and others. Because they didn't see the value of dealing with a human being, they cut them out and did it themselves online, and in most cases saved money (e.g., travel agencies). Businesses recognized the growing trend and put more money and resources into their e-commerce presence and less toward customer service training. In fact, with more customers going online, businesses were able to dramatically reduce their front-line payroll. All of this has caused an even larger reduction in face-to-face interaction and an increase in dissatisfaction for the consumers who do choose to deal with employees at brick-and-mortar merchants versus online shopping. Now the stores have fewer people working, giving less assistance in finding products and longer checkout times. Companies need to humanize their systems. (See Chapter 8.)

## Inability to Connect Employees and Jobs to Success

All employees, regardless of their seniority, department, or title, need to understand how their positions and contributions impact the overall success of the company and its service vision. Without clearly drawing that connection, many times the vision becomes transitional and temporary. A solid service vision is the foundation of the business, it represents what the company stands for, why it exists, and how all employees can play a part in that vision. (See Chapter 5.)

## Poor Hiring Standards

Nearly every company's number one obstacle is finding enough talented people. Most companies hire reactively, trying to fill openings caused by either turnover or growth. When companies reactively hire, their objectivity is distorted, and their hiring standards are compromised, which always results in a poor corporate culture made up of a group of individuals versus a synergetic team. (See Chapter 6.)

## Lack of Ongoing Experiential Training

On average, a company devotes more than 90 percent of its training to hard skills (such as technical and operational skills and product knowledge) and less than 10 percent to soft skills (such as customer service, relationship building, role playing, service recovery, and experiential training). It is impossible to be world-class unless you are totally committed to extensive and continuing training in soft skills.

As a result of low service aptitude and declining people skills, the top customer service companies have an extremely thorough orientation training on customer service that is separate from the rest of their orientation training for new employees. We like to call it *Secret Service* Boot Camp. It is a scheduled and nonnegotiable training that every new employee must go through and test out of before being allowed to interact with any customers.

Most companies devote almost no time to training staff on an ongoing basis. *Secret Service* Boot Camp is only part of the training in soft skills. Existing employees need refreshers and reminders. Many of the top customer service companies in the world reorientate all employees on a regular basis, requiring all employees to retake *Secret Service* Boot Camp every year alongside those newly hired people. Is it any wonder these companies have legendary customer service delivered by their entire staff consistently? (See Chapter 9.)

## Not Letting Employees Have Input on Systems

Many organizations hold senior-level executive meetings to address the constant erosion of their customer service. Then management returns to the front line fired up with dozens of new ideas and orders from the CEO to fix the problem. They want it implemented immediately, only to find resistance from the ranks, who are used to the strategy of the month. Eventually the ideas of top management lose their steam.

Companies that excel at customer service have workshops with different departments of the organization, allowing staff to have an opportunity to share their thoughts and their front-line expertise on how the company can deliver better service to its customers.

Not only do you get some incredible ideas from people who are in the trenches every day, but also and more important, you get commitment and buy in from the people who are responsible for delivering these new ideas. (See Chapter 9.)

## Failure to Implement and Execute Consistently

There is no shortage of great ideas. If anything, there are too many great ideas.

The problem is how to take a great idea and transform it into a non-negotiable system that gets executed regularly by every employee at every location. Most ideas fizzle after a few months because management can't possibly monitor all the new initiatives.

A rock-solid implementation process forces you to put every single idea through a *drill-down*. This process involves closely scrutinizing the idea to be sure it should be implemented, and then creating the training, systems, and support needed to fully implement the idea.

If an idea adds cost or complexity to current systems or processes, you must be sure it is worth it before you proceed to implement it. There are two reasons for this. First, your company needs to make a profit, and second, you need to ensure that you are being realistic in your intention to execute it consistently. (Not all great ideas are simple, but you would be amazed at how simple and effective most are.)

A company that tries to implement a dozen great ideas at once is asking to fail. A better approach would be to create a realistic roll-out calendar. Start with two or three ideas and then, 90 days later, introduce the next two or three. In about 18 months, all 12 of those great ideas will likely be implemented successfully. (See Chapter 10.)

## Lack of a Strong Employee Culture

Too often a company spends all its resources trying to get its employees to provide better service, yet fails to lay the groundwork, namely devoting resources and effort to provide legendary service internally to its teams. This does not work!

Lacking an internal world-class culture, these companies fail to provide the best lesson possible on how to go above and beyond for the customer. Employees who do not receive unbelievable service cannot deliver it. Also, these companies will not attract employees who have an outstanding aptitude for delivering world-class service.

If you look at any world-class service organization, you will find a common thread: The organization is a world-class place to work, it is world-class in its community, and it helps its employees lead world-class lives.

Secret Service is not just something that happens between your front-line staff and your customers. It also has to exist vertically and horizontally within your organization. The great customer service companies have as many systems in place internally to exceed team (employees') expectations as they have in place to exceed their customers' expectations.

Those in management positions are sometimes the worst role models. With all the responsibility and stress they experience, they often forget the need to treat employees as customers as well The best leaders worry about motivating just one person: themselves. They know that if they have their "A" game on, and their vision is obvious, they will succeed in inspiring their people, and employee satisfaction is dramatically higher. (See Chapters 6 and 14.)

## Lack of Measurements and Accountability

Companies need to see the impact that customer satisfaction has on their key metric drivers (i.e., customer retention, average ticket, re-sign rates, referrals, average contracts, frequency of visits). This demonstrates the critical importance and focus necessary. This also allows management teams to hold employees accountable for providing a great customer experience at every level of the organization. If you don't measure the results, how will you ever know if you are achieving them consistently? How can you remedy the inconsistencies and celebrate the successes? It is imperative to have several tools in place to track and measure the consistency and results of your customer service systems. Once these tools are in place, you can hold people accountable for any system inconsistencies until the system inconsistencies become a rarity. Equally as important, you need to celebrate the success of the systems and the employees who are delivering them.

Measurement tools can be anything from customer surveys, third-party companies that measure customer satisfaction or secret shoppers to statistical benchmarks (such as the average ticket or the number of referrals) that provides a benchmark to measure the impact of the new systems and to determine whether they are being consistently executed. (See Chapter 13.)

# Focus on Artificial Growth

Companies are under tremendous pressure to cut costs. Growing your business artificially may satisfy shareholders and investors short term, but it is rarely effective over the long term. Examples of artificial growth are mergers, acquisitions, price cutting, and novelty marketing promotions. But, typically, none of these result in higher customer satisfaction, loyalty, repeat business, referrals, or sustainable growth.

# Service Blunder: An Example

I, too, have been guilty of cutting costs that resulted in *reducing service*. A few years ago, my management team at John Robert's Spa and I were reviewing our current P&L, and I started demanding we find ways to increase our bottom line 3 percent.

So out came all the ideas. We justified some of them to ourselves and rolled them out. We said things like, "We can save thousands of dollars if we stop accepting American Express credit cards," and, "We can save thousands of dollars if we don't let customers put their tip on their credit card" (a common salon practice). Things like that sounded great in the conference room, but did they ever infuriate our customers! We lost some of our customers as a result. We eventually changed our policy back, but not before the damage had been done.

Unfortunately, this wasn't the first time that we, like so many other companies, have been guilty of becoming overly focused on the bottom line without realizing the impact it makes on our customers. We tried a number of other ideas that made sense dollar-wise in the conference room but ended up alienating our customers.

Most penny-pinching ideas result in squeezing service, which kills sales in the long run. In our case, our managers focus less on cost cutting and more on increasing the average customer spending, increasing new-client retention, cross-marketing our services to our existing customers, and branding incentives for new customer referrals.

All of this can only be executed by focusing on the fundamentals of world-class service, which always makes our bottom line much stronger than spending our time talking about purchasing sundries for 3 cents less from a new vendor.

Twenty-five years ago, we had employees with excellent people skills working with marginal technology. Today, we have employees with marginal people skills using excellent technology.

The pendulum has swung so far to the high-tech side that customers are now starving to be recognized as individuals with preferences. Here's what Adam Eisenstat, Director of Communications for (Donald) Trump University, says:

People are our greatest resource. It's worth taking a second look at this marketing cliché in our automated age. Automation has too often resulted in less customer service and more mechanized commercial interaction. The signature cliché of this new, dehumanized environment is "Please hold, your call is important to us."[2]

People often complain that it's hard to get a real human being, but in certain areas of business, getting the best people [employees] is a secondary concern. Rather, the emphasis is on finding ways to eliminate people and having machines do their jobs. The advantages seem obvious: Machines work at super human speed; they don't get salaries or benefits; they aren't prone to mood swings, injury, illness, and all the other complications that make humans less than perfect units of productivity.

No matter what your process is, it cannot compensate for low-quality people implementing the process. Remember: people before process. Despite the preeminence of technology in today's world, the old saw still applies: Get the best people you can get.[3]

## World-Class in Action

### e-Service

Zappos.com has grown into a billion dollar online brand through customer service. "We are a service company that just happens to sell shoes," says Zappos.com CEO Tony Hsieh.[4]

Besides a pretty extensive inventory, 3.5 million items, 1,200 brands and 150,000 styles, they offer free overnight shipping, both ways, on all orders. "Our philosophy is to spend the money that would've put towards marketing into the customer experience, which includes free overnight shipping, free return shipping, and offer 24/7 customer service. By doing so, we end up with more repeat customers and word-of-mouth, which we believe is the best form of marketing."

The company is so committed to providing superior service that all Zappos.com employees must complete 1,200 hours of customer loyalty training, regardless of their position. And Zappos.com loves returns. "We want first time customers to return something, just so they can figure out how easy it is," says Christopher Peake, senior buyer. Zappos.com trusts their customer. If the shoes you ordered don't fit, the customer loyalty center will immediately send you out the right size before the customer sends the original pair back.

The company started in 1999 and in just nine years has grown to nearly a billion dollars in revenue, with over six million customers and over 2 percent of Americans having purchased from them.

## Scenography

The Ritz-Carlton is never content and is always raising the experience bar. Executives decided they needed a scenographer, which is someone who, as with a play, could help them direct scenes for the customer, but through customized service, rather than lighting or props. The luxury chain tapped Palo Alto, California, design firm IDEO. "We wanted to bring a little something extra out of each hotel that helps to make the experience personal, unique, and memorable," says Len Wolin, Senior Director of Program Management for The Ritz-Carlton. "But most of all, we wanted it to be subtle."[5]

IDEO went to work creating a set of scenography workbooks. These books helped a group of the most creative staffers at each hotel brainstorm localized service scenes, such as a warm, personalized check-in process or a big night in, in which the executive chef might send up a handwritten note, a champagne toast, and a sample from the night's menu for guests with restaurant reservations. At San Francisco's Half Moon Bay hotel, guests are now invited to an intimate wine tasting at check-in. The localized touches "should be almost subliminal," says IDEO's Dana Cho, who led the project.

# Experiential Reports

Companies like Lane Bryant, Chick-fil-A, and Hallmark Gold Crown stores have hired me to provide an experiential report for their businesses. Some suggestions made by The DiJulius Group to these retailers include:

- On employee nametags, add the school they attend or the city they are from. This opens up customers to engage a friendly comment like, "Do you know so-and-so from Progressive?" or "My sister lives in Aurora. Maybe you know her."

- Create new titles and job descriptions for employees, such as:
  —Director of Romance
  —Hallmark Concierge
  —Special Occasion Consultant

  These new titles can be given to associates. No pay difference is necessary, but which would you rather be: a part-time associate at the local card store or the Hallmark Concierge or Director of Romance? Each position could have specific duties or things to know or study up on, such as contacts, networks, and extensive knowledge of specific Hallmark inventory. Anyone who is super-busy appreciates having the name of someone to call to place an order and have it shipped or ready to be picked up.

- Hallmark Special Occasion Club where Club validation can be either a laminated wallet card or monthly notification, or both.

  —Display beautiful wallet cards available for customizing with a list of holidays and special personal occasions, including birthdays and anniversaries, so customers are more likely to carry it as a reminder to get a present or card for important people in their lives.

  —Make it easy to apply for this card, by filling out a form in the store or by going online.

  —Send Club members an e-mail reminder when a special occasion is coming up, with a reminder, "We have great gift ideas . . ."

  —In November, remind the customer to update the card for the new year. Customers can also add names and dates at any time, and each time a new card is sent within 7 days. Lost cards will be replaced. Imagine the wallet advertising for Hallmark if thousands of people carried these cards around with them.

# Notes

1. Dan J. Sanders, *Built to Serve* (New York: McGraw-Hill, 2007).
2. Sanda Blakeslee, "Say the Right Name and They Light Up," *New York Times*, December 7, 2004.
3. Adam Eisenstat, "The Role of People in an Age of Automation," *Inside Trump Tower*, issue 34 (April 11, 2006), www.trumpuniversity.com/connect /newsletters/itt/issue34.cfm.
4. Joshua Hunter, "Internet Service Provider," *Transworld Business*, October 6, 2007, www.twsbiz.com/twbiz/features/article/0,21214,1679153,00.html.
5. Jena McGregor, "Customer Service Champs: *BusinessWeek*'s First-Ever Ranking of 25 Clients," *BusinessWeek*, March 5, 2007.

# Service Aptitude Level

*What level is your company?*

*The customer sets the pace, you capture the moments. You are in charge. Your ultimate responsibility is that each guest feels well when they leave because of how you enhanced their life in the moment that you had to serve them.*[1]

—Horst Schultze, Former President
of The Ritz-Carlton

There are five levels of customer service:

**Company Service Aptitude Levels (C-SAT)**

| Level | Description |
|---|---|
| Level 1 | Unacceptable |
| Level 2 | Below Average |
| Level 3 | Average |
| Level 4 | Above Average |
| Level 5 | World Class |

The defining characteristics of companies at each of these levels apply to all organizations, regardless of what the product is or who the customer is. A brief description of the levels is:

## Level 1: Unacceptable

- It is very difficult to do business with the organization: hours of operation are limited, policies are not consumer-friendly, and it is impossible to get a call returned.
- No training is provided.
- Can't hire new staff fast enough.
- Technical skills are limited to minimal product knowledge.
- The company competes by having the cheapest price or has no competitors.
- Turnover is high at all levels, including management.
- Employees think customers are rude.

## Level 2: Below Average

- The company is difficult to do business with. The company has stringent policies (such as for returns or cancellations), and it is difficult to speak to a human being.
- Training is limited to technical and operational training.
- Employees may be technically proficient but have minimal soft skills, such as dealing with customers and service recovery.

- Service is extremely inconsistent and totally dependent on who the customer deals with.
- If a customer is inconvenienced, management gets defensive with customer; little or no attempt is made to rectify the situation.
- Turnover is high.
- Only the owner or senior management has the authority to fix a problem.

### Level 3: Average

- Employees are technically proficient.
- Customer service is consistent; with some flashes of above average service and below average level service.
- Some employees will occasionally go above and beyond in a situation.
- The majority of training is devoted to technical and product knowledge.
- Many great ideas exist on paper but are not always implemented.
- Only managers have the authority to make things right for the customer.

### Level 4: Above Average

- Technically, in areas such as product knowledge and equipment, the company is the best in the industry.
- Employees perform some great acts but sometimes lack day-to-day consistency.
- Experiential training is provided, including soft skills, how to deal with customers, and service recovery.
- The company is able to charge above-average prices compared to the competition.
- The company has a strong inspirational service vision.
- Above-and-beyond situations occur often.
- New employees receive solid training in customer service.
- Lower than normal turnover.
- All front-line employees have the authority to make the situation right for the customer.

### Level 5: World Class

- It is extremely easy to do business with the company. Policies are customer-friendly, and when they aren't, front-line associates can override them.

- Technically, in areas such as product knowledge and equipment, the company is the best in the industry.
- Experiential training is provided, including soft skills, how to deal with customers, and service recovery.
- Employees are taught and tested on standards for every point of contact with the customer.
- Employees are trained on possible service defects and on above-and-beyond opportunities.
- The company has certification training, which employees must pass in order to advance in the company.
- The company has a strong inspirational service vision.
- The company profiles its customers and shares guest information internally.
- Daily pre-shift huddles are held.
- There is a strong above-and-beyond legacy.
- Great systems are designed and implemented.
- The company has a reputation for great customer service.
- The company has typically higher prices than its competitors do.
- Customer service training is constant, and there is awareness of it daily.
- New employees receive solid training in customer service.
- Very little compromise occurs in the hiring of employees.
- Turnover is extremely low and the company has a great corporate culture.
- There is a strong implementation process and follow-through on initiatives.
- The company hires only those people who are fanatical about customer service.
- All departments know how supporting each other affects the customer.

## What's the Real Service Aptitude Level of Your Company?

When it comes to customer service, do you know the rating for your company, location, or department? The DiJulius Group has created an incredibly powerful tool called the Company Service Aptitude Test (C-SAT, see Figure 4.1). The C-SAT not only pinpoints the service

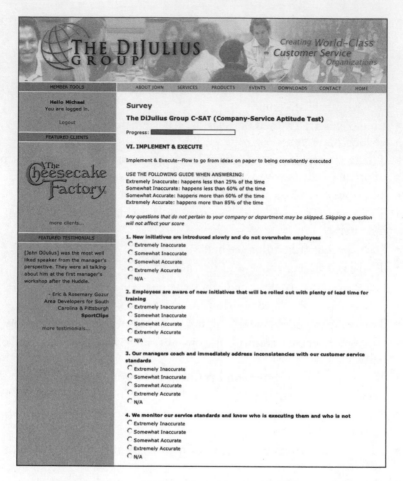

**FIGURE 4.1** Company Service Aptitude Test (C-SAT)

aptitude level of your organization, but even more important, it lets management know where the strengths and opportunities are to get to the next level. The C-SAT is based on the "Ten Commandments" of providing a world-class customer experience. These are the 10 principles shared by every great customer service organization. Now your management can take the C-SAT.

You can determine the service aptitude of your organization by going to www.thedijuliusgroup.com/SAT and taking the C-SAT. Upon completing it, you will receive a report on how your organization fares, its strengths and weaknesses, and other information. There is no charge, and you can take this test online as many times as you want. No results are ever shared; your results are confidential.

This test is designed so that individual departments may take it and score themselves independently. It will take approximately 15 minutes to answer all the questions. If you are taking it to determine the level of customer service delivered by your company, there are two approaches you can take: (1) look at your entire organization's customer service as a whole, or (2) look at the customer service of each individual department (i.e., sales, technical support, call center) or location. If you choose to take it by department or location, you will obviously have to take it once for each department or location you have. This allows you to determine which departments, managers, and front-line employees are stronger and which are weaker. Department scores may then be averaged to find an overall company score.

Answer the questions as honestly and critically as possible, so that your score can be determined accurately.

You can take the test as often as you like. You can always re-take the test as you progress and implement new strategies. Set yourself a goal to be at a higher level in four months, and at that point, retake the test. Use it as a benchmark for where you ultimately want to be.

> Whenever in doubt between two answers, opt for the lesser (the more conservative) answer. It is much more advantageous to rate yourself slightly lower.

## C-SAT Report

Within seconds of completing the test, you will receive a C-SAT report emailed directly to you, sharing your company's service aptitude level based on your answers. (See Figure 4.2.)

Direct Opinions, a leading market research and performance measurement studies company headquartered in Beachwood, Ohio, helped The DiJulius Group create the following C-SAT.

THE DiJULIUS
GROUP

*Creating World-Class Customer Service Organizations*

**The DiJulius Group C-Sat (Company-Service Aptitude Test)**
RESULTS

| | |
|---|---|
| **Test taken for:** | Overall Company Standards |
| **Pre-test prediction:** | Level 4, Above Average |

| | CATEGORY | SCORE |
|---|---|---|
| I. | Service Vision | Above Average |
| II. | World Class Internal Culture | Average |
| III. | Non-Negotiable Customer Service Standards | World Class |
| IV. | Secret Service Systems | Unacceptable |
| V. | Training to Deliver the Ultimate Customer Experience | Below Average |
| VI. | Implement and Execute | World Class |
| VII. | Zero Risk | Average |
| VIII. | Creating an Above & Beyond Legacy | Above Average |
| IX. | Measuring Your Customer's Experience | Above Average |
| X. | World Class Leadership | Average |
| XX. | Comprehensive | Average |

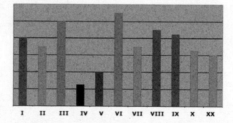

Final Service Aptitude Score for Habernathy Insurance Company
**LEVEL 3, AVERAGE**

To view a full report, please visit the following link:
http://www.thedijuliusgroup.com/sat/view.php?munid=136&atunid=166&unid=5

Visit our website to find out how to improve your Company's Service Aptitude www.thedijuliusgroup.com

**FIGURE 4.2** Typical C-SAT Report

# Company Service Aptitude Test

## Intro Questions

Please select how your answers will be applied when taking
this test. I am answering the questions based on:                    _____

1. Overall company standards
2. My specific department's standards
3. My location's standards

    Before beginning, please select which answer you believe
best describes your company's current customer service level:    _____

    Level 1 Unacceptable
    Level 2 Below Average
    Level 3 Average
    Level 4 Above Average
    Level 5 World Class

    For the following questions, select the statement that applies:

A. Extremely Inaccurate
B. Somewhat Inaccurate
C. Somewhat Accurate
D. Extremely Accurate

## I. Service Vision

### A clear purpose of why the business exists

1. Our company has a strong service vision which
   instills service passion in all employees.                     _____
2. Our employees can articulate what our service brand
   promise(s) is.                                                  _____
3. Our employees are educated on how critical their
   role is in successfully delivering our service brand promise.   _____
4. Our company constantly articulates our service brand
   promise and vision to all NEW employees during
   their orientation.                                             _____
5. Our company constantly articulates our service brand
   promise and vision to all EXISTING employees through
   various communications (i.e., signage, meetings).              _____

## II. Creating a World-Class Internal Culture

**Attract, hire, and retain only the people who have the Service DNA**

1. We have a daily staff meeting with employees, in person or by phone, at the start of each workday/shift. _____
2. Our company's culture was created intentionally by design with constant focus on company values, not just announced. _____
3. Our employees police each other on meeting customer service standards. _____
4. Our internal/employee culture is very strong. _____
5. Prospective employees go through multiple interviews before being offered a position. _____
6. It is more difficult to obtain a position in our company than our competitor's because of our strict hiring process and expectations. _____
7. Our company/department is not understaffed. _____
8. Turnover at our organization is significantly better than our industry standard. _____
9. Customer service skills are a major part of our hiring, screening and selection process. _____
10. Customer service is a key factor in our review and promotion process. _____
11. All applicants are prescreened with a required customer service test. _____
12. Customer service standards and expectations are discussed during the interview process. _____
13. It is clear to prospective employees that failure to meet customer service standards will prohibit long-term employment. _____
14. Our company is proactively hiring. _____

## III. Nonnegotiable Experiential Standards

**Experience standards everyone must follow**

1. Our organization is excellent at creating relationships. _____
2. Our personal service is not overshadowed by our technology (i.e., automated services). _____

3. Our company distinguishes between operational standards and experiential standards. _____

4. Our company has nonnegotiable customer service standards at every point of customer contact. _____

## IV. *Secret Service* Systems

Utilizing customer intelligence to personalize their experience and engage and anticipate their needs

1. Our employees use positive language and always avoid saying "no" to the customer. _____

2. Employees are warm and welcoming and smile during customer interactions. _____

3. We use a unique process to manage new customers differently than existing customers, i.e., provide additional information, directions. _____

4. Employees introduce themselves to each customer they have an encounter with. _____

5. Employees mention the customer's previous purchase history, personal preferences or other information that has been acquired in the past. _____

6. Our employees record customer preferences. _____

7. Employees remember and use the customer's name 2 to 4 times during each encounter. _____

8. Our company has a clear system for acknowledging VIP customers that even new employees are able to follow. _____

9. We have a VIP program to provide special perks for our top customers. _____

## V. Training To Provide a World-Class Customer Experience

Systems and processes that remove variation and provide a consistent customer experience

1. Employees are trained in the classroom on customer service as well as on the job service training. _____

2. Our employees are fully trained on customer service skills before they are permitted customer interaction. _____

3. Our employees are screened and tested on their service aptitude. _____

4. Our customer experience standards, for each point of customer contact, are documented and used to train every new hire. _____

5. All employees are tested and certified on our nonnegotiable customer service standards. _____

6. We provide soft-skill customer service training for all NEW employees regardless of their position. _____

7. We provide soft-skill customer service training and recertification for all EXISTING employees at least annually. _____

8. Our customer experience cycle is well outlined and our employees understand each stage. _____

9. How many hours of CUSTOMER SERVICE TRAINING, soft skill, nontechnical training, does your company provide to each NEW employee? _____
   • 0   • 1–5   • 6–10   • 11–15   • 16 & up

10. How many hours of CUSTOMER SERVICE TRAINING, soft skill, nontechnical training, does your company provide to each EXISTING employee per year? _____
    • 0   • 1–3   • 4–7   • 8–11   • 12 & up

## VI. Implementation and Execution

**How to go from ideas on a paper to being consistently executed**

1. New initiatives are introduced slowly and do not overwhelm employees. _____

2. Employees are aware of new initiatives that will be rolled out with plenty of lead time for training. _____

3. Our managers coach and immediately address inconsistencies with our customer service standards. _____

4. We monitor our service standards and know who is executing them and who is not. _____

5. Our organization consistently follows through on the execution of new initiatives. _____

## VII. Zero Risk

**Anticipating your service defects and having protocols in place to make it right**

1. Our company receives very few complaints concerning our customer service. _____
2. Any of our employees would know how to make it right if we dropped the ball on a VIP customer. _____
3. Our website includes a direct number, on each page, for customers to contact a person directly if they have a challenge. _____
4. Any employee who answers the phone can satisfy a customer challenge. _____
5. Employees use the protocol we have in place to resolve the most common reoccurring service defects. _____
6. Employees know they are empowered to do what it takes to make things right. _____
7. Employees know how to make things right without guidance or approval. _____
8. Our employees trust our customers. _____
9. Our employees make our customers feel that the Customer is always right. _____
10. Every member of our staff delivers outstanding customer service, even when difficult challenges arise. _____
11. All employees are aware of potential service defects at every point of customer contact. _____
12. All employees are tested on their awareness of potential service defects at every point of customer contact. _____

## VIII. Creating an Above-and-Beyond Culture

**Constant awareness and branding of how to be a hero**

1. Our employees are aware of opportunities to go above and beyond with customers. _____
2. Our employees buy into the concept of going above and beyond for the customer. _____
3. Our employees are willing to do whatever it takes to outperform our customer's expectations. _____

4. Employees constantly seek ways to go above and beyond for the customer. _____

5. We publicize above-and-beyond stories back to our employees. _____

6. All employees are tested on their ability to recognize above-and-beyond opportunities at every point of customer contact. _____

7. Our organization has an established award to recognize employees that go above and beyond on a regular basis. _____

## IX. Measuring Your Customer's Experience

**What gets measured gets managed**

1. We have a formal process in place to follow up with each and every customer challenge. _____

2. We have a clearly defined means of measuring customer satisfaction objectively. _____

3. We have a defined process to track customer comments and trend issues for internal process improvement. _____

4. We use results from our customer service measurement program to consistently improve our service. _____

5. Our company has an established process to follow-up with every inactive customer to understand why they haven't purchased recently. _____

6. We use information from our lost customers to improve our processes or service. _____

7. We have a formalized contact plan to communicate with all customers on a regular basis. _____

8. We use a third-party service to conduct customer satisfaction surveys with our customers. _____

9. Customer satisfaction results impact our managers' compensation and incentives. _____

## X. World-Class Leadership

**Walking the talk**

1. The service aptitude of our management team is very high. _____

2. All of our managers—regardless of location/department— know how to create a world-class culture. _____

3. Our company has training programs that coach managers in monitoring the employee lifecycle. _____

4. Our company's senior management has regular contact with our customers. _____

5. Customer service performance is a component linked to management compensation. _____

6. All managers are empowered and trusted to use their best judgment when handling a customer crisis. _____

7. All managers are aware of potential service defects at every point of customer contact. _____

8. All managers are tested on their awareness of potential service defects at every point of customer contact. _____

## XI. Comprehensive

1. I am extremely satisfied with the level of customer service our organization delivers. _____

2. Our customer service is better today than it was a year ago. _____

3. If we continue our current practices, I am 100% confident that our customer service will be better a year from now than it is today. _____

4. It is extremely easy for our customers to do business with our organization, with regards to technology, payment methods, policies, use of website, phone systems, traffic flows, availability of product and hours of operation. _____

5. Our employees' levels of expertise with regards to product knowledge, competency of equipment, product knowledge, and industry awareness are very high. _____

6. Our organization is excellent at cleanliness, dress code, following systems and processes, tasks, stocking inventory, attention to detail, etc. _____

7. The service aptitude of our employees is very high. _____

8. Our company does not outsource customer service departments. _____

9. Deficient customer service by any employee is immediately addressed. _____

10. Unacceptable behavior to a customer has led to employee dismissal. _____

11. Our company's customer service is stronger than our major competitor's.        _____

12. Our company will refuse business if it compromises our quality of service.        _____

Examples of online report issued are shown in Figure 4.2.

## Recommended Action Plan

Everyone in your organization should take this test so that you get a cross section of feedback on how your internal employees feel your service is and you also gain many other insights. For example, your managers may rate your customer service a level 4, while your front-line employees rate it a 3. Whose perspective would be more accurate in this case? The front-line employees, since they are the ones interacting with the customers the most. This report also tells you specifically what areas are holding you back from being a level IV or V customer service organization. Although you may be only a level III customer service company, you may have strengths in hiring, customer recovery, above-and-beyond service and your weaknesses could be in training, culture, and customer service measurements. By getting those three factors up a certain percent, you would elevate your company to the next level (see sample report in Figure 4.2).

It is recommended that this test be taken quarterly, so you can uncover the areas you need to address, create a strategy to improve each area, and retake it the following quarter. You can also compare departments and averages of managers' scores. Obviously this test is only telling you what your internal people feel about your customer service. To learn more about what your customer feels about your customer service, see Chapter 13, "Measuring Your Customer's Experience."

It is estimated that the following percentages are how companies would fall into the appropriate levels of customer service:

**Company Service Aptitude Levels (C-SAT)**

| Level | Description | Companies (%) |
| --- | --- | --- |
| Level 1 | Unacceptable | 12 |
| Level 2 | Below Average | 29 |
| Level 3 | Average | 38 |
| Level 4 | Above Average | 18 |
| Level 5 | World Class | 3 |

## The Next Step

Once you determine your service aptitude level, you can begin applying the 10 Commandments to provide a world-class customer experience. This is the focus of Chapters 5 through 14.

# Notes

1. Richard K. Hendrie, "The Why, What and How of WOW" *ehotelier.com*, March 25, 2005, http://ehotelier.com/browse/news_more.php?id=A4593_0 _11_0_M.

# The Customer
# Service Revolution

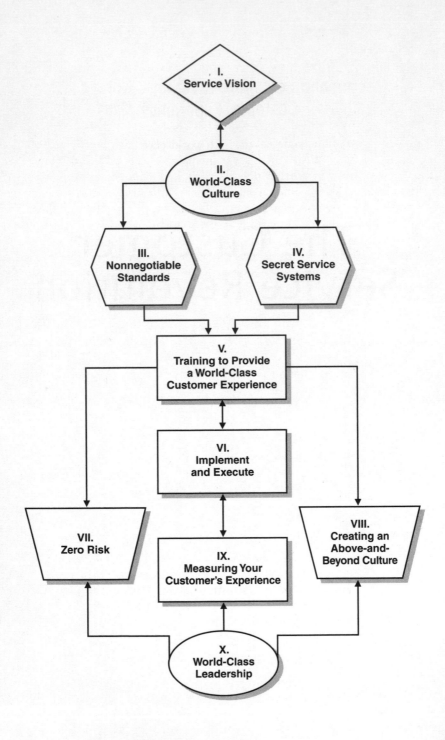

# X Commandments for Providing a World-Class Customer Experience

From years of studying and working with world-class customer service organizations, I have found that there are principles they all have in common that differentiate them from other organizations and elevate them to a different customer service level. These commandments of world-class service are irrefutable. There are not nine or eleven, there are ten. They do not change, or become obsolete. Just as important as the commandments themselves, is the order of the commandments, here, referred to as the *Chain of Commandments*. The commandments are arranged in the precise sequence necessary for an organization to provide a world-class customer experience. It is impossible for an organization to reach its optimum level of service attitude and customer satisfaction without proficiently executing each commandment.

I. *Service Vision:* A clear purpose of why the business exists.

First and foremost every organization that provides superior service has a strong Service Vision that creates a clear direction for everyone in that business—the true underlying purpose of what an organization brings to the community and why your customers buy from you that they couldn't get elsewhere (Chapter 5).

You must start with a Service Vision before anything else can take shape in your organization. The Service Vision drives hiring, standards, training, leadership philosophies, and so on. Without the Service Vision, you are like a pilot without a flight plan. How will you know where you are headed?

II. *Creating a World-Class Internal Culture:* Attract, hire, and retain only the people who have the Service DNA.

Creating a world-class internal culture that only attracts, hires, and retains the people who are capable of upholding the Service Vision of the organization (Chapter 6).

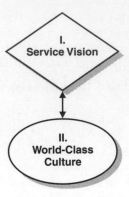

Building your culture using your Service Vision to guide you will make or break the success of the following eight commandments.

III. *Nonnegotiable Experiential Standards:* Experience standards everyone must follow.

Have nonnegotiable experience standards for each stage of the organization's customer experience cycle. These experiential standards allow employees to provide a consistent engaging experience that is unlike the majority of competitors. Employees must consistently execute each of these standards (Chapter 7).

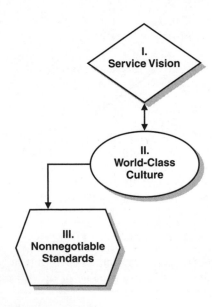

Your Service Vision is clear and you are adding the people that truly share in that vision; now you have to create experiential standards that will allow that Service Vision to be of value to your customer.

IV. *Secret Service Systems:* Utilizing Customer intelligence to personalize their experience and engage and anticipate their needs.

Create Secret Service systems that easily enable front-line employees to personalize the customer's experience by engaging them and anticipating and delivering on their needs (Chapter 8).

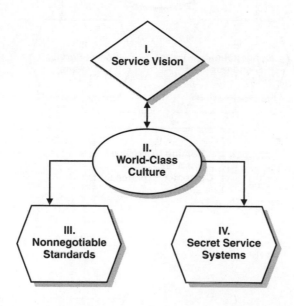

Having great standards is not enough, you now need to systemize those standards in order for them to be realistically delivered on a consistent basis.

V. *Training to Provide a World-Class Customer Experience:* Systems and processes that remove variation and provide a consistent customer experience.

Create an incredible training program for all new and existing employees consisting of soft-skill training that increases their service aptitude, giving them the knowledge and tools to provide a world-class customer experience (Chapter 9).

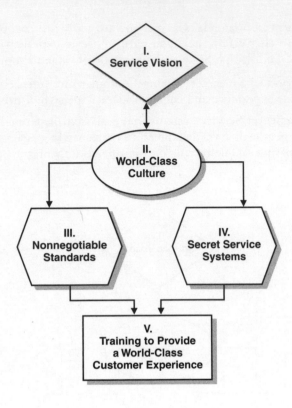

You have turned standards into systems, but who knows about them? It is critical to ensure every new employee gets trained on these standardized systems, otherwise the next generation of employees will dilute your Service Vision.

VI. *Implementation and Execution:* How to go from ideas on a paper to being consistently executed.

A solid process that allows the realistic implementation of the customer service initiatives and systems that are executed consistently by front-line employees (Chapter 10).

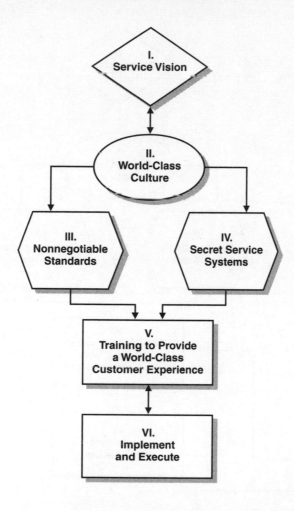

Without execution, systems in manuals are nothing more than ideas on paper. This is where most companies fail, the execution of these systems. The implementation and accountability for these standards and systems are every manager's responsibility.

VII. *Zero Risk:* Anticipating your service defects and having protocols in place to make it right.

All employees must have full awareness of the potential common service defects that can arise at each stage of the customer experience cycle and be trained and empowered to provide great service recovery when defects arise, so your company is known to be zero risk to deal with (Chapter 11).

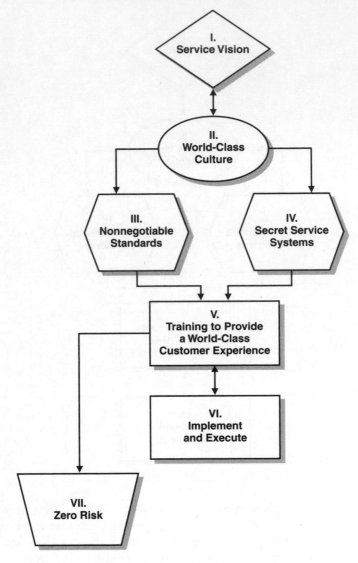

Everyone's service aptitude appears strong when things are going smoothly, an employee's or company's true service aptitude is revealed when things don't go as planned and service defects arise.

VIII. *Creating an Above-and-Beyond Culture:* Constant awareness and branding of how to be a hero.

Create an awareness of the most common opportunities where employees can really deliver heroic service for the customer that creates an above-and-beyond culture (Chapter 12).

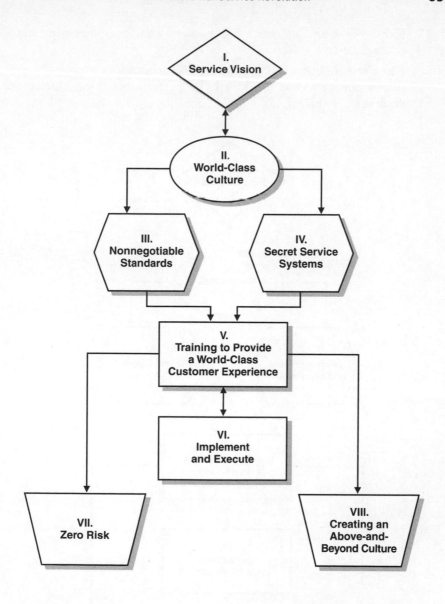

Are your employees empowered and inspired to exceed customer expectations? Do you have mechanisms in place to collect and redistribute above-and-beyond stories to constantly remind your employees of the Service Vision?

IX. *Measuring Your Customer's Experience:* What gets measured gets managed.

Use a scientific method to measure your customer's experience and satisfaction, providing benchmarks for performance in each location/department (Chapter 13).

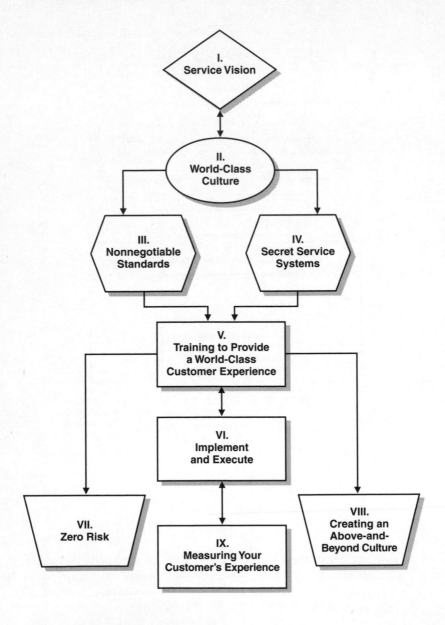

Your goals must be measurable, tied to a specific metric that lets you measure: how satisfied your customers are with you, who is clearly doing it, who is inconsistent, are you keeping your Service Brand Promise to your customers, how effective your service recovery is, and how do you stack up against your competition.

X. *World-Class Leadership:* Walking the talk.

Every world-class customer service organization is world-class to work for. It takes world-class leadership to provide the passion, inspiration, and discipline to all employees (Chapter 14).

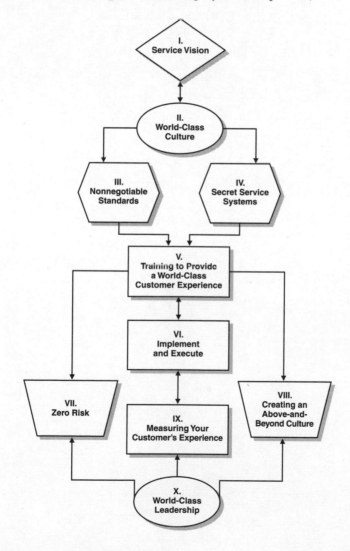

While this is the final commandment, it is the most important, having the most impact and responsibility for the success of all 10.

Chapters 5 through 14 cover one of the commandments in detail sharing how the top customer service companies possess these traits.

# 5

# Commandment I: Service Vision

## A clear purpose of why the business exists

*A company's Service Vision serves as a rallying point across the organization by being the one thing that all employees have in common no matter what the individual job or title may be.*[1]

—Disney Institute

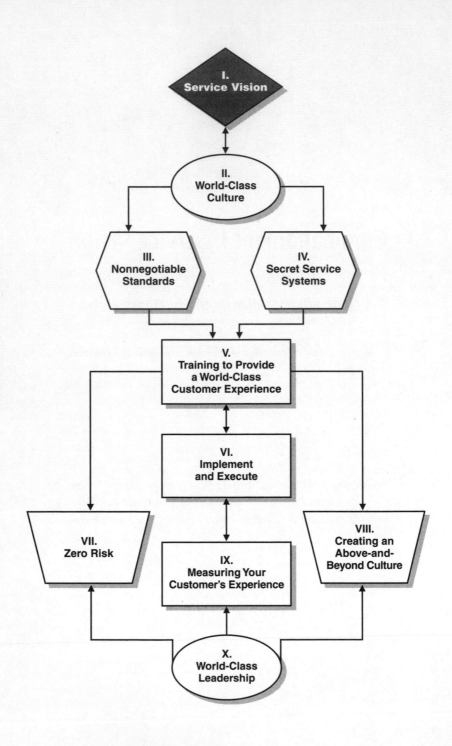

First and foremost an organization must have a strong *Service Vision* that communicates clearly the type of service culture to all of their employees. The vision articulates the true underlying purpose of why your organization exists and offers customers what they can't get elsewhere.

The level of service you wish to provide must be established before many other aspects of your organization can take shape. The Service Vision influences hiring standards, training, leadership philosophies, and your overall business model.

When James McManemon, General Manager of The Ritz-Carlton was asked, "If you were starting a new business, any business, and wanted to make customer service your value proposition, what would you do first?" His response, "The first thing I would do is create the Service Vision for the company. Be crystal clear with what the company's Vision is and be able to articulate that extremely well. Then I would hire talent based on that same belief, only adding employees that share those service values, and finally create the processes and training to achieve that Service Vision."

Sounds pretty simple: (1) create the Service Vision (Commandment I), (2) hire talent that aligns with that Vision (Commandment II), (3) create the processes (Commandments III and IV), and (4) train to achieve that Vision (Commandment V). In my experiences, every world-class service organization does all that extremely well. However, many companies do not. The 79 percent of companies operating at levels 1, 2, and 3 on the service aptitude scale never truly create a Service Vision for their company. They may use words like "service" and "experience" and "client first," but without a true Service Vision, these slogans are stale slogans that everyone else is using as well.

The global business culture that prevails today is broken. What it needs is a radical transformation, a monumental paradigm shift that will reshape our present understanding of the true purpose of work.[2]

Many entrepreneurs open a business, find a niche, start growing, and one day have a business that hits a wall because they have added so many people, none who share a common focus or direction. "A Service Vision is like a flight plan for a pilot, without it he has no idea where he is headed," says McManemon. "People want to be led by someone they trust and who has a vision. It is about employee engagement, making your employees a part of the success of the organization."

> An organization's vision represents the purpose of its existence, the
> heart of what it is as an entity.[3]
>
> —*Dan J. Sanders, Author*

**Service Vision:** The true underlying value of what your organization brings to your customers, that provides a meaningful purpose
for your employees.

## Creating a Successful Service Vision

There are two critical parts in creating a successful Service Vision:

1. Finding a way to articulate your company's purpose and vision.
2. Analyzing how well you consistently market that vision internally to
   your employees and how well you make the connection between how
   your employees' roles impact and support that Service Vision.

## Disney's Service Vision

Disney calls it a "Service Theme." According to Walt Disney himself, a
Service Theme is the basis of its mission as a business; it represents what
the company stands for and why it exists.[4] "Leaders die, products become
obsolete, markets change, new technologies emerge, and management fads
come and go, but core ideology in a great company endures as a great guidance and inspiration," appeared in a *Harvard Business Review* article.[5]

Many Service Visions become stale, lose their meaning, or become
something to which no one pays attention to anymore. The *Harvard Business Review* article goes on to say that a Service Theme is not something
that can simply be declared, but it reflects existing truths about a company.

Disney's Service Theme: *To create happiness by providing the finest in
entertainment, to people of all ages, everywhere,* creates a clear focus, commu-
nicating an ultimate goal to their 100,000+ people who work for the company. It serves as a rallying point across the organization by being the one
thing that all employees have in common no matter what their individual

job or title may be. Tom Peters wrote in his landmark book, *In Search of Excellence;* "Excellent companies all seem to have service themes that pervade the institution."[6]

## How to Create a Service Vision

Creating a Service Vision is a lot like creating a mission statement for the organization. It should be a brief concise sentence; think back to Disney's Service Vision: *To create happiness by providing the finest in entertainment, to people of all ages, everywhere.* A word of caution: If it takes your leadership team less than 30 hours to develop, it probably will just be a bumper sticker with no meaning. To be successful, it requires the correct effort. This is so much more difficult than it appears. It is never the product or service that you sell, it is the underlying purpose of why your company is in existence.

A Service Vision should be something senior management debates heavily. It must be created from the legacy of the company. Every great service company is a storytelling company. It constantly tells folklore stories over and over again about how employees deliver on their Service Vision to the customers. In the daily preshift huddle, these stories keep the service philosophy front and center in every employee's mind and put a burden on both existing and new employees to continue that legacy.

## Creating a Service Brand Promise

Once you have a strong Service Vision, you want to support it with Service Brand Promises, which are keywords, phrases, quotes, and "isms" that are repeated over and over again in your company that reinforce your Service Vision.

A few ways to create your own Service Brand Promise can be accomplished by the following exercises:

- Asking "What business are we in?"
- Asking "What do we sell?"
- Determining what is "Priceless" to your customer.
- Answering "What is the long-term benefit of doing business with us over many years?"
- Determining how you can make price irrelevant to your customers.

> What business are you in?

If you ask anyone at Nemacolin Resort, "What business are you in?" you should hear: "Making friends and creating a lifetime of memories is our business."

# How Inspirational Are Your Service Brand Promises?

Do you even have one? Some companies do not see the value in developing a Service Brand Promise because they feel it is just warm and fuzzy words that have no meaning. I disagree!

Every world-class customer service company I have ever studied has an inspirational Service Brand Promise that reminds how it wants employees to care for its most important asset—its customers.

The most common answers I hear when I ask businesses what they sell are:

- We sell ourselves.
- We sell service.
- We sell an experience.
- We are in the people business.

These Service Brand Promises are overused and stale. A Service Brand Promise does not always have to be something you advertise to the public. Some companies make it public others do not. Regardless, it is an internal marketing tool that, if advertised continuously to your employees, reinforces your Service Vision.

## Powerful Service Brand Promises

See if you can guess which company has each of the following Service Brand Promises:

### Service Brand Promise
Whatever/whenever
The answer's "yes" . . . what's the question?

No rules

Nothing is impossible

Perfect night out

Making price irrelevant

We are ladies and gentlemen serving ladies and gentlemen

What does each of these Service Brand Promises advertise to its employees?

- *Whatever/Whenever:* This says it all. This company does a fantastic job of advertising this promise to its people, who are required to answer every phone call by saying "Whatever/Whenever." After answering the phone this way, how can an employee possibly say "no" to a customer?
- *The Answer's "Yes":* This communicates a few concepts to employees: (1) No is not an option. (2) Be creative and find a way to make it happen.
- *No Rules:* This says, "Just ask us. However you want it, you get it."
- *Nothing Is Impossible:* This tells employees that no request is too ridiculous. Find a way to make it happen. This promise also works internally for the newly hired employee who dreams of heading a department or even the company.
- *Perfect Night Out:* This reinforces (1) the customer's entire reason for dealing with the company, and (2), the objective of every employee, regardless of his or her position in the company. Every employee plays a part in this promise.
- *Making Price Irrelevant:* Based on the experience they received, customers feel your prices are an incredible value.
- *Ladies and Gentlemen Serving Ladies and Gentlemen:* As service professionals, we treat our guests and each other with respect and dignity.

## The Answers

| Service Brand Promise | Company |
|---|---|
| Whatever/whenever | W Hotel |
| The answer's "yes" . . . what's the question? | Cameron Mitchell Restaurants |
| No rules | Outback Steakhouse |
| Nothing is impossible | Nemacolin Woodlands Resort |
| Perfect night out | The Melting Pot Restaurant |

| Service Brand Promise | Company |
|---|---|
| Making price irrelevant | The DiJulius Group |
| We are ladies and gentlemen serving ladies and gentlemen | The Ritz-Carlton |

## Is It Expensive Coffee—or Inexpensive Rent?

Recently, I had the pleasure of working with Starbuck Corporation's subsidiary, Seattle's Best Coffee Company. This is a very impressive organization that does all the right things to produce a strong service culture. While researching them, I found that one hurdle for their front-line employees was that they might need to overcome feeling guilty for selling a cup of coffee for over $4. So I started thinking about what they *really* sell. I remembered one of my favorite sitcoms, *Friends*, and how Ross, Rachel, and Chandler hung out at Central Perk, their favorite coffeehouse, for hours laughing, having a good time, and being friends.

I thought about all the times I meet people at places like Seattle's Best Coffee or Starbucks. It may be an old friend from school, a potential client, a neighbor, or a relative. Our 15-minute get-togethers turn into two-hour sessions. Then it hit me: What a deal! Places like Starbucks and Seattle's Best Coffee aren't selling an expensive cup of coffee; they are selling really inexpensive rent. Think about it, a living room for people to connect, hang out, and enjoy each other's company, all for under $10 to $15 is a bargain.

Starbucks envisions local outlets as a "third place" (besides home and work) to spend time, and their store design is intended to achieve this. The café section of the store is often outfitted with overstuffed chairs and small tables with hard-backed chairs. Most stores provide wireless internet access.[7]

What does your company sell? Fully develop a value proposition that is so strong that your newest employee runs home to tell a parent, spouse, or neighbor, "Hey, do you know what business we are really in?"

## What Is Your Company's Priceless?

I have found a very effective way of helping organizations figure out a Service Brand Promise by borrowing from the MasterCard "priceless" commercials. Picture MasterCard using your organization in their next priceless commercial. What would be your company's priceless tag line? Let's look at a few examples.

## A Couple Dining at the Melting Pot Restaurant

| | |
|---|---|
| Babysitter | $45 |
| Dinner for two with a bottle of wine | $125 |
| The perfect night out | PRICELESS |

## John Robert's Spa

| | |
|---|---|
| Precision haircut and styling with Master Hair Designer | $100 |
| Carmel blonde highlights | $125 |
| Makeup, manicure and spa pedicure | $110 |
| Being called a Hottie! | PRICELESS |

## Secret Service Workshop

| | |
|---|---|
| Attending a workshop by THE authority on world-class customer experience | $500 |
| Autographed copy of *What's the Secret?* | $20 |
| Making Price Irrelevant to your customers | PRICELESS |

### Have a Five-Year-Old's Mentality

This is another way to figure out your organization's higher purpose. I have found that when doing this exercise, most companies don't think big enough and come up with bland Service Brand Promises. For instance, I was working with a financial services company, helping people plan for their retirement, and their first attempt at their priceless tag line was "20 percent annual return on your retirement investment." Boring! So I started thinking like my five-year-old son, Bo, who always asks, "why" to everything.

> Why do your clients want a 20 percent annual return?
> They responded, "So they can create wealth."

> Why do they want to create wealth?
> "So they can have something to retire on."

> Why do they need something to retire on?
> "So they don't have to work till the day they die and so their standard of living doesn't change."

After having this type of dialogue, they created a new purpose for their customers:

> Being able to retire five years earlier than you expected and maintain your standard of living . . . PRICELESS.

# A Few of My Favorite "isms"

A company can have several Service Brand Promises. They can also be a company's "ism"—a saying that gets repeated over and over again, that instills the service philosophy the company wants every associate to have. Does your company have an ism?

### Levy-isms

Started in Chicago over 25 years ago, Levy Restaurants have 100 locations such as in sport stadiums, arenas, convention centers, zoos, racetracks, and many free-standing restaurants around the country. Today, the company generates $1 billion in annual revenue.

- WOCAAT—Winning One Customer at a Time.™
- We can't be 100 percent better than our competition, but we can be 1 percent better in a 100 different ways.

### The Ritz-Carlton-ism

- Anticipate and fulfill the unexpressed needs of our guests

### Disney-ism

- Creating Magical Moments

### Starbucks-ism

- We are not in the coffee business serving people; we are in the people business serving coffee.

### John Robert's Spa-ism

- We are people's trips to Paris.

# Personal Service Brand Promises

I have seen people have their own Service Brand Promises, which work in exactly the same way as they do for companies. The individual uses the promise to keep focused on his true underlying purpose and on the value proposition of the role he plays for his customers. Here are a few of my favorites.

## Daymaker

Several years ago, David Wagner in Minneapolis changed his title from that of hairdresser to Daymaker. He even put Daymaker on his business cards under his name. His card prompted people to ask, "What do you do?" and he replied, "I make people's day." Who would you rather go to, a hairstylist or someone who calls himself a Daymaker? Today David Wagner is the owner of JUUT Salonspa, which has nine locations, and he has written a successful book, *Life as a Daymaker.*[8]

## Your Best Friend

Tom Smith's official title at Nemacolin Resort, is National Sales + Indulgence Officer. But ask him what his title is, and he will say, "Your Best Friend." That's exactly what he means to his customers. Whatever you need, Tom Smith delivers it. He lives by Nemacolin's Service Brand Promise: "Nothing's impossible." If you want to take someone on a romantic getaway, he will see to it that you look like the most romantic person in the world, from rose petals all over the room to a warm bubble bath waiting and your significant other's favorite bottle of wine uncorked. If you want to impress a customer you send to Nemacolin, Tom Smith and his team will find out her preferences, have them waiting for her, and of course give you the credit.

> You do not merely want to be considered just the best of the best. You want to be considered the only ones who do what you do.[9]
>
> —*Jerry Garcia*

## THE Authority on World-Class Customer Experience

This is my personal Service Brand Promise to my clients. As an author, speaker, and consultant, customer service is all I do. I turn down over 25 percent of business opportunities a year because it is not a fit for what I do best. If you want a sales speaker or a leadership consultant, I can recommend some good ones, but I am not your guy. I focus totally and constantly on studying, researching, and working with the best customer service organizations on what works and doesn't work for companies with regards to being world-class. If you want someone to take your organization's customer service to a whole new level and make price irrelevant, you can't find anyone better to do it.

One of my clients, cj Advertising has a similar focus. cj Advertising, headquartered in Nashville, Tennessee, is the largest full-service direct response advertising firm exclusively serving personal injury attorneys in the United States. They do an amazing job for their clients and it is not difficult to figure out why. First, they only work with law firms. If you are an accounting firm or doctor's office and you want to hire them to do your web site or a marketing project, they will have to turn you away. Their clients, the law firms, can trust that cj Advertising knows the legal industry and the legal complexities of advertising and marketing, as well as, if not better than their own law firms do. And second, they offer market exclusivity with every client. They do not have or will not take on as clients, two law firms from the same city that compete against each other. That's the kind of vendor/partner you want for your business.

The Melting Pot Restaurants, 110+ franchised locations, not only have several great Service Brand Promises, but Kendra Sartor, Vice President of Brand Development, does an incredible job of marketing to the outside world, while being equally effective at articulating the franchise vision internally through The Melting Pot MVP card (Figure 5.1). The MVP card is something that you will find on most managers, and they really live it. It is a compass that guides them to accomplishing their mission: "To provide our guests a chance to escape, create memories, and pursue their dreams" by creating the perfect night out by having happy team members, genuine hospitality, immaculate, inviting surroundings, and exceptional food and beverage.

One of the clearest Service Visions I have come across is Sport Clips, headquartered in Georgetown, Texas, which created a strong Service Vision that is unique to moderately priced models. But through the uncompromising focus of their Service Vision, Sport Clips has grown to over 500 locations throughout the United States.

"Our value system is composed of our mission statement, our Heart of a Champion, and our three key questions," says Clete Brewer, President of Sport Clips. "These serve as our foundation for team members and franchisees. It allows us to get the right folks to service our clients with a Championship Experience."

**MVP**
MISSION · VISION · PRINCIPLES
MOST VALUABLE PLAYER

The Melting Pot.
*a fondue restaurant*
*Dip into something different*

**What It Takes To Be A Most Valuable Player At The Melting Pot...**

We believe that you are the key ingredient in our mission to provide the Perfect Night Out for our guests. Everyone is capable of being an MVP. Here are just a few examples of how each of us can give an all-star performance:

**The Entire Team**

- Know everything about the food and beverages we offer our guests
- Be the final check in quality control
- Take care of every guest's needs as a team
- Show our commitment to providing the Perfect Night Out through our commitment to the four key ingredients
- Strive for ways to always go above and beyond for our guests and your fellow team members

**Front Of The House**

- Smile, make eye contact and warmly greet every guest
- Have impeccably neat and clean uniforms, tables and stations that are always set and ready to go
- Anticipate our guests' needs before they realize the need
- Make each guest feel important and special
- Create an emotional attachment to our restaurant by helping our guests create great memories
- Strive for ways to always go above and beyond for our guests and your fellow team members

**Heart Of The House**

- Make sanitation and food safety your first priority
- Provide exceptional food every time
- Never compromise for the sake of time
- Strive for ways to always go above and beyond for our guests and your fellow team members

**Management**

- Take ownership of the Perfect Night Out mission
- Lead by example and attitude
- Set a high standard for performance and hold yourself and others accountable
- Provide feedback and listen to your team
- Help others grow, advance and achieve great rewards
- Strive for ways to always go above and beyond for our guests and your fellow team members

The Melting Pot restaurants were built on ambition, resolve and passion. We are empowering you to use that same motivation to do whatever it takes to deliver the Perfect Night Out for our guests!

**FIGURE 5.1** The Melting Pot MVP Card

*(continued)*

**YOU ARE THE KEY INGREDIENT IN OUR RECIPE FOR SUCCESS!**

The Melting Pot is more than a restaurant—it's a movement of incredibly passionate people providing our guests a chance to escape, create memories and pursue their dreams. Whether it's a special celebration, time spent with good friends or an opportunity to WOW a business partner, we are giving our cherished guests a chance to dip into something different!

At The Melting Pot, we fight for this cause every day. Our management teams are a faithful, dedicated group that guides our fondue ambassadors. These hard-working, devoted team members spearhead our movement, and we call them our Most Valuable Players – those of you who are committed to promoting our Mission, sharing our Vision and living our Principles. You are the future of our business!

**MISSION**

To create the Perfect Night Out for our guests by bringing each of these four key ingredients to the table: Happy Team Members, Genuine Hospitality, Immaculate, Inviting Surroundings and Exceptional Food and Beverage.

Genuine Hospitality

Happy Team Members

**PERFECT NIGHT OUT**

Immaculate, Inviting Surroundings

Hospitable Food & Beverage

The Perfect Night Out is not possible without our four key ingredients!

**VISION**

To be the restaurant of first choice

**WE WILL REALIZE THIS VISION WHEN WE DO THESE THINGS...**

For Our Team Members...
- Provide a fun place to work
- Recognize and reward each other
- Make decisions based on our Principles

For Our Guests...
- Deliver the Perfect Night Out
- Anticipate our guests' needs before they realize the need
- Make them feel important and special
- Create an emotional attachment to our restaurant by helping our guests create great memories

For Our Vendors...
- Treat our vendors as our partners
- Be fair in all business dealings
- Expect the best so we can be the best
- Communicate honestly and directly regarding their services and products

**PRINCIPLES**

**PRIDE**
Passion and enthusiasm for our rich guest service tradition

**QUALITY**
Putting your five senses in

**LEADERSHIP**
Inspiring others by example and attitude

**ACCOUNTABILITY**
You see it, you own it

**TEAMWORK**
There is no team without ME

**LEARNING**
Four courses for life

**HOSPITALITY**
Service from the heart

**FAMILY / BELONGING**
Caring for those around you

**INTEGRITY**
The moment of truth

**FIGURE 5.1** *(Continued)*

*Heart of a Champion:* Sport Clips ask their team members and franchisees to:

- Do what's right,
- Do your best, and
- Treat others the way they want to be treated.

*3 Key Questions:* Sport Clips asks of each person we hire and each team leader who comes into the system:

1. Can I trust you?
2. Do you care about me?
3. Are you committed to excellence?

And last and most important, *the Sport Clips' Mission Statement:* To create a championship haircut experience for men and boys in an exciting sports environment.

"The best thing about this is I would bet that 85 percent of our store managers can recite all three of these. It is really a part of us," says Brewer. In January 2007, *Entrepreneur* magazine named Sport Clips the 72nd best franchise in America and the 49th fastest growing franchise.

Lexus cars are about living the elegant, good life; Nike's shoes represent the possibility of Olympian achievement; Disney's theme parks conjure magic, dreams, and fun; and Harley's bikes are about freedom and brotherhood. A powerful Service Brand Promise brings the consumer to a deeper state of pleasure, satisfaction, and comfort. Service Brand Promises should not be just clever ads and creatively scripted personas.[10]

Harley-Davidson enjoys one of the strongest emotional connections with its customers. What other company has customers who have tattoos of the company's brand name on their body, permanently? Harley-Davidson sells more than motorcycles. The company sells a lifestyle of adventure and excitement—universal ideals that appeal to hardcore bikers and accountants.[11]

Most service oriented organizations have multiple Service Brand Promises. I believe each department should create their own that supports the overall Service Vision of the business. Just as important as the inspiring Service Brand Promise is the self-awareness exercise your employees go through to establish it, thus giving it real meaning to them.

## Changing the Mindset

Elevating an organization's customer service is not an event or flavor of the month. It is a process that needs a commitment from the top down.

Numerous internal components have to be examined and addressed, from creating the Service Vision, hiring standards, and training, to measurements and execution. To truly improve a corporation's customer service there must be a long-term commitment that builds each year. I have found that organizations that have successfully improved service and made it their value proposition did all this and also had an internal champion dedicated to ensuring the momentum didn't die down, but actually grew stronger. Companies have key executives such as sales directors, marketing managers, and people development coordinators, but many times, do not have an executive in charge of the most important aspect of their business—the customer's experience.

### Chief Xperience Officer

If you are really serious about customer service in your organization, then take the advice of my good friend Jim Gilmore, co-author of *Experience Economy and Authenticity*, who recommends having a Chief Xperience Officer.[12] To eliminate confusion with the CEO, Gilmore recommends using the acronym CXO. It is a total paradigm shift in the way corporations think and view their level of customer service. Instead of it being an expense, they need to view it as a necessary investment.

This position and title would be oversee the company's most important function: the satisfaction of their customers and the future direction of the organization's customer service evolution.

The CXO should be responsible for:

- Ensuring that service is one of the company's hiring standards.
- The development and marketing of the Service Vision.
- Ensuring the equal representation of the experiential component along with the other five: physical, atmosphere, functional, technical, and operational. (See Chapter 7.)
- The creation and evolution of all the company's customer experience cycle and nonnegotiable standards.
- The service training of new and existing employees.
- The implementation and execution of these standards.
- Service recovery training and systems to ensure the organization is zero risk.
- Creating an above-and-beyond legacy.
- The measurement and accountability of customer experience.

Basically, these are all of the 10 commandments to providing a world-class customer experience that customers are willing to pay a premium for.

*A Title with a Promise*

Some companies give people titles that reinforce their purpose. Here are some additional examples of job titles that demonstrate a promise to the company's Service Vision:

- Director of First Impressions
- Director of Customer Loyalty
- Director of Satisfaction
- Experience Guide
- Secret Service Agent
- Secret Service Specialist
- Head of Secret Service
- Director of Secret Service
- Secret Service Ambassador
- Chief Customer Officer
- Director of WOW
- Daymaker
- Indulgence Office
- Your Best Friend
- Head of Customer Intelligence
- Director of Employee Loyalty
- Chief Visionary Officer
- Director of Employee Morale
- Chief Brand Officer
- Head of Customer Intelligence
- Chief Visionary Officer
- Chief Brand Officer
- Your Escape Ambassador
- Rejuvenation Specialist
- Director of World Class
- Overachiever Specialist
- Director of World-Class Experiences

*A Greeting with a Promise*

I also love greetings that reinforce the company's Service Vision. Here are some examples:

- Whatever whenever
- How can I make you a raving fan?
- At your service
- Anything is possible
- How may I start your world-class experience?
- How can I make you a customer for life?
- Yes is the answer
- World class starts here

If you are a guest at W Hotel, and you call the front desk from your room, the front desk answers, "Whatever, whenever." If it happens to be 10:35 AM, and you want breakfast but breakfast ends at 10:30, how can they say, "Sorry you are five minutes too late," after answering the phone "Whatever, whenever"?

> You can't change the experience until you change the paradigm.

I have worked with several hospitals and medical facilities over the years and I don't think there is any tougher or more important jobs out there than taking care of people's health. Their Service Vision, however, is one of the easiest and clearest to figure out, yet I have found that the medical industry typically does a very poor job in connecting the roles of their employees to that Service Vision.

## The DiJulius Group Hospital

This is an exercise I do when working with hospitals and medical centers: Imagine The DiJulius Group has decided to open and manage a hospital. What would that look like? How would they approach things differently? Let's look at some of the titles hospitals use for their employees: (1) tray passers, (2) receptionists, (3) nurses, and (4) patients.

The person who is in charge of delivering food to the patient is a Tray Passer. I asked why are they called that, and the response was, "That is what they have always been called." How proud would you be if someone asked, "What is it that you do?" How difficult is it to get Tray Passers to realize the part they play in the company's Service Vision? I found that

Tray Passers are pretty important in educating patients on proper nutrition for the most rapid recovery. If this person's expertise can have a big impact on a patient recovering fully and sooner rather than later, they play a major role in any hospital's Service Vision. How about we rename Tray Passers "Chief Nutritionist Officers" or "Directors of Patient Diet"?

Upon arrival at a hospital, the person that you go to for information and directions is called the "Receptionist." And most of the time they act like receptionists, by providing the least information they can, and only when asked. What if we changed their title to "Director of First Impressions"? Wouldn't that title make them rethink the role they play in the experiences of all the visitors to the hospital?

Let's talk about the toughest job in the world, nursing. Most hospitals today will tell you how nurses are underpaid, understaffed, overworked, and as a result, many are burned out. What if we called them "Daymakers"? Because that is what they actually are.

If they were constantly referred to as Daymakers and they had to introduce themselves as Daymakers, wouldn't that make them reconsider their role and the sensitivity they must have with every patient and family member they come in contact with? Who do you think are happier with their jobs, nurses or Daymakers?

And finally the customers, who are the people who come to us for our services, whom we have always called "Patients." Why? Probably because the first hospital that ever opened called them that and since then everyone else just did the same. Any employee of a hospital will tell you that after dealing with hundreds of patients per day, over time, the employees can become desensitized and numb. Especially when dealing with a new patient that has, what a nurse considers a minor, temporary condition, compared to the patient down the hall, who may only have a few days left to live. However, it is all relative to the patient and the "minor," temporary condition may be the worst thing that has ever happened to that person and has him or her scared to death. Most nurses and doctors will also admit that instead of referring to patients as "Ms. Daniels in room 201," they just refer to them as "201b" (meaning room 201, second bed). With that perspective, it can make it more difficult to provide a world-class patient experience.

Any good hospital will tell you that they have two external customers: (1) the patient and (2) the patient's loved ones. Again, what if we thought outside the box and renamed patients, "family members," and the loved ones "relatives"? In many situations, hospital customers are like hospital family members and hospital relatives, where the employees get to know them very well, even if it is just for a few days.

Like anything else, just giving new titles doesn't change the culture, it is an aid in reminding that person of the role that comes with his or her position. But it is ultimately management's daily responsibility to constantly demonstrate how each department supports and impacts the Service Vision of the organization, which drives the customer's experience and level of satisfaction.

> If you can't change the people, change the people.

Afraid your Service Vision will be met with some "rolling of the eyes"? You can't let that stop you. One hospital that was committed to changing their culture was met with resistance by their 15 receptionists. So they asked all 15 to reapply for their existing jobs. Only three members of the original crew survived.

## Marketing Your Service Vision

There are two parts to creating a successful Service Vision. The first part is finding a way to articulate your company's purpose and vision—coming up with what business you are in, what you really sell, and inspirational Service Brand Promises that reinforce that Service Vision. Doing that the proper way requires a great deal of time, thought, and hard work; that is the easier part. The second part of a successful Service Vision is analyzing how well you market that vision internally to your employees and make the connection between how your employees' roles impact and support that Service Vision. Like any great marketing, just coming up with clever slogans is not enough, instead, it is getting that message out consistently to your target audience that seals the deal. In this case, your target audience is every employee in your organization.

Having a great inspirational Service Vision is important, but what makes it inspiring is how the leaders of a company make it come to life— with storytelling and constant references to how your organization is living their Service Brand Promise. Otherwise it is just a warm and fuzzy bumper sticker that has little meaning. Once you have your Service Vision established, you need to make it come to life. It has to be much more than a slogan or words on paper. This is done by linking it to folklore stories, by branding it daily, and by presenting annual awards for achieving it.

Like anything else, phrases, slogans, and creative titles don't change the culture. The company's Service Vision reminds all employees that they play an important role in achieving and maintaining that vision. But it is ultimately management's daily responsibility to constantly demonstrate how each department supports and impacts the Service Vision of the organization, which drives the customer's experience and levels of satisfaction.

## What We Do Today Impacts Our Customers' Lives

You don't have to be a Ritz-Carlton Hotel, Starbucks, Disney, or Nordstrom to create inspirational Service Visions, any company in any industry can do it. I have worked with all types of companies from all types of industries, but probably no phone call ever surprised me more than when I received a call from A-T Solutions, headquartered in Fredericksburg, Virginia. A-T stands for "anti-terrorism" training and consulting. I was positive that this company, run by ex-military personnel, mistook the title of my first book, *Secret Service*. However, I soon realized that the owner, Ken Falke, was well aware of what my version of *Secret Service* was and was very serious about making A-T Solutions a world-class customer service organization. In the two years I have been working with them, their growth has been phenomenal. Like any other company, growth can be difficult when you are trying to get 400+ employees to buy into your organization's philosophy.

One of my projects was to help tie all their departments together and demonstrate how all—receptionists, salespeople, trainers, human resources, marketing, accounting—contributed to the overall purpose of the company. Being a receptionist of an anti-terrorist training company probably isn't the sexiest job in the world. So, during one of my workshops, I showed a picture of an A-T Solutions trainer conducting a typical training program; I then flashed to a picture of a soldier disposed in Afghanistan. Next I showed a picture of a soldier stepping off a plane, being greeted by his wife and nine-month-old son, whom he had never met before. I followed that photo with a family vacationing on a beach somewhere. These were very powerful images. A-T Solutions doesn't "sell" anti-terrorist training. As a result of what they provide, soldiers come home safely to their families and Americans travel safely together without a second thought of danger or fear. So now, even the receptionist can be proud because she sees the part she plays in the underlying purpose of what A-T Solutions provides.

## Everyone Plays a Part in the Success of the Service Vision

Dan Sanders, author of *Built to Serve*, shares a great example of this. Medtronic is a leader in medical technology, manufacturing prosthetic valves for use in hearts. Shift workers spend long hours on assembly lines producing these valves. Medtronic employees did not see themselves as producing heart valves, rather they believed they were helping save lives. Medtronic holds an annual event where employees can meet patients who are alive because of transplanted artificial hearts containing Medtronic technology. That realization allowed Medtronic to provide a context of higher purpose for its workforce, resulting in focused and fulfilled employees.[13]

Teaching your front-line employees how valuable their roles are and the integral part they play in providing your customers with your company's underlying purpose is crucial. The Nemacolin Resort, a five-star property in Farmington, Pennsylvania, has done a very good job of making their front-line employees realize the part they play in the overall satisfaction of their guests. A group of managers from a Fortune 50 company were having a retreat at Nemacolin and arrived at the shooting range about an hour and a half later than the range had them scheduled. As a result of the miscommunication, they were unable to hold their activity because the range had just closed. The group was disappointed and a little upset.

On their way back to the hotel, the shuttle bus driver overheard their conversation with each other, and after he dropped them off, he called and alerted Dennis Noonan, the Director of Sales. Noonan immediately arranged for a shooting guide to come to the range, Noonan then found the group in the lobby of the hotel and asked, "Who's up for an activity?" Noonan apologized and said, "Let's go shoot." He went with them, helped get them set up, opened the five shooting stands just for them, and they blasted a ton of clay targets. "They had a ball, we bought them drinks afterward, and they raved and said this is above and beyond service," said Noonan. This Nemacolin customer recovery story is now something this company uses in their customer service training, and to no one's surprise, Nemacolin Resort has seen repeat business as a result. None of this would have been possible without a little detective work by the shuttle bus driver, who understood the importance of his role in the company's Service Vision.

The following is an example of a Service Vision with supporting Service Brand Promises:

**John Robert's Spa**

*Service Vision:* To enhance the quality of lives around us

*The business we are in:* THE Experience

*We sell:* Fashion ~ Rejuvenations ~ Escape

*We make price irrelevant by:* Enabling our guests' to look and feel AMAZING

*Service Brand Promises:*

- We are a guest's trip to Paris.
- We are 60-minute vacations.
- The answer's yes. . . . Now what is the question?
- The better the experience, the less price becomes an issue.
- While they may complain about the service defect, they are going to rave about how we handled it.
- Daymakers who also do hair.

The following is a template to create your Service Vision and supporting Service Brand Promises.

### Service Vision

Service Vision                    _____

The business are we in           _____

We sell                          _____

We make price irrelevant by      _____

Service Brand Promises           _____

# Notes

1. The Disney Institute and Michael D. Eisner, "Be Our Guest" (Disney Institute Leadership Series), *Disney Editions*, May 1, 2001.
2. Dan J. Sanders, *Built to Serve* (New York: McGraw-Hill, 2007).
3. See note 2.
4. See note 1.

5. James Collins and Jerry Porras, "Building Your Company's Vision," *Harvard Business Review*, September–October, 1996.

6. Thomas J. Peters and Robert H. Watermark, *In Search of Excellence* (New York: HarperCollins, 1982).

7. http://en.wikipedia.org/wiki/Starbucks#The_Third_Place.

8. David Wagner, *Life as a Daymaker* (San Diego, CA: Jodere Group, 2003).

9. Jerry Garcia *BrainyQuote.com* www.brainyquote.com/quotes/quotes/j /jerrygarci163269.html.

10. Richard K. Hendrie, "The Why, What and How of WOW," *Remarkable branding.com*, issue 68 (March 2005).

11. See note 2.

12. James H. Gilmore and B. Joseph Pine II, *The Experience Is the Marketing* (Louisville, KY: BrownHerron, 2002).

13. See note 2.

# 6

# Commandment II: Creating a World-Class Internal Culture

*Attract, hire, and retain only the people who have the Service DNA*

---

*We don't put People in Disney, We put Disney in People.*[1]
—Disney Institute

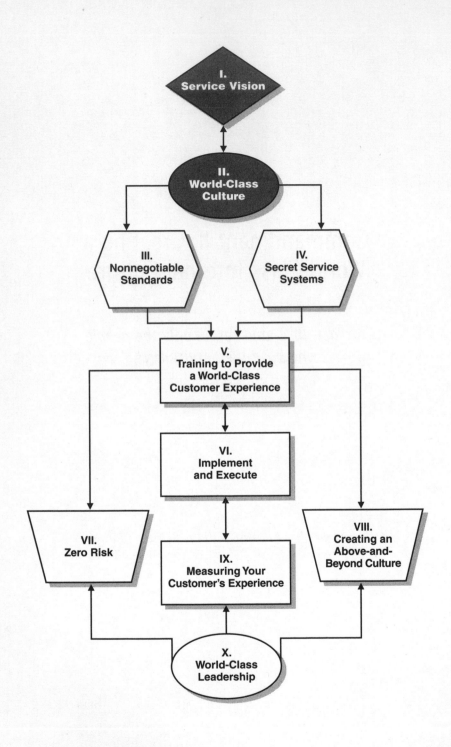

Creating a world-class internal culture that attracts, hires, and retains only the people who are capable of upholding the Service Vision of the organization is the second step in achieving world-class customer service. Building your culture using your Service Vision to guide you will make or break the success of the following eight commandments.

## Why People Leave

According to a Gallup survey, the top three reasons why employees leave their jobs are:

1. Lack of faith in the leadership or vision of the company.
2. Concern with the way management is treating people.
3. Lack of management support in areas such as performance reviews and employee development.

The single most important determinant of an individual's performance and commitment to stay with an organization is the relationship the individual has with his or her immediate manager. People leave their manager far more often than they leave the organization.[2]

The cost of replacing an employee is somewhere between 1.75 to 2.5 times his or her annual salary. High turnover can cause remaining employees to question their loyalty. Studies prove that the reasons why people leave their jobs is directly related to how connected people feel at work. A study done by the Family and Work Institute found that compensation and benefits have a 2 percent impact on job satisfaction, while quality and workplace support have a combined 70 percent impact.[3] Retaining employees is not a function of the human resources department. Employees are most engaged when they feel as though their work is important, feel appreciated, learn and grow, and feel they are part of a great team.

According to a report by the U.S. Bureau of Labor, in the next decade, there could be as many as 10 million more jobs available than there are employees in the United States due to the Generation X population being considerably smaller than the Baby Boomers.[4] Jeff Taylor, CEO of Monster.com, warns, "We'll be facing the worst labor shortage in our lifetime within the next five years."[5]

The better the culture, the less pay becomes an issue.

By far, finding quality people is the number one struggle in every industry. When I speak on building a world-class internal culture, I get many "our situation's different" comments, how they think my information is great, but it doesn't apply to their industry because it is so much harder to find good people and how unrealistic it is for them to create a world-class employee culture.

In the early days at both of my companies, John Robert's Spa and The DiJulius Group, we struggled with this as much as everyone else. We made the exact same mistakes that most other companies who have poor cultures make. We were hiring reactively, never able to find good applicants, always understaffed, not thrilled with some of the employees we did have because they didn't get it, or take pride in their job. We had high turnover and an overall average level of morale.

Since then, I have studied many of the organizations that truly have world-class cultures and found out there was a formula to their success. If you gradually implement a similar approach, you will get similar results. It won't happen overnight, but within a few months you will start to see significant results.

This second commandment—to provide a world-class customer experience, Create a World-Class Internal Culture—means that in order to be a truly world-class customer service organization, you must attract, hire, and retain only those people who have *Service DNA*. The best service companies do an incredible job achieving this goal, starting with the process of recruiting and hiring and extending through orientation and continuing throughout the entire employee career experience.

Most companies hire reactively, racing to fill openings caused by either turnover or growth. When companies reactively hire, their objectivity is distorted, and their hiring standards are compromised. When you convert your company to operating on a schedule where the hiring process begins three to six months ahead of time, *before* the openings occur, you allow your organization to get to know the employment candidates and reduce the risk of a wrong fit. It's the difference between a courtship and a shotgun wedding.

Businesses need to do a better job of screening applicants, and then need to follow up with mandatory training that includes teaching the soft skills that will help increase your new employee's service aptitude. The need for good training is not a generational issue or a work-ethic issue; we as leaders need to be clear about our expectations, by setting standards and sufficiently training employees to deliver unforgettable customer service.

People need to earn the right to work for you.

As business leaders, we need to have standards that require prospective employees to earn the right to be part of our company. Having a set of nonnegotiable hiring standards, characteristics an employee must embody that are clearly defined and articulated, will turn your prospective employees either on or off.

One of the things I am proudest of is that in an era when most companies can't find enough good help and are willing to hire anyone who walks through the door, John Robert's Spa turns away 24 out of 25 applicants. If we find five great candidates in a row, we will certainly hire all five, but on average, we hire 1 out of 25. Of the other 24, more than half *don't want* the job after the first interview, where we go over our nonnegotiable employment standards. We haven't always been that way; ten years ago, we probably needed employees more than they needed us and it showed.

During the interview process, many businesses paint rosy pictures of what it is like to work at their organization, which can lead to high expectations on the part of the employee. If the position is dramatically different from how it was presented, the new hire becomes disenfranchised, either quits or gets fired, and both the company and the ex-employee are back to square one, with all that time and training (hopefully they were trained) wasted.

At John Robert's Spa, just as we have Service Vision for our customers, we have an Employee Vision; we want employees for life who regard the decision to have a career at John Robert's Spa as one of the best decisions he or she has ever made. However, a career at John Robert's Spa is certainly not for everyone. We have learned from our past mistakes, and now we do a much better job of weeding out candidates who are the wrong fit. While not necessarily bad candidates, they just are not the right fit for our culture. Today, with the beauty industry's turnover topping 100 percent annually, John Robert's Spa has a turnover that consistently runs 12 to 14 percent because we do such a good job on the selection process.

We are not for everyone, nor do we want to be. We are for the 2 percent who want to emerge as the best of the best, who are not afraid to work hard and challenge themselves to see how much greatness they actually have inside.

We don't make it easy to get hired. Unlike many businesses, who hire candidates before they have completed their applications, we make job candidates come to at least three interviews, possibly four, over the course of several weeks. We also want to make sure that our job candidates are not running up and down the street looking for the best deal because, on paper, we are not the best deal.

# Disney's Approach to People Management

I had the pleasure of attending the Disney University in Orlando, Florida, where I took Disney's Approach to People Management course. Where better to learn how to create a world-class culture than Walt Disney World. The concepts and principles I learned there totally redefined how both my companies, John Robert's Spa and The DiJulius Group, created our corporate cultures and helped us go from a company that hires reactively and compromises standards to a company that builds a strong corporate culture by design.

When Disney hires new "cast members" (their terminology for employees), both the employment expectations and service standards are clearly defined to potential candidates to ensure they understand how critical these elements are to being a part of the Disney culture. When Disney managers conduct initial interviews with prospective hires, they detail their nonnegotiable employment standards, referred to as PATA (pay, attendance, transportation, and attitude), and their service standards (safety, courtesy, show, and efficiency).

Shortly after completing the Disney course, I created a position within both my companies called the People Development Coordinator. This was the person who would be responsible for defining our corporate culture and making sure we added and retained only people who were a right-fit.

> A culture is not announced. It is created by a constant focus on values.[6]
>
> —*Brenda Harris, President, Talent Tree*

## Scare Them Away

The main objective of the People Development Coordinator, who now conducts first interviews with prospective hires, is to scare the applicant out of working for us. If she can't do that, chances are very good that the applicant will be successful at John Robert's Spa. What "scare" really means is to help candidates recognize that a job at John Robert's Spa may be either a much bigger commitment than they wanted, or exactly what they have been looking for. Our People Development Coordinator inspires this thinking by effectively articulating in full detail our employment standards, known internally by the acronym SEATCAP:

S = Secret Service

E = Education

A = Attendance

T = Team

C = Community Involvement

A = Attitude

P = Purpose

SEATCAP is an employment standard specific to the hiring values at John Robert's Spa, but may apply to many companies. To elevate the quality of prospects you hire, you must first determine your company's nonnegotiable hiring values, then develop a way to articulate the significance of those values to your applicants in those first interviews. Like a company's Service Vision, just creating some hiring standards or characteristics is not even half of the issue, it is how you can make those characteristics come to life, making them black and white to your potential employee candidates that really makes a difference.

Let's explain what we mean by these standards:

*Secret Service:* This clearly communicates our standards for how our guests are to be treated by every team member at John Robert's Spa. Every applicant is expected to read both of our service bibles, *Secret Service* and *What's the Secret?* and provide book reviews. Every applicant must attend the mandatory Secret Service boot camp training prior to the technical job training. Every new team member must study the *John Robert's Guest Experience Cycle Handbook* and be tested on the service defects, standards, and above-and-beyond opportunities for each stage of interaction with the guest. Every new team member must take the Service Aptitude Test, the 75-question multiple-choice quiz on how to handle customer service situations.

*Education:* In the first interview, every applicant learns about the amount of training necessary to work at John Robert's Spa. Unlike the salon industry standard, which is typically about three hours of training per year per employee, our employees receive anywhere from 75 to 800 hours of training per year, which averages out to about 175 hours per employee per year. (We have 140 employees and our training hours per year exceed 25,000 hours.) We want to make sure that every applicant understands his or her commitment to training and not only is it a requirement for advancement but also for continued employment.

*Attendance:* Many businesses, especially salons, have constant attendance issues. Not at John Robert's Spa! We make sure that applicants understand that if they are 14 minutes early for their shift, they are a minute late for the preshift huddle. (They get paid for those extra 15 minutes.) We are not about to hold our breath each day hoping employees will be on time or even show up. We do not want employees who do not respect the company they work for, the teammates they work with, or the customers they work on. Our employees know there is zero tolerance for poor attendance.

*Team:* At John Robert's Spa, your fellow team members are number one, even before your guests. We understand that if our team members are treated with world-class respect, they in turn will treat their customers with world-class respect. Internal world-class respect occurs both vertically, management-down, and horizontally, from employee-to-fellow-employee. As I stated earlier, people don't quit companies; they quit managers or coworkers. If coworkers are miserable and in turn make their teammates miserable, a company will experience a lot of turnover. We educate all applicants about our "10-feet greet," which means that whenever you come within 10 feet of a guest or coworker, you smile and say hello, even if it's the tenth time that day.

*Community:* What we do within the community is critically important to us. John Robert's Spa's mission statement is: *To Enhance the Lives around Us,* and we take that very seriously. We inform our candidates of all the contributions we make to the community: We provide services every month to patients in the local children's hospital; over the holidays, we take them hundreds of gifts donated by team members and guests; we provide free haircuts during prom week for all seniors who sign the John Robert's Prom Promise that they won't drink and drive; the list goes on and on. We want to attract people who believe in that degree of community involvement. We know that if they believe in giving back to the community, we don't have to worry about what type of team member they will be or how they will take care of the guest.

*Attitude:* This is the topic we spend the most time on in the first interview. We explain that employees who drop the ball on customers won't get fired, but will be coached on how to do it right the next time. But if employees come to work repeatedly with poor attitudes, we will encourage them to find employment elsewhere, demonstrating our commitment to a positive work environment and culture. We are very compassionate employers. We will hold someone's hand, go to therapy with her, even write a check, or offer time off if a personal problem is overwhelming. But she has to leave her problems at the door when she comes to work, or else she will be out the door. We want to be a "negative-free" facility, where negative people are uncomfortable working.

*Purpose:* Whether you work 44 hours per week or 4, you should have passion and enthusiasm for what you do. It's about making people's days, creating value over and above the product you are selling. Front-line employees are empowered when they have a sense of purpose and ownership in their job.

> Each of your jobs have functions which you have to perform, as does the chair you are sitting in. It has a function. The only difference between that chair and you is the chair has no purpose. You and the way you perform your job does. Choose to come to perform your work with a purpose, know what your purpose is.
>
> —*Jim McManemon, General Manager, The Ritz-Carlton*
> *Sarasota, in a speech to his staff*

Each SEATCAP value has stories behind it, and halfway through an interview, it's very easy to see how a candidate is responding. Some candidates get glassy-eyed and look at our interviewer as if she is nuts. Other candidates nod their heads, saying, "I know. I've heard about all this. It's why I am here. I thought you said this was going to be tough."

A world-class culture does not compromise values, rather, it remains faithful to values, even when remaining faithful means doing things differently from everyone else. A legendary culture is created in the head and the heart of the leader and passed from team member to team member.[7]

We even give our applicants a list of the area's top salons that they should consider interviewing with. We want them to make sure they are making the right decision and finding the best fit for their career goals.

## Build the Culture and the Customers Will Come

If you truly want to be a world-class customer service organization, then you have to be the employer of choice. And to do that, you need to be known for four things:

1. Being a great place to work.
2. Providing great training.
3. Having superior customer service.
4. Offering unlimited opportunity.

If you can create that type of reputation, you will never have a shortage of applicants. People will wait months to get hired because they know that merely by having your company on their resumes, they will be significantly more attractive if they ever find themselves in the job market again.

Ask yourself: If you had 10 applicants for one job, and one of them had worked at Nordstrom or Disney or The Ritz-Carlton, wouldn't you immediately give that candidate a closer look?

Create your own simple acronym of your hiring nonnegotiable standards. Then you can easily and passionately share your standards, and you can send the wrong-fit candidates running for the door.

> World-class service is not something you deliver, it is a result of something you are.

Too many companies believe they are unable to implement high hiring standards because of the nature of their business or the limitations of their industry. I have heard the following excuses repeatedly:

- There is a labor shortage.
- We can't be picky when we only pay our employees so little.

If those excuses apply, how are companies like Starbucks, Disney, and Nordstrom so successful at hiring good people and retaining them? They do not pay more than the industry standard, yet all of those companies turn away far more applicants than any of their competitors.

In the past, we made the same hiring mistakes many businesses do. Since then we have created a reputation for being an employer of choice in our area; as a result most applicants are aware they have to earn the right to be a part of the John Robert's family.

This hiring model can work for any company in any industry. If you create a reputation for being a great place to work, that provides unbelievable training, that delivers fanatical customer service, and offers unlimited opportunity, your company will be sought after and have an abundance of applicants to choose from. That last one—offering unlimited opportunity—is where many companies fail. The reason businesses have short-term, transitional employees is because that is all they are offering them. Nearly every great company has countless stories of people who started off sweeping floors, parking cars, or washing dishes, and today are senior level management. Why limit the vision of your newest employee and what they can become by helping your company grow?

What people can achieve will shock you as long as you allow them to be part of a cause or a purpose and you give them an opportunity to feel like they are making a difference.

Howard Schultz, CEO of Starbucks, advised his managers to, "make sure people's jobs aren't too small for their spirit by stifling them or making their position robotic; make sure there is always a vision of growth in the company."[8]

> We don't hire people with more winning qualities than our competition; we just bring out their winning qualities.

I have never come across a world-class customer service organization that wasn't a world-class company to work for. In my work as a consultant, I have encountered many companies where my efforts to improve customer service would be futile unless we first addressed and improved their internal corporate culture.

The scope of the consulting we do with organizations who want to take their service to the next level has numerous phases, including assessing their current service systems, developing more effective training programs, delivering customer experience workshops, creating measurement and accountability protocols, and defining employee career experiences. Many times when I explain the phases of my consulting, and define the employee experience as the most critical element to the success of creating a world-class customer service organization, the CEOs choose to omit that phase from our proposal. This is where I find myself in a difficult situation because although I know we provide the absolute best customer service consulting, I also realize that when the "employee career experience" phase is omitted, we dramatically reduce the long-term success of the project.

I was consulting with a large chain and their Secret Service project team (a group of franchisees and corporate resources of the franchisors) was creating some great customer service standards. Instead of getting excited about all the progress and systems being created, the franchisees started commenting about how they knew they didn't have the culture that would allow for this project to be successful. They felt the turnover was too high at the front-line levels, and the managers were not trained on how to create high morale or buy in. Finally, everyone on the Secret Service project team, including the CEO, realized that we had to first create a blueprint for creating a world-class internal culture. This is what we did and it has had an incredible impact on the roll out of their new customer service program.

*What's in It for Me?*

Leaders of companies must emphasize to their colleagues the importance of their internal culture. A strong culture is 10 times more likely to embrace the change necessary to shift from an average (level 3) to above average (level 4) customer service company (see Chapter 4). Employees must experience world-class before they are capable of delivering it. Training existing and future managers how to do this isn't simply common sense. Morale is dependent on who their boss is and it should be every leader's first-order of responsibility to have extremely high morale among their employees.

You can have the greatest Service Vision in the world, but if you don't consistently make the connection of how each level of your team participates in the purpose of that vision, and just as important, how each employee benefits from executing that vision, it becomes just a stale slogan. The old adage: "What's in it for me?" still applies. How does your Service Vision tie into your Employee Vision? "There has to be a win in it for everyone; the guests, employees, and managers," says McManemon.

THE Ritz-Carlton EMPLOYEE PROMISE

- At The Ritz-Carlton, our Ladies and Gentlemen are the most important resource in our service commitment to our guests.

- By applying the principles of trust, honesty, respect, integrity, and commitment, we nurture and maximize talent to the benefit of each individual and the company.

- The Ritz-Carlton fosters a work environment where diversity is valued, quality of life is enhanced, individual aspirations are fulfilled, and The Ritz-Carlton mystique is strengthened.[9]

## The Employee Career Experience

When I hire someone, that is the time when I go to work for them.

In creating the Employee Career Experience, you have to break down each stage of an employee's career with your company. These stages are quite consistent from company to company:

1. Recruiting.
2. Screening and hiring.
3. Orienting and training
4. 90 days after hire.
5. 6 months after hire.
6. 1 year after hire.
7. 2 years after hire.
8. 5 or more years of employment.

I will be upset if any of my employees go through tough times alone, without coming to me for help.

> —*Maggie Hardy Magerko, Owner and President,*
> *84 Lumber and Nemacolin Woodlands Resort*

Because the employee's mentality is different at each stage, the manager needs to emphasize and avoid certain factors at each stage. When creating this with The Melting Pot Restaurants, we designed a model for their franchisees and managers to follow, a blueprint on how to create a positive working environment. This blueprint teaches new managers (because we can't assume they know how to do it), and reminds experienced managers how to create a great culture throughout an employee's career in a way that continually reinforces their emotional capital in the company.

We identified three components of each stage: service defects, standards, and above-and-beyond opportunities. Service defects are the things that the company and management need to avoid at each stage because those things can cause the employee's morale to take a nose dive. Standards are actions we want the company and management to deliver at each stage because those are the things that will differentiate the company from any other company the employee has ever worked for. And finally above-and-beyond opportunities allow management to demonstrate a culture of going out of their way to care about the individual employee, leaving a reoccurring impression that this company is unlike any other they have ever worked for.

Take for instance the recruiting stage. This has nothing to do with interviewing, it is how well a company is marketing itself to get right-fit candidates. The service defects and standards at this stage address how well we are branding our company as the employer of choice to prospective right-fit applicants. Many companies hire poorly because they are casting their bait in the wrong ponds and getting the wrong applicants.

Examples of service defects in the recruiting stage include:

- Attracting wrong-fit candidates.
- Recruiting reactively (only when short-staffed).
- Failing to articulate clearly the type of employee we want.

Examples of standards at the recruiting stage include:

- Constant (ongoing) recruiting and brand awareness regardless of staffing needs.
- Strong relationships with local schools and guidance counselors.
- Incentives for team members and guests to refer right-fit candidates.

### Scavenger Hunt

I have learned many techniques from working with Nemacolin Woodlands Resort in Pennsylvania, a great service organization. One of my favorite is the scavenger hunt they have their new associates experience. It is a competitive scavenger hunt on this huge resort where each new associate has a list of 50 things they have to discover, find the answers to, and take pictures of (disposable cameras are provided). In the course of the scavenger hunt, I realized two things: it is a lot of fun, and the new associates are learning a lot about the history of Nemacolin. What a great idea!

Any time I hear a great idea, I replicate it within my organization. The John Robert's Spa orientation now includes a scavenger hunt across all our locations. We take a group of new employees, typically eight to twelve in a group, pair them up, give them a list of about 30 things to discover or get the answers to, and have them get pictures of every item on the list. This achieves many things: The new employees have a great deal of fun, they work with another team member, and in the process they learn a lot about our culture and legacy and heroes, visiting all of our locations and meeting many existing John Robert's employees who go out of their way to help the new employees get their answers and pictures.

### Re-Orientation

I learned another great lesson from working with The Ritz-Carlton Hotels: They put all their existing employees through the orientation process again. I immediately brought this idea back to John Robert's Spa, and we instituted a re-orientation for all our existing employees every other year, meaning if you were hired on in 2007, you would retake our orientation training in 2009, 2011, etc.

Mixing experienced employees with new hires has had so many incredible benefits we didn't even anticipate. During key points in the orientation, experienced employees shared great testimonials, telling stories of what it was like when they joined the company. This immediately created a bond between new and seasoned employees, which resulted in new employees having friends at work, and reducing the typical anxiety of being a new employee.

Most of all it reinvigorated our seasoned staff. Many experienced employees expressed great surprise at how much the orientation had improved, and how much of our legacy they had forgotten about. They were reinspired by the John Robert's story—where we came from, what it took to get us here, and where we are headed.

Service Management Group (SMG), headquartered in Kansas City, a customer satisfaction measurement company, is well known for helping companies measure and improve their customer experience, but they work just as hard at creating a world-class internal culture. They use Talent Plus to screen potential SMG employees, as does The Ritz-Carlton and Cheesecake Factory. Additionally, SMG has a rigorous internal interview process as well, that makes it even more difficult to get hired, and allows them to choose individuals who are a great fit for SMG.

SMG's focus on their internal culture doesn't just stop at the hiring process. Andy Fromm, the President, also supports health and fitness among SMG employees. For example, anyone interested in competing in the corporate challenge bike race, triathlon, or duathlon receives a racing bike. He recently replaced all the vending machine junk food with fresh fruit and more healthy snacks—and those are all free.

SMG also gives an extra week of vacation to all employees by splitting the company departments into Red and Green teams around the holidays. Red Team employees can take off the week before Christmas and Green Team employees can take off the week between Christmas and New Years. It's up to the employees and department managers to ensure they maintain excellent client service at this time. "It is not uncommon for a SMG employees not to take all their time off to meet the needs of our clients," says Vice President Jack Mackey.

SMG also understands how much employees love time off in the summer, so they offer Friday afternoons off if employees complete a 40-hour work week by noon and clients' needs are satisfied. Each employee can take up to half the summer Fridays off.

SMG treats all employees to lunch on summer Fridays. Each department takes a Friday and serves as the lunch host, lining up the food and helping to serve. SMG provides the budget and the departments choose the menus.

Winter isn't so bad either. Every Friday, SMG has Pours at Four. Beer is served, people take a break, and visit. Amazingly, you will see people visit for 15 minutes or a half hour, then take their beer back to their desks, voluntarily, and keep working.

## Everyone Plays a Part in Delivering an Experience

You can't be world-class unless every department in your organization is world-class, from front line to back office, from support staff to management. What if your job is loss prevention? I left The Ritz-Carlton Sarasota in such a rush for the airport that I forgot my laptop charger in my room. I planned to call when I got back into my office, but before I could, I received a next-day air package from The Ritz-Carlton Sarasota. In it was my charger, with a note saying, "Mr. DiJulius, I wanted to make sure we got this to you right away. I am sure you need it, and, just in case, I sent you an extra charger for your laptop." The note was signed by Larry K. Kinney, in Loss Prevention. Just as he said, in the box was a second charger. Obviously, Kinney doesn't think like many other employees who are behind the scenes and don't come in regular contact with the customer. Take for example how The Ritz-Carlton trains employees who work in accounting: These employees go through room charges and other items on their guests' bills, noting guests' purchases. It provides a significant opportunity to record guests' preferences for future visits. So when a guest returns, the database may tell them this person loves Canada Dry ginger ale, so The Ritz-Carlton can stock it in the room's mini bar.

### Engagement Scoreboard

At The Ritz-Carlton, they use an Engagement Scoreboard that tracks and posts how many times employees are engaged with guests. This scoreboard is posted for all to see. Some of the things the scoreboard tracks are:

- Each time an employee records a guest preference
- Each time a MRBIV is identified, meaning:
  —Mistakes
  —Reworks
  —Breakdowns
  —Inefficiencies
  —Variations
- Recognition of an employee by a guest or fellow employee
- Hazards
- Innovation

This engagement scoreboard makes it obvious which employees are engaged and which are not. "Our goal is to have everyone at least 90 percent engaged, then I know I have a boat where everyone is rowing in the same direction," says McManemon.

Cameron Mitchell, president of Cameron Mitchell Restaurants, knows how to build a brand: "It's amazing the power of the concept. Any organization needs to define itself and say: Who are we? You need to be able to answer that basic question. We answer that by saying we are great people delivering genuine hospitality. We all have the same role in the company. To make raving fans of the five groups of people we do business with: our fellow associates, our guests, our purveyors, our partners, and our community. That is why keeping your company's philosophy in the forefront at all times is imperative. Anyone involved in working in your company has to know your Brand Promise and be able to articulate that." It is a formula that's allowed Cameron Mitchell Restaurants to grow from a single restaurant in 1993 to a 30+ location, multibranded empire that had receipts over $125 million in 2007.[10]

cj Advertising, Nashville, Tennessee, is known for the excellent customer service they deliver to their clients, however, they are also a great company to work for and have a fine reputation with (vendors) as well. They have many internal standards they deem nonnegotiable. For example, the standards that relate to job candidates and vendors are:

1. Return all phone messages within same day.
2. Return e-mail messages within same day.
3. If a job candidate is rejected by cj, send them correspondence and give them the names of the other top agencies in Nashville to check out.
4. Let people know where they stand in the interview process in a timely manner.
5. When candidates come into the office, offer them a beverage as they wait.
6. Validate all parking for interviewees.
7. Streamline the interview process to ensure that candidates get handled in a timely manner.
8. Treat all vendors with respect and return their calls even if we know that we will not use their services.
9. E-mail a thank-you note when vendor went above-and-beyond to provide us with excellent customer service.

cj Advertising's nonnegotiable standards for internal customers include:

1. Answer employee benefit questions the same day they are received.
2. Hand out paychecks by 3:30 PM on the Thursday before payday.

Most companies worry about their customers' first impressions but don't think about how important new employees' first impressions are. Another best practice at John Robert's Spa is to provide Secret Service to our interview candidates. Their second interview is always an observation day where they come and observe our operations in action and interact with an existing team member. We try to give the employee who the potential candidate may be shadowing information on that candidate, such as where they went to school or worked previously, so the employee can personalize their observation experience and make them feel even more comfortable.

Everyone has heard that loyal employees create loyal customers. But do you have any idea how important employee loyalty is to customer satisfaction? A study conducted by Service Management Group shows the higher the employee turnover, the lower the customer service satisfaction levels (Figure 6.1).

Employee loyalty also produces more brand marketing. Extremely satisfied employees instinctively spread the word about how great their company is to not only buy from, but to work for.

Brand loyalty begins at home; if you can't sell it on the inside, you won't sell it on the outside. "Customer loyalty is driven by employees. Engage your employees. Your success depends on cultivating a cohesive team

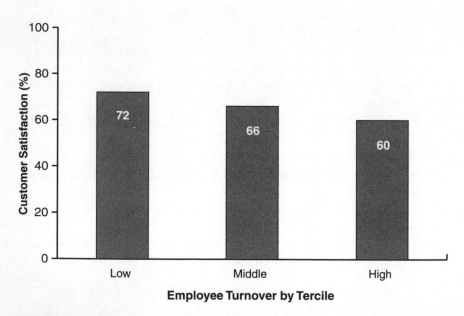

**FIGURE 6.1** Employee Turnover Impact on Customer Satisfaction (Service Management Group Client Data). *Note:* **Higher employee turnover reduces customer satisfaction.**

of individuals who share your passion for the business," says Jack Mackey, SMG Vice President (Figure 6.2).

In March 2007, *BusinessWeek* launched their "Customer Service Champs," a list of their top 25 customer service companies. One of the criteria for making the list was emphasis on creating exceptional employee loyalty as much as customer loyalty, keeping their people happy with generous benefits and perks. For instance, since 1984, Wegmans (ranked #5 by *BusinessWeek*) has given away $59 million in scholarships to 19,000 employees. And senior management log many hours on the front lines, listening in on phones in the call centers, and working by staffers' sides.[11]

### *Employees Need to Experience World-Class Service before They Deliver It*

At most of the Four Seasons' properties, the final stage of the seven-step employee orientation is something the chain's executives call a "familiarization stay" or "fam trip." Each worker in these hotels, from housekeepers to front-desk clerks, is given a free night's stay for themselves and a guest, along with free dining.[12]

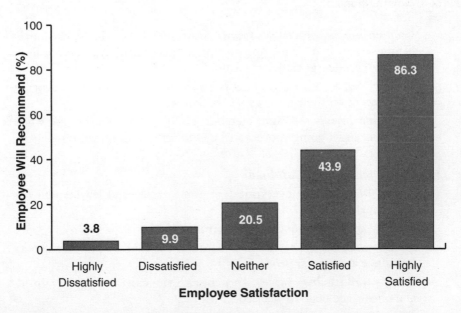

**FIGURE 6.2** **Employee Satisfaction Impact on Whether Employees Will Recommend Their Company to Potential Customers (Service Management Group Client Data).** *Note:* **Loyal employees recommend their company as a great place to be a customer.**

While there, employees are asked to grade the hotels on such measures as the number of times the phone rings when calling room service to how long it takes to deliver items to a room. "We bill it as a training session," says Ellen Dubois du Bellay, Vice President of learning and development. "They're learning what it looks like to receive service from the other side."

Understanding the meaning of exceptional service is key when your product or service is out of range for many employees—a $400 per night room rate isn't easy to swing on a housekeeper's budget. But the Four Seasons doesn't stop at orientation: After six months of service, employees may stay at any property up to three nights a year for free. By 10 years, they get 20 free stays. As you'd imagine, "there's a very healthy uptake," says du Bellay. Four Seasons' creative but practical approach reveals one of the most powerful secrets of world-class service: helping employees understand what it feels like to be a customer.

### The Cake

The Cheesecake Factory does an incredible job at keeping the focus on the guest experience by rewarding and recognizing their staff members with the following honors:

- *Commitment to Excellence Award:* Staff members who consistently demonstrate their dedication to uphold and fulfill the service mission of "absolute guest satisfaction."
- *100 for 100:* $100 in gift cards is awarded to staff members scoring 100 percent on their mystery guest scores.
- *Above-and-Beyond Pins:* Staff members are given pins on the spot when they are caught going above-and-beyond for guests or team members.

### Disney Tips for Culture Building[13]

1. *Keep it simple.* Make everyone feel comfortable and leave room for individuality.
2. *Make it global.* Everyone must buy into it.
3. *Make it measurable.* Create specific guidelines that are part of the performance assessment process.
4. *Provide training and coaching.* Incorporate the culture in the training and encourage peer-to-peer coaching.
5. *Solicit feedback and ideas from the team.* Foster a sense of ownership and expand creativity by allowing employees to contribute.
6. *Recognize and reward performance.* Build employee motivation through reward and recognition.

## Humanizing Lawyers

Injury lawyers have been called many things, most notably, ambulance chasers. But what about injury lawyers who are called life savers, community activists, or who have genuine concern for people's well-being? Don't laugh; some law firms are not only breaking the stereotype of their profession, they are having an impact on their communities that Oprah would be proud of.

### Safe and Sober

Alcohol-related crashes are responsible for a death every 31 minutes and an injury every single minute. Three out of every 10 Americans will be involved in an alcohol-related crash at some point in their lives, and in 2006, 18,000 people were killed in alcohol-related crashes.

As a result of this, Berg Injury Lawyers of Northern California have created the Safe and Sober Free Cab Ride Home Program, which seeks to raise community awareness of the dangers of drunk driving and to encourage individuals to make responsible choices by providing a safe transportation alternative on many of the traditionally high, alcohol-consumption holidays. Cab rides are made available within certain cities to area residents who otherwise might attempt to drive home after drinking. Rides are provided to an individual's residence, not to other drinking locations.

The law firm teamed up with Veterans Cab. "Now all someone has to do is call a taxi cab and say the 'Ride is on Berg Injury Lawyers.' We get drunk drivers off the road," says William Berg, Managing Partner.

### Child Safety

Thousands of parents put their children at risk every day without knowing it.

- Motor vehicle crashes are the leading cause of death for children ages 3 to 14.
- 1,500 children are killed every year, 50 percent are unrestrained.
- Out of 100 children, only one is properly restrained in a child's seat in a vehicle.

As a result of a 99 percent misuse rate of children's safety seats, Daniel Stark Injury Lawyers, a Texas law firm, got involved and started holding Child Passenger Safety Days to make sure as many children as possible are properly safe in a vehicle. It is a time to not only raise awareness about the importance of using child safety seats, but also to educate the community about how to properly install and maintain this lifesaving equipment.

During this event, certified child-passenger safety technicians under the supervision of Passenger Safety, Texas Cooperative Extension are on hand to inspect child safety seats and to help parents and caregivers learn how to properly install child safety seats in their vehicles. In addition, technicians provide basic child safety seat training and answer questions. During inspections at one such event, the technicians found only 1 child out of 48 were correctly restrained. Twenty-two replacement seats were given out and 15 old or unsafe seats were discarded.

# Notes

1. The Disney Institute and Michael D. Eisner, "Be Our Guest," (Disney Institute Leadership Series), *Disney Editions*, May 1, 2001.

2. http://gmj.gallup.com/gmj_surveys, as quoted in The Ken Blanchard Companies, www.kenblanchard.com/ignite/ignite_volume7_2005.html.

3. Family and Work Institute, as quoted in www.kenblanchard.com/ignite /ignite_volume7_2005.html.

4. U.S. Bureau of Labor, 2000, as quoted in The Ken Blanchard Companies, "The Retention Challenge," www.kenblanchard.com/img/pub/pdf_ignite _retentionchallenge.pdf.

5. *Harvard Business Review* (November 26, 2003), as quoted in The Ken Blanchard Companies, "The Retention Challenge," www.kenblanchard.com/img/pub /pdf_ignite_retentionchallenge.pdf.

6. Meredyth McKenzie, "Smart Leaders: Brenda Harris, President and Chief Operating Officer, Talent Tree," *Smart Business Houston*, November 2007.

7. Dan J. Sanders, *Built to Serve* (New York: McGraw-Hill, 2007).

8. John DiJulius, personal communication.

9. http://corporate.ritzcarlton.com/en/About/Default.htm.

10. Nancy Byron, "Running the Table: How Cameron Mitchell Builds Brands that Set Him Apart in a Crowded Industry," *Smart Business Columbus*, May 2007.

11. Jena McGregor, "Customer Service Champs: *BusinessWeek*'s First-Ever Ranking of 25 Clients," *BusinessWeek*, March 5, 2007, www.businessweek.com /magazine/content/07_10/b4024001.htm.

12. See note 11.

13. See note 1.

# 7

# Commandment III: Nonnegotiable Experiential Standards

## Experience standards everyone must follow

---

*Because of the shift to the Experience Economy, goods and services are no longer enough; what consumers want today are experiences—memorable events that engage them in an inherently personal way. People now decide where and when to spend money and their time—the currency of experiences.*[1]
—James H. Gilmore and B. Joseph Pine,
*Authenticity: What Consumers Really Want*

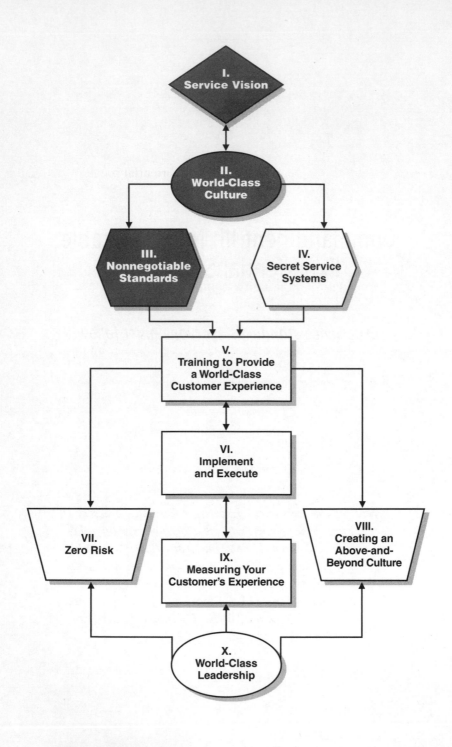

Having nonnegotiable experiential standards for each stage of your organization's customer experience cycle enables employees to provide a consistent engaging experience that is unlike the majority of your competitors.

If your Service Vision is clear and you have hired people that truly share in that vision, now you have to create experiential standards that will allow that Service Vision to become a reality.

## Experience Tax

What if your company actually applied an experience tax to everything you sold to your customers? Think about it for a moment. Similar to a sales tax, regardless of what you sell or which department you work in, at the bottom of the sales slip or the monthly invoice, you would have a experience tax in addition to the original price. What if it was an extra $5.00, or even an extra $500? Would you do anything differently? What would you add to your product or service to justify the price?

If you had to justify to your customers the reason for an experience tax, you would start to analyze and quantify each stage of your customer experience cycle (points of contact), and understand how important it is to be consistent in delivering your nonnegotiable standards.

### Do You Swear to Tell the Truth, the Whole Truth . . .

Imagine that your company's customer service is on trial. You (the manager) are the main witness:

PROSECUTOR: Do you have competitors who charge less for the same service or product?

MANAGER: Yes, plenty of them.

PROSECUTOR: Then why would your customers purchase from you and pay more?

MANAGER: We give better service. We greet customers immediately and call them by name. We treat them like a valuable person, not like a transaction or a number. We build relationships with them. We meet deadlines and deliver on what we say . . . things like that.

PROSECUTOR: That's great. Is there ever a time you don't do these things? Say, you don't recognize them immediately or don't give them more attention or don't run on time?

MANAGER: Yes, of course those things happen. We're human.

PROSECUTOR: I thought so! Let me ask you one final question: When you miss a deadline or run late, or when you treat customers like a transaction, you obviously charged them less—correct?

MANAGER: Uh . . . no, we don't.

PROSECUTOR: What! You don't charge them less? You just told me your customers come to you because you deliver all those things. Are you saying you charged full price for your product and service, but you didn't deliver the full-service portion?

MANAGER: Ah, I guess so.

PROSECUTOR: I rest my case.

## People Want Either the Best or the Least Expensive

The truth of the matter is, unless you are the cheapest in your industry, many businesses already charge an experience tax. The only difference is nobody is brave enough to break it out, but it is in there, buried in your total price. If we were not charging an experience tax, then everyone's prices, for a given product or service, would be exactly the same. But they are not because some companies promise to provide more of an experience than their competitors.

The point is this: Every employee, associate, partner, and shareholder must realize that your company needs to actually deliver whatever it is you promise. Otherwise, your customers can go down the street to a competitor who doesn't promise or charge for those things.

# Teacher Becomes the Student

Smart Business Network, one of the nation's fastest growing publishers of local management journals in over 20 major cities throughout the United States, asked me to emcee and be a judge for their annual World-Class Customer Service Awards. Knowing that I would learn a great deal, I gladly accepted. What I thought I was going to learn was different customer service practices, however, what I ended up learning, actually changed my perspective of customer service.

Being one of the judges, I got to review dozens and dozens of companies' customer service best practices. After narrowing the group of candidates down to about 20 finalists, the judges got to personally interview each one before choosing the final winners for each category. During the finalist's 10-minute presentations on how their customer service stood apart, I heard things like how the Regional Transit Authority had state of the art technology that made life simpler for their customers; how customers at the zoo could get closer to the animals; and how an airport offered traveler-friendly amenities such as Wi-Fi and child-friendly areas.

I found myself mentally questioning them, thinking to myself: What about how friendly your staff is, or how well you trained them to be interactive, and what about your service recovery systems. That judging experience made me realize that customer service does extend beyond the level of hospitality of employees. In order to really assess how good your customer service is, you need to examine six different components of your business, each one having a major impact on the customer's level of satisfaction.

## The Six Components of a Customer's Experience

In order to create brand loyalty and customer evangelists, you must (1) operate at a high level in six distinct areas of business and (2) constantly evaluate your company's customer service across each category, separately, and as categories overlap (see Figure 7.1):

1. *Physical:* Deals with the actual brick-and-mortar component of your operation. These are the physical elements that are more permanent or long term, that cannot be changed daily.
2. *Setting:* Refers to the controllable setting you create daily. As Disney says, "Everything speaks from the doorknobs to the dining rooms

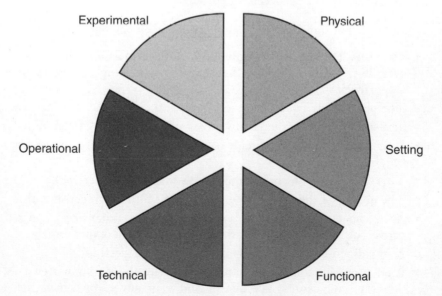

**FIGURE 7.1** Customer Experience Components

sends a message to the guest."[2] The setting communicates a message about what you can provide your customers. This isn't always visual, it may be the music your customers hear when they call and are placed on hold or the mood your web site creates. The setting reveals the characteristics of your business as they appeal to the five senses of your customer: sight, sound, smell, touch, and taste.

3. *Functional:* Refers to the ease of doing business with you—return policies, hours of operations, and other factors. Functionality has nothing to do with human interactions, such as being pleasant or saying please or thank you.

4. *Technical:* Refers to your staff's level of expertise in their particular skills and in the company's systems and equipment, such as product and job knowledge. Again, this has nothing to do with whether they are nice.

5. *Operational:* Refers to the actions that team members must execute behind the scenes before, during, and after a customer's experience. These actions assist in the day-to-day transactions with customers, the tasks, compliances, and duties of our jobs.

6. *Experiential:* Refers to the actions that team members execute while interacting with the customer. Those actions that make the customer say "WOW!" The customer is delightfully surprised. Experiential actions are the reason why customers return, refer others, and become brand evangelists. These include Secret Service, personalization, anticipating customer's needs, and others.

Let's look at some real-life examples of these components:

- Your server is the most incompetent waitress (technical) you have ever met, but she is trying her hardest and being extremely nice (experiential).
- The place needs a good paint job (physical).
- The store where you shop is always out of what you want (operational).
- Your favorite store is difficult to get to and has barely any parking (physical).
- This salon has high energy and always smells great (setting).
- The quality of the food (technical) is unfit for human consumption.
- An associate overheard that you really wanted a diet drink and ran across the street to the drugstore to get it for you (experiential).
- At the diner, everything is themed 1950s style (setting).
- It is impossible to get a human being on the phone. No matter what you try, you cannot get out of the company's voice-mail maze (functionality).

- The company has a 24-hour answering service and guarantees a call back within 60 minutes (functionality).
- My sales rep always screws up my order (technical).

Specific examples of each of these six components are:

**Physical**

Brick and mortar
Building
Structure
Architecture
Location
Accessibility
Parking availability
Design
Décor
Public areas
Floor coverings
Signage
Spaciousness
Handicap accessible

**Setting**

Ambience
Candles
Theme
Lighting
Acoustics
Grounds
Furnishings
Comfort of chairs, beds, etc.
Mood
Signage
Sound system
TV placement
Noise level

**Functional**

Policies
Hours of operation
Ease of doing business
Accessibility to a human being
Product selection
Design of your web site
How well you are staffed
Reliability of vendors
Security
Payment options
Phone number on web site

**Technical**

Employees level of expertise
Speed of your technology
Computers
State of the art technology
Ability to use your web site
Equipment
Phone system
Software
Product knowledge
Quality of product
Timeliness
Knowledge

**Operational**

Daily tasks
Cleaning
Dress code
Preparation
Answering the phone
Duties
Checking people out
Processing orders
Functions of the job
Compliances
Paperwork

**Experiential**

Hospitality
Customer engagement
Personalization
Above and beyond
Using the customer's name
Remembering preferences
Presentation of food
Verbiage/vocabulary of staff
Congeniality
Willingness to help
Anticipating needs
Service recovery
Soft skills

An example of physical excellence would be the beauty of Disney parks or how The Cheesecake Factory restaurants are designed. Starbucks has mastered setting, from the comfortable, inviting furniture to how well they merchandise their cafes, just as Disney has mastered how well they theme their parks and hotels. A couple of great examples of Functional excellence are Nordstrom department stores and Zappos.com who have simplified the process of returning merchandise.

Cleanliness is a great example of operational excellence. When you are considering your customer's experience, you need to put yourself in your customer's shoes. Consider a hospital room, or massage or facial room. Because patients and customers are lying down for extended periods of time, they may notice the condition of areas of the room employees never look at.

As for the sixth component of the customer's experience, experiential excellence, there is no need to provide specific examples here because the rest of this book is focused on experiential standards.

Keep in mind that it is important to constantly review how customer friendly your company is in each department. With regards to training of new and existing employees, the majority of your training will deal primarily with technical, operational, and experiential.

The vast majority of companies focus their training on the technical with very little if any emphasis on the experiential. Having been fortunate to work with some of the best customer-service companies in the world, I have both learned and helped create some amazing training that truly prepares new employees to be able to provide a world-class experience, regardless of their backgrounds.

> People don't remember what you said as much as how you made them feel.

Are any of the components more important than another? No, all are critical and all need to be reviewed and tweaked on a regular basis. The components differ significantly in terms of required people skills training. Physical, setting and functionality have little to do with training or people skills, but the other three components absolutely do involve people skills and training. There is a difference, however, in the training required for each component. It is much easier to train employees on technical and operational skills; they are job-specific, and they include easy-to-train subjects, such as product knowledge, and checklists. Also, technical and operational skills tend to be present and thorough because of prior education, degrees, licensing, certifications, and trade schools. Many industries today mandate continuing education credit hours. The vast majority of companies are weakest in the experiential category.

> Ask your customer to describe the most memorable thing that took place during their last transaction with you.[3]
>
> —*Jeffrey Gitomer*, *Author*, Customer Satisfaction Is Worthless

## Task Focused versus Customer Focused

Secret Service focuses on the experiential. But it is important that a company be technically and operationally excellent before they can be experientially excellent. While your emphasis on experiential skills should not come at the cost of technical or operational, being only technically and operationally focused results in employees losing sight of the customer. As Amy E. Mendenhall, Customer Experience Manager of Hallmark Gold Crown Stores, says, "We have to work hard at not becoming overly task focused and make sure we are being more customer focused." This challenge is not unfamiliar to world-class service companies. Jim McManemon, General Manager of The Ritz-Carlton Sarasota, says, "We have to constantly make sure we are keeping our employees engaged with the guest, otherwise they could easily focus on the technical aspect of their jobs."

Disney educates cast members about the importance of courtesy over efficiency. If a company is strong technically, and operationally, many times that may go unnoticed by your customers. Very few customers ever call their friends and say, "You wouldn't believe how clean their restrooms are," or, "everyone was in the proper dress code." However, if any of those things are not in place, it becomes a "veto" and results in customers not returning or providing word-of-mouth advertising.

Neither technical nor operational excellence will create brand loyalty the way experiential excellence will. Experiential training is the least-provided and hardest-to-teach of the components. But it is also the most rewarding because it provides the largest return on investment (ROI). Experiential training is about making the customer's day. It is about creating value over and above the product you are selling. It clearly sets you apart from you competition. It is about empowering your front-line employees to have a sense of purpose and ownership in their jobs.

# Focusing More on What Drives
# Customer Satisfaction

To demonstrate the importance of experiential standards and how critical it is to incorporate them into your training, let's look at a client of The Di-Julius Group, Summa Health Systems, a network of hospitals. Summa, like many hospitals is focused on increasing their patient satisfaction scores, which they called "Service Excellence" scores. They hired me to help them create additional systems that would have a dramatic impact on their patients' experiences, thus affecting their Service Excellence scores. When reviewing the key drivers, experiences that determined how satisfied their patients were with Summa, it was interesting to see that 10 out of 14 (71 percent) of the key driver questions fell under the experiential category:

| Service Excellence Key Drivers | Category |
|---|---|
| 1. Staff concern for your privacy | (Experiential) |
| 2. Skill of the nurses | (Technical) |
| 3. Staff worked together to care for you | (Experiential) |
| 4. Staff sensitivity to inconvenience | (Experiential) |
| 5. Friendliness/courtesy of the nurses | (Experiential) |
| 6. Courtesy of the person who took blood | (Experiential) |
| 7. Concern and comfort during test and treatment | (Experiential) |
| 8. Staff address your emotional/spiritual need | (Experiential) |
| 9. Explanations during test and treatment | (Operational) |
| 10. Staff included you in decisions regarding treatment | (Operational) |
| 11. Staff attitude toward visitors | (Experiential) |
| 12. Responses to concerns/complaints | (Experiential) |
| 13. Nurses attitude toward requests | (Experiential) |
| 14. Nurses kept you informed | (Operational) |

Yet, experiential is the most overlooked part of most companies' training. It is always about technical and operational training.

## Humanize

Another reason why experiential training is lacking and desperately needed in business today, is that many professionals, such as accountants, doctors, and technology professionals, are heavily trained technically, but have virtually no soft/people skill training. All this results in a very sterile customer experience by the majority of these industries. In many cases, these respected professionals are the worst offenders at providing disappointing customer service.

In order to create a world-class service organization, you must have nonnegotiable experiential standards at every stage (point of contact) of your customer experience cycle. Nonnegotiable means front-line employees understand that these standards are mandatory. It will not be acceptable for employees to pick and choose. All standards are an equal part of the experience.

## World-Class Service Is Not Restricted to Upscale Businesses

Too often, one of the most common reasons I hear businesses use for why they can't deliver exceptional customer service is because they do not charge premium prices. Therefore their model doesn't allow for all the extras needed to provide service at a higher level, such as paying people more, having extra support staff to dote on customers, using sophisticated point of sale systems, and so on. These are not excuses. None of that is necessary to deliver superior service. They are nice to have, but are not necessary. Companies like Chick-fil-A, Panera Bread, and Sport Clips are fantastic examples of companies that do not have extremely high prices but still provide great customer service.

Sport Clips is a chain of moderately priced men's salons throughout the United States. Founder and CEO Gordon Logan created a strong Service Vision that is unique to moderately priced models. Sport Clips has remarkably grown to over 500 locations. They have done this by delivering a superior client experience in a unique and entertaining atmosphere at modest prices.

First off, Sport Clips is no ordinary hair salon or barbershop. They call it "The Championship Experience." Themed like a men's locker room, they display sports memorabilia all over the walls, sports magazines, every hair station has its own TV monitor playing ESPN, and there is memorabilia you can purchase. Everything is sports themed; for example their menu of services is called the Service Lineup and it includes the different haircut packages: The MVP, Triple Play, Varsity, and Jr. Varsity. They also offer Extra Innings (massaging head shampoo, a hot towel around the face, neck and shoulder massage, and free neck trim between haircuts) and the All-Star Treatment. They call their franchisees Team Leaders and employees are Team Members. But they don't rest on just the physical and atmosphere components of providing an experience. Even with their incredible growth, Sport Clips is very selective about who they award a franchise to.

They have extensive customer service training and nonnegotiable standards for each stage of their Five-Point Play.

Sport Clips didn't look at their remarkable sales and stay content. Sport Clips hired The DiJulius Group to help create the training systems and processes to ensure that the consistency of these standards didn't get diluted as the brand grew. As Clete Brewer, President of Sport Clips points out, "Sport Clips was not executing at a high level consistently across all of our stores and we felt we needed to make sure that our system was (1) the right one, and (2) transferable to 500 plus stores, and finally (3) layers could be added as we grow to continue to make Sport Clips the premier place for men and boys to get a great experience and haircut."

The key to the Sport Clips Secret Service project was helping their Championship Experience evolve into much more than the technical part of the customer's experience. It was ensuring that every Team Member knows how to personalize their client's visits, by engaging them, remembering their names, some personal history, haircut preferences, and creating a genuine relationship.

"It [the Secret Service project] gave our team more confidence that we are doing it right; we just need to simplify the training and make it easier for a new Team Member to get the high level of service we are looking for," says Brewer. "We also were able to take away some great ideas that we all want to do once we master the basics of our five-point play. We are rolling out the new simplified training and development program in our Corporate Stores and, after proper testing, it will be rolled out nationwide next year."

Here is one client's response to their great service:

> I'm addicted to Sport Clips. Yes, I like to watch ESPN while I'm getting my hair trimmed. That's an obvious plus. But here's the little thing that keeps me coming back. Every time I walk in they ask for the last four digits of my telephone number. They enter it into the computer and then they say "You usually get a number two (clipper) guard on the sides and a scissor cut on top. Is that what you want today?" "Yeah, that's great," I say. They even keep up with my preference on hair gel.
>
> Their little system of record keeping has saved me a lot of stress and a lot of bad haircuts. I could never remember which size guard I liked. Was it a number 4 or a number 1? Geez, I never got it right it seemed and my haircut has never looked right at other salons. But at Sport Clips, they take notes, they keep stats. My hair looks the same every time I walk out of there. It's easy, I don't even have to think.

"We are all about Secret Service. Our clients think it is amazing what we deliver in our haircut experience. Secret Service just validated much of what Gordon Logan and Sport Clips have been doing over the past 13 years and most importantly helped us take it to the next level by engaging our whole organization. Sport Clips is positioned to do even more in the years to come," says Brewer.

## Examples of Nonnegotiable Standards

A sample of nonnegotiable standards at John Robert's Spa is called Always and Never Standards:

### Never Standards

- Point.
- Say, "no."
- Say, "not a problem."
- Make blind phone transfers internally.
- Overshare with guest.
- Gossip.
- Criticize other team members.
- Show frustration publicly.
- Criticize competitors.
- Accept fine or okay from a customer who is asked how was everything today.
- Only say, "I don't know."
- Have a conversation with a coworker, in front of a guest, that is unrelated to the guest.
- Make the customer wrong.

### Always Standards

- Take them there.
- Do warm transfers.
- 10-feet greet.
- A smile is part of the uniform.
- Greet by name after you learn it.
- Say name two to four times.
- Genuinely say, "certainly, absolutely," and "my pleasure."

- Do what it takes to make it right!
- Own it—even if it is not your fault.
- Focus on what you can do, not what you can't.
- Anticipate and deliver on the guest's needs.
- Deliver at least one Secret Service to every guest.
- Be a detective.
- Acquire, document, and share customer intelligence.
- If you know it, use it.

There is a reason why The Ritz-Carlton is one of the best hotel chains in the world. Even if you have never been to one of their properties, it is obvious that these are not just words on paper. The Ritz-Carlton Credo demonstrates the importance of experiential standards their employees need to deliver in order to create the level of service their guests have become accustomed to:[4]

## THE CREDO

The Ritz-Carlton Hotel is a place where the genuine care and comfort of our guests is our highest mission. We pledge *to provide the finest personal service* and facilities for our guests who will always enjoy a warm, relaxed, yet refined ambience. The Ritz-Carlton experience enlivens the senses, instills well-being, and *fulfills even the unexpressed wishes and needs of our guests.*

### Three Steps of Service

1. A warm and sincere greeting. Use the guest's name, if and when possible.
2. Anticipate guest needs.
3. Fond farewell. Give them a warm goodbye and use their names, if and when possible.

They didn't just stop there; a summary of their Basics (standards) shows how they get specific, detailing exactly how their employees provide the finest personal service for their guests, by incorporating experiential standards in conjunction with the critical operational standards that must be executed:

BASICS

1. Each employee is empowered. For example, when a guest has a problem or needs something special you should break away from your regular duties, address and resolve the issue.

2. To provide the finest personal service for our guests, each employee is responsible for identifying and recording individual guest preferences.

3. Whoever receives a complaint will own it, resolve it to the guest's satisfaction, and record it.

4. "Smile—we are on stage." Always maintain positive eye contact. Use the proper vocabulary with our guests. (Use words like "Good Morning," "Certainly," "I'll be happy to," and "My pleasure.")

5. Escort guests rather than pointing out directions to another area of the hotel.

6. Answer within three rings and with a "smile." Use the guest's name when possible.

## Can We Learn from Junk Collectors?

I had the pleasure of being the opening keynote speaker at the annual 1-800-GOT-JUNK? conference in Vancouver, Canada. What an eye-opening surprise this was!

In 1989, Brian Scudamore started a little business, originally named The Rubbish Boys, that came and removed any junk taking up space at your home or business. This simple concept has now become a $100+ million annual sales empire called 1-800-GOT-JUNK? They have over 300 locations and are the largest junk removal service in the world. How did they do it? You guessed it—the company is recognized for outstanding customer service by being unique and doing things nobody else in their industry is willing to do. Their trucks are fresh, colorful, and spotless. Their drivers are clean-cut and neatly dressed in uniform. But that's not all. They do what they say they will. For example, if they say they will arrive between 9:30 and 10 AM, they do. (How many companies do that?) Some drivers call en route and say, "I should be at your house in 15 minutes. Can I stop and get you a cup of coffee?" This company is creating a buzz and getting people talking about 1-800-GOT-JUNK? I can tell you that I certainly learned something from this junk removal company!

### e-Experience

Amazon.com is the leader in providing quality customer service for a company with very few face-to-face interactions with their customers. They certainly personalize it. When you log onto their web site, they greet you by name, have product recommendations by using customer intelligence they have collected from your purchase history. Now when you order a product, you have the ability to purchase it through them and go pick it up at a nearby store that has the product in stock instead of having it shipped. That is right, you order it and pay for it on Amazon and within a few minutes the local store sends you a confirmation e-mail informing you your product is ready to be picked up. Amazon has changed the time it takes to get the product in its customers' hands from a few days to less than 30 minutes, and it saves the customer shipping costs. One of Amazon's Service Brand Promises is "Obsess Over Customers."

# Notes

1. James H. Gilmore and B. Joseph Pine II, *Authenticity* (Boston, MA: Harvard Business School Press, 2007).
2. The Disney Institute and Michael D. Eisner, "Be Our Guest" (Disney Institute Leadership Series), *Disney Editions*, May 1, 2001.
3. Jeffrey Gitomer, *Customer Satisfaction Is Worthless, Customer Loyalty Is Priceless* (Austin, TX: Bard Press, 1998).
4. http://corporate.ritzcarlton.com/en/About/Default.htm.

# Commandment IV: *Secret Service* Systems

*Utilizing Customer Intelligence to personalize their experience and engage and anticipate their needs*

---

*Secret Service creates an emotional bond between customer and company that transcends the product or service.*

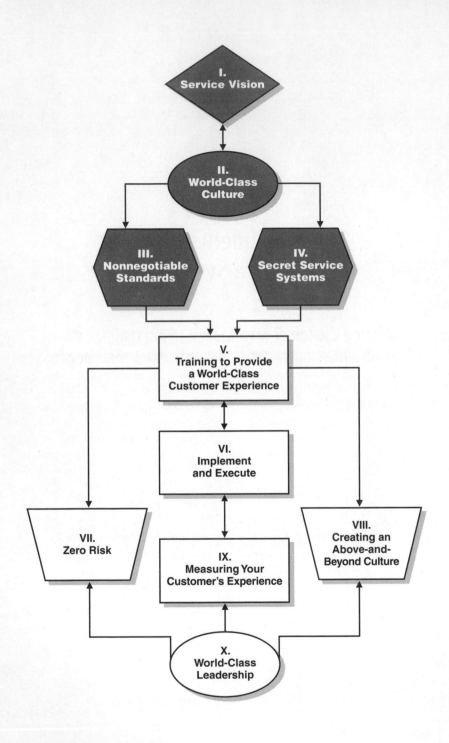

Creating Secret Service systems that allow front-line employees to engage and interact with customers enables them to personalize the customer's experience by anticipating and delivering on their needs. Having great standards are not enough (Commandment III). You now need to systemize those standards in order for them to be realistically delivered on a consistent basis.

> Commodities are fungible, goods tangible, services intangible, and experiences are memorable.[1]
>
> —B. Joseph Pine and James H. Gilmore,
> The Experience Economy

*Secret Service* creates an emotional bond between customer and company that transcends the product or service. That bond, that feeling becomes sought after again and again. It requires a personal connection between customer and employee, and often the lowest paid and least appreciated employee is the best source of this bond.

In Chapter 7, we demonstrated how critical experiential standards are to creating customer loyalty. In this chapter, we detail what experiential actions are and the systems behind them that can make them a standard.

## Brief Review

*Secret Service* means using *hidden systems* to deliver unforgettable customer service. By obtaining *customer intelligence* and utilizing it to *personalize* their experience, you leave the customers asking:

"How'd they do that?"

"How'd they know that?"

Secret Service is behind-the-scenes systems that team members use to anticipate and deliver on the unexpressed needs of the customer by using a system of *silent cues*, *visual triggers*, and *visual aids*.

*Customer intelligence* includes customer data (i.e., buying habits, purchasing history, referrals, personal preferences, where they live, and work).

# Giving a Customer a Memorable Experience

*Secret Service* actions are all experiential components. *Secret Service* is all about personalizing a customer's experience, engaging your customer, and anticipating their needs, thus making a memorable customer experience.

As a result of providing *Secret Service*, companies:

- Create stronger relationships with their customers.
- Build emotional capital and brand equity with their customers.
- Turn their customers into brand evangelists.
- Make price less relevant to their customers.

> We want our standards to be what our competition considers above and beyond.

When John Rolfs was the General Manager of The Ritz-Carlton in South Beach, Florida, he hired me to work with his staff and different departments (valet, bellman, restaurants, housekeeping, and others). Having worked with Rolfs in the past when he was General Manager of The Ritz-Carlton in New Orleans, I jumped at the chance. I enjoy working with any property that he is associated with because he makes my job so much easier. I know his staff gets it. It's no accident that the properties he manages consistently earn five-star status.

While discussing Rolfs' needs for this workshop, I hear familiar requests: "We need a refresher, a shot in the arm about what it is we are actually providing our guests. We need an increased awareness among our front-line associates about the need to go above and beyond, and why it is so important to address service defects and guest challenges immediately." I hung up the phone smiling ear to ear, feeling great about this workshop. You couldn't tee it up any better. He had asked of me exactly what I do: increase the service aptitude of his teams.

I arrived by prearranged car service to the hotel. As I got out of the car, the valet greeted me, "Mr. DiJulius, my name it Scott, I would like to welcome you to The Ritz-Carlton. We will get your luggage for you. Please walk this way." Wow! I was impressed. They knew who I was. They must have recognized me after reading my book and seeing my picture on the back cover. Was I finally becoming a national celebrity?

The bellperson, who was standing inside the door, 10 feet away from us, greeted me in the exact same way, as did the person behind the check-in desk, who already had my room keys ready. The bellperson then accompanied me on a detailed tour of the hotel and showed me to my room.

I decided to call for room service, and the operator answered with, "How may I help you, Mr. DiJulius?" I placed my order and she said, "Would you like bottled water with that?" I said, "Sure, thanks," and she completed the call with, "Certainly, it was my pleasure." My room service arrived about 10 minutes earlier than estimated.

Next I walked around the hotel to observe all the activity in the lobby and the restaurant, and to watch the concierges at work. This is always my best research, I typically get dozens of ideas of missed opportunities and material to include in my upcoming presentations. As I moved from one part of the property to another to observe more, I started to get a nauseous feeling in my stomach and went to my room to lie down. I wasn't coming down with a bug—I was starting to panic. As I had watched the hotel operation unfold, it was like a well-choreographed Broadway play. All the employees knew their roles and lines and executed them flawlessly.

All I could think was, "What do they need me for? All I could do is screw this up!" Then I thought, "Wait a minute, this is what I do. Heck, I've spent the past 10 years of my life researching this stuff."

Once I stopped to think about what was happening, it all started to come to me. First the limo ride: the driver, who was not a Ritz-Carlton employee, got out and whispered my name to the Ritz-Carlton valet. This started the chain of communication that was always one step ahead of me.

I was really impressed by how well The Ritz-Carlton has trained its third-party vendors, such as my limo driver, to deliver *Secret Service* to its guests. The Ritz-Carlton valet, who was wired, communicated my name to the doorman, who greeted me and then directed me to the front desk, where the staff had prepared for my arrival.

The room-service operator knows by the caller ID which room is calling and the guest's name the reservations are under. If more than one person is in the party, the operator changes the greeting to, "How may I help the DiJulius party?" Equally important, when the operator transfers the caller to another department, such as the concierge, the operator notifies that person who is calling. And in this way, the personalized greeting and service continue (which is called a "warm transfer" versus a "cold or blind transfer").

That is literally *Secret Service*. It is a simple, no-cost system at work behind the scenes, wowing you the customer and personalizing your experience. None of that is hard to execute. However, that is what makes The Ritz-Carlton unique. That is why it's not uncommon for The Ritz-Carlton to be fully booked, charging more than $700 a room during peak season.

That day my focus was to help the staff take what they were already doing extremely well, which was executing operational excellence, and to focus intensely on making it experientially superior. For example, I helped them find even more ways to profile their guests and share that information across all their departments. For instance, their restaurants worked on a system to distinguish between new and returning guests. Maintenance worked on "making it right" when someone was inconvenienced because something was not working properly in their room, such as the movie channel or the air conditioning.

The Ritz-Carlton doesn't just hope that front-line associates understand it: The Ritz-Carlton ensures it by performing all the principles a world-class organization observes. Stringent hiring standards weed out applicants who don't have service DNA. From day one on the job, every associate knows what world-class service is, how to correct a service defect, and how to recognize the opportunity to go above and beyond. A great training program starts with the hire and continues throughout employment. No excuses are accepted.

## Cheat Sheets

It is ironic how so many things I did in my youth were really indications of what my adult life would be like. For instance, I was constantly reprimanded by teachers for talking all the time in class. They would kick me out of class, call my mother, but nothing worked. Today, I am a professional speaker.

I was also known to be a poor student or worse. And I am not proud to say that I cheated more than once in school. It turns out, however, that my cheating may have been a positive influence on my specialty of customer service. When I went into business, I always kept cheat sheets on customers and employees to help me remember exactly who they were and what their preferences were so I could personalize their experience by being more engaging and relating to them as individuals. I am positive that my intense focus on this concept is more responsible than anything else for the rapid and continued success of both my companies, John Robert's Spa and The DiJulius Group. We have made personalization an integral part of our training. We teach all employees how to personalize each customer's experience.

# If You Know It, Use It

The thing that amazes me the most is how much money companies invest in sophisticated customer relationship management (CRM) systems, yet they utilize very little of what they learn. Customer relationship management systems facilitate the "relationship," but very few companies require that employees learn and utilize the capabilities of their databases. Utilizing your database is the easiest and most powerful way to provide *Secret Service* and engage customers (versus making them feel like a transaction). By doing things such as updating personal and professional preferences, checking buying history, and so on, you can personalize the service you deliver.

> Knowledge is worthless if it is not utilized.

## Personalize the Customer

This concept is not as obvious as you might think, especially to front-line employees. Failing to personalize happens at John Robert's Spa more than I want to admit. A service provider will read a popup note about a guest coming in, maybe where they work or that they are celebrating something, but won't proactively use that information in their conversation. Information and knowledge of the customer (customer intelligence) is worthless if we don't use it to build the relationship with the customer. We have found out that engaging customers is not common sense and front-line employees need to be trained on how to incorporate usable, customer intelligence (customer information) into their dialogue.

The following principles are nonnegotiable standards for how employees can personalize existing customers anytime they come in contact with them. This applies to conversations that take place in person, on the phone, or at any stage of your customer experience cycle.

### Customer Personalization

- Acknowledge their name immediately.
- Recognize their special occasion immediately—if that is the reason for their visit.
- Demonstrate your Secret Service awareness of at *least* one thing that is specific about them as your customer and/or about them personally. For instance:
  —Ask how their last (specific) purchase, from you, worked out.
  —Thank them for their referral.
  —Mention their profession or where they work.
  —Acknowledge a preference of theirs, for example, "I know you like your orders to arrive on Mondays."
  —Make mention of family members, kids, spouse, or others.
  —Recognize any recent special occasion (i.e., birthday, promotion).
  —Mention the city they live in.

—Mention the school they attend.
—Mention where they work.

A good example of a missed opportunity to personalize a customer's experience occurred when I had a meeting at a financial services company I use. When I walked in, the receptionist was on the phone, so I sat down and waited till she got off. A few minutes later, the person I was meeting with appeared in the lobby to greet me. I asked, "How did you know I was here?" He said, "The receptionist just notified me." I didn't realize that she even knew who I was, but she missed a great opportunity to deliver some Secret Service by saying, "Welcome, Mr. DiJulius. I have just notified Bob that you are here. He will be here momentarily. Is there anything I can get you?" Instead, she said nothing; I didn't even know she was off the phone.

## Walking the Talk

This applies to business-to-business (B2B) companies as well. I own both types of businesses, John Robert's Spas, which is business-to-customer (B2C) and The DiJulius Group, which is B2B. The Service Vision of The DiJulius Group is "Creating World-Class Customer Service Organizations," which means we have to walk our talk and make sure we are delivering world-class service to our customers. We have customized the program Outlook, by adding an area, so we can track both personal and professional information on our speaking, consulting, and prospective clients. Figure 8.1 shows the area where employees at The DiJulius Group can update and access personalized information on their clients. Information such as their

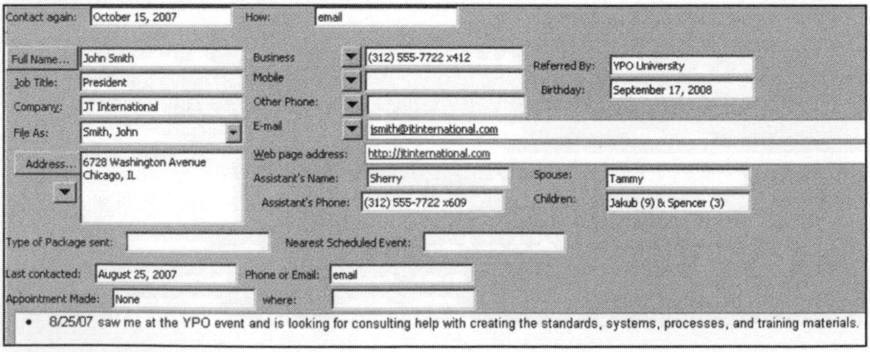
Contact again: October 15, 2007
How: email
Full Name... John Smith
Job Title: President
Company: JT International
File As: Smith, John
Address... 6728 Washington Avenue Chicago, IL
Business (312) 555-7722 x412
Mobile
Other Phone:
E-mail jsmith@jtinternational.com
Web page address: http://jtinternational.com
Assistant's Name: Sherry
Assistant's Phone: (312) 555-7722 x609
Referred By: YPO University
Birthday: September 17, 2008
Spouse: Tammy
Children: Jakub (9) & Spencer (3)
Type of Package sent:
Nearest Scheduled Event:
Last contacted: August 25, 2007
Phone or Email: email
Appointment Made: None
where:
• 8/25/07 saw me at the YPO event and is looking for consulting help with creating the standards, systems, processes, and training materials.

**FIGURE 8.1** Personal and Professional Information

company history, assistant's name, spouse's name, kid's name, birthday, past communication history, and so on. This file is shared with everyone in our office and whoever is speaking to a client can access this information to personalize the conversation.

I have a philosophy I share with all my people at the corporate offices. When they transfer a call to me, if the person doesn't immediately tell me how impressed they were with the person who they just spoke to, we are not being world-class.

## The Norm Factor

If you take away nothing else from this book, teach your employees how to master the *Norm factor*. This is a reference to the character Norm in the old sitcom *Cheers*. When he walked into the bar, everyone yelled "Norrrm!" Would Norm have frequented Cheers if he had not been so recognized? Developing this technique—teaching your front-line employees how to do it consistently—is probably the most important Secret Service system your company can create.

Mastering the Norm factor should be an integral part of your soft-skill training. Many companies let this happen by chance, typically a few long-term employees create relationships with regular customers and this naturally happens. You have a high degree of inconsistency when it is only contingent on long-term employees and regular customers. The best customer service companies train all their employees, even their newest employees, how to make everyone feel like Norm. A good system with the proper training allows even the newest employees to personally engage and recognize even those customers who come less frequently.

Customers should not have to expect or receive less of an experience because they are dealing with a new employee. It is important that your newest employees be extensively trained so they hit the ground running.

# Distinguish New from Returning Customers

This Secret Service system identifies new from existing customers. For instance, at John Robert's Spa, returning customers are draped in black capes for haircuts, and new customers are draped in white capes. Every team member throughout the salon knows this fact and can address our guests accordingly. The color of the capes is the silent cue and visual trigger.

In some fine restaurants, everyone from the bus staff to the server knows that a customer with a red napkin has never been to the restaurant before. This ensures that new customers are greeted correctly, receive more details about the menu, learn about the chef's credentials, and benefit from any other service protocol for new customers. A black napkin means they are an old friend and a gold napkin means they are one of the restaurant's top 50 guests. The server should be bringing them their favorite drink before they even ask.

I love it when I hear people say, "We treat all our customers the same, and they all deserve to be treated like royalty." I am not saying the "white capes" are treated better than "black capes," they are just treated differently. New customers could be experiencing a level of anxiety and uneasiness. The top customer service companies literally have the white cape system at every stage of their customer experience cycle—on the phone, check in, check out, and follow up. It should be a totally different experience for new customers than it is for returning customers. More information shared, baby steps, versus anticipating the needs of a returning customer based on his or her past preferences and sales history.

Returning customers should be treated like "old friends." We actually have included this in the customer service training for companies, role playing an old friend. Picture this: you are traveling, walking along the street and you bump into your old friend, whom you haven't seen since high school. Your eyebrows go up, you're genuinely excited to see them, and you ask them about something you remember they told you. Our existing customers need to be made to feel like "old friends" and it is critical that you don't assume front-line employees will naturally do that.

A "white cape" system doesn't necessarily have to be their first visit or experience. For many businesses, it might be the first three months we do business with them. For instance, a dry cleaner has red bags for newer customers (less than 90 days), black and blue bags for regulars, and yellow and gold bags for VIP customers, thus notifying everyone internally what type of customer they are dealing with. This way, if you are a new counter clerk and you see someone walk in with a red bag, you give them more information on how their clothes will be cleaned and when they will be ready, you also tell them about additional services you offer (i.e., tailoring, the storing of gowns and dresses). If a customer brings in a dark color bag, you know he has been a customer for a while and you treat him as such, welcoming him back. If you see a customer parking their car and you notice a yellow or gold bag in the back seat, you run out there and carry the bag inside for them.

Some hotels vary the color of the "Do Not Disturb" sign on the door to distinguish new from returning customers. This way housekeeping will notice if you are first-time visitor at the resort, and tell you a lot more about the activities available, offer directions to surrounding attractions, offer suggestions on places to dine, and provide other services that will add value to the experience. Other hotels use different color valet tickets that hang from the guest's rearview mirrors, to notify the valet and security guard at the gate anytime a guest is coming and going during their stay. This allows the hotel associates to personalize their interactions, depending on whether it is a returning guest or one who has never been to the property before.

All of these examples demonstrate how customer service systems go beyond the initial greeting. These systems also allow your team to tailor the information to meet the customer's needs.

### Color Cues

You need to create a system of silent cues, visual triggers, that enable all employees, even the newest, to distinguish between new and returning or VIP customers and to personalize the customer's experience accordingly. Color is a quick and easy way to identify a new customer, whatever your industry or business.

### Silent Cues

It is important to distinguish between new, returning, and VIP customers at every stage of the customer experience cycle. For instance, Figure 8.2

**FIGURE 8.2**  John Robert's Spa Software, Salonbiz, Prompting Front Line Employees That the Customer Is New

shows the software that John Robert's Spa uses, Salonbiz, which notifies the call center and front desk that this guest is new when their name is clicked on. This is crucial because new guests need more direction and more information than existing guests.

Another example of visual aids is our appointment book that is color coded. This allows the service providers to immediately know if a guest is a first time, returning, or VIP customer. If it is a returning guest, the service provider can click on the guest's name to get additional information, sales history, personal notes, referrals, where they live, or work, to then personalize the guest's experience (Figure 8.3). Anytime any employee interacts with one of our VIP guests, our software immediately notifies them (Figure 8.4).

## Secret Service Lawyers

Carter Mario Injury Lawyers, with four offices throughout the state of Connecticut, has an average annual growth of at least 20 percent over the past five years. Revenues have grown from $2.5 million in 2002 to over $8

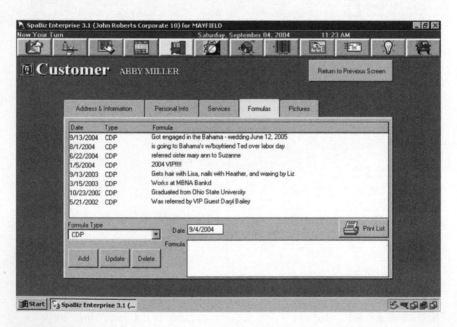

**FIGURE 8.3**  John Robert's Spa Client History and Personal Notes Section

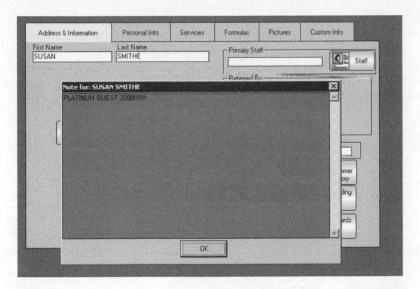

**FIGURE 8.4**   John Robert's Spa Software Notifying Employees of VIP Customers

million in 2007. However, sales were not always strong. In 2002, the law firm was stagnant largely due to low service aptitude. That is when Carter Mario, CEO and President, a person who is passionate about service, decided to buy out his partners in the law firm. "Our service culture had to change in order for us to differentiate from the rest of the pack and to survive," says Mario. "We adopted a service culture that has enabled us to become one of the fastest growing law firms in the state. Most law firms still do not understand the service nature of our business and really do not understand that people have a choice. We have identified all of the traditional problems within our profession from a service perspective and have successfully branded ourselves as a firm who cares for our clients."

One of the single biggest complaints in the legal industry from clients is poor communication between clients and lawyers. "We made this the number one priority in our office: client contact. We guarantee we will return the client's call the same day or lunch is on us. It is a nonnegotiable part of everyone's job here," says Mario.

Many organizations attend my Secret Service workshops and have had great success at going back and implementing their own Secret Service systems. However, not many have been as successful and committed as Carter Mario. After returning from attending a Secret Service workshop, the management team at Carter Mario instituted a procedure for capturing information about each client in a format that allows everyone access. They were able to customize the software they use, which was made for attorneys, by adding a "Secret Service Tab" (see Figure 8.5). This tab contains vital customer intelligence, such as preferred refreshment, client's eye color, birth date, spouse and other family members' names, children's ages, hobbies, past vacations, even pet's name.

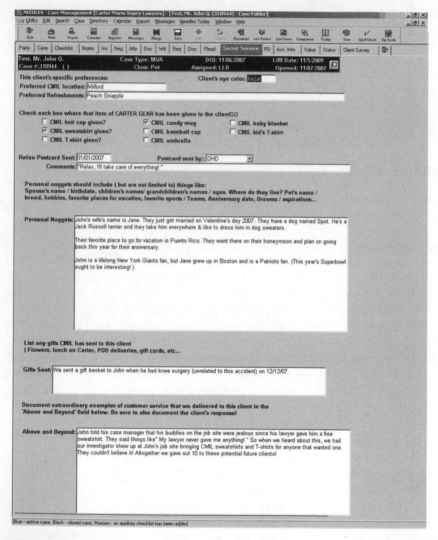

**FIGURE 8.5** Carter Mario Law Firm—Customized Secret Service Tab Tracking Their Clients Personal Preferences

The use of personal information literally blows clients away. They use the Secret Service tab to execute what Carter Mario calls "drive-bys," where a staff member makes a seemingly spontaneous visit with a client who is in the office, just to say hello and say something personal, which is retrieved from the client's Secret Service tab. Mario says, "By knowing names of their spouse, kids, hobbies, and any other personal nugget, it helps build our client equity. We do this with everyone we come in contact with—claims adjusters, opposing attorneys, judges, court reporters, everyone." It is not uncommon for a Carter Mario employee to leave the building and go to the deli to get their client their favorite drink. "We have continuously received great responses from our clients, and a collateral benefit has been that our staff members doing the drive-bys really enjoy the responses they've received, and it pumps them up," says Mario.

# Guestology

*Guestology* is another Disney term meaning: understanding our guests' expectations.[2] Profiling your customer's preferences allows you to anticipate their needs. An employee of a coffeehouse may notice a regular customer pulling into the parking lot. And before the customer can get to the counter and order, her drink is ready and waiting.

I have worked with some resorts that provide a returning customer's favorite cocktail as the customer is being seated for dinner or have their favorite soft drink ready in the vehicle upon departure.

By collecting and storing preferences and other personal information, your staff will be able to personalize future visits. Staff can ask the customer specific questions, such as "How are little Billy and Suzi?" or "How did you enjoy your trip to the Bahamas last month?" This system is also great for noting what the customer does not like.

When a customer calls in to place an order, within seconds, the call center representative should be able to pull up their database and historical information and be able to personalize their experience, citing things such as, "I know you like your orders to arrive at the beginning of the week."

Obviously, not every business has the advantage of knowing who is coming in on a given day. Fast-food restaurants and retail stores generally do not take appointments and therefore cannot use a database. However, they still can provide Secret Service effectively.

### Club 100
This is a phenomenal technique for retail and fast-food restaurants. I'm not sure where CLUB 100 originated, but it is an extremely effective way

to get front-line employees to remember and recognize an incredible number of customers' faces and names. Make a contest out of it and call it something like CLUB 100. Challenge your employees to demonstrate that they know 100 different customers who walk through the door and can greet every one of them by name.

### Panera Warmth

I shared the CLUB 100 idea with nearly 2,000 managers of Panera Bread at their annual convention in Charlotte, North Carolina. I was a fan of Panera Bread long before they became a client of mine. I think they are the twenty-first century *Cheers*. They have front-line people who are friendly and mature, in their 30s and 40s, and Panera's atmosphere makes you want to stay there all day instead of going back out into our crazy, hectic world.

Within weeks after the convention, I started getting feedback on how managers had already instituted variations of the CLUB 100 approach and with great success. At one location, a manager offered a $50 gift certificate to anyone who could demonstrate the ability to learn 50 names and faces and a $100 gift certificate to anyone who learned 100 names and faces. There was no limit on how many employees could win.

You would be amazed at how quickly employees grasp this technique. As employees join the club, their name goes on the CLUB 100 board in the breakroom, they receive a CLUB 100 T-shirt and pin, and so on. Pretty soon you will have a Club 200 and a Club 500, and you will have accomplished two things: (1) your employees make a conscious effort to associate customers' faces with their names and recognize them, and (2) a lot of customers now feel like "Norrrm!" Companies have found that their staff are amazed at what a positive motivator it is to use a customer's name and how much fun it is and how many friendships are formed.

Training your employees to remember their regulars allows them to provide superior service more often.

## It's a Two-Way Name Game

If you really want to make people feel like Norm, remembering customers' names is not enough. Norm also knew everyone's name that worked and frequented Cheers. Think about yourself as a consumer. The places you feel like Norm, the businesses you have the strongest relationships, are places where you know the names of numerous people. There is no such thing as a one-way relationship. Another simple technique is training your front-line employees to *always* introduce themselves in every interaction, to wear their name tags, and to repeat their names.

Relationships are what make people feel like human beings. We stop being a transaction or an account number and we start to have human interactions. Relationships build emotional brand capital. Upset customers have no problem leaving companies. They have a *much* harder time leaving Nicole or Eric. Customers who are treated like mere transactions view the companies as big and cold, with unsympathetic policies. By contrast, customers who have relationships with associates think about how much Nicole has done for them over the years, how well she knows them and their preferences, and that her son Dave just entered college.

# Secret Service for Retailer

Having worked with companies like Lane Bryant and Hallmark Gold Crown stores, I learned how critical building a rapport was prior to trying to sell someone something. Both Lane Bryant, a woman's clothing retailer, and Hallmark have hundreds of stores across the United States, and have made a significant investment in improving their customer's experience. While observing their customer interaction, I noticed, like many retailers, they had associates working as a greeter up front. The associate greeted the customer immediately with a promotional pitch.

Rarely did I see customers "bite" on this type of greeting. They just nodded and walked away, and none of them re-engaged the associate. Some customers found what they were looking for on their own and made a purchase; others looked around a bit and left without purchasing. The floor greeter had almost no impact on sales. This is an ineffective use of resources: Most retailers are very limited in how many staff they can schedule at one time, so it is critical to get maximum productivity out of every associate.

I felt the model of a greeter was right; the approach just needed tweaking. Many consumers perceive employees at retail stores as aggressive salespeople who are trying to make commissions and score big rather than actually wanting to help you. When I walk into a store and someone says, "Can I help you?" I immediately respond, "No, thanks," even if I actually do need help.

## Building Rapport

I suggested to Lane Bryant that, first of all, the greeter waiting at the front of the store should be busy, for example, folding sweaters. Then, when someone enters, the associate should act as if the customer is an old friend—stop the busy work and give a sincere greeting. Given the fact that many consumers are cynical and suspicious of being approached, it is critical that associates are trained to first build rapport, long before any sales pitch is made. Actually, if rapport is built, no sales pitch will ever be needed because the customer will ask for help. For Lane Bryant, I suggested their greeter open with, "What's the occasion?" because a woman always has a reason for shopping: going on vacation and needing some warm-weather clothes, or getting a new job and needing some professional clothes, or even just having some free time. More important, it is the next thing the associate says that builds the relationship and breaks down the customer/salesperson barrier: "Excellent! Where are you going on vacation?" or "Congratulations! What is your new position?" People love to talk about what they do, and by getting the customer to share and talk, and by finding commonalities, the associate immediately builds trust and finds out what is needed. Now it becomes more like helping a friend rather than making a sale.

Similarly, Hallmark Gold Crown stores have their greeters ask, "Who are you shopping for?" which I think is a great ice-breaker and rapport-building opening. Associates should be trained to follow up that question with another ice-breaker/rapport question:

- *My husband:* How long have you been married?
- *Someone I work with:* Where do you work?
- *My daughter:* How old is she? Where does she go to school?

This rapport- and relationship-building accomplishes your goal of connecting with the customers through genuine conversation rather than just jumping in for the sale.

When retailers use these techniques, their conversion rate (percent of customer who purchase) doubles, and the average ticket dramatically increases.

- Teach front-line personnel to be detectives. Pay attention to what the customer is wearing: name tag or employment badge, a hat or shirt with a slogan or logo, great clothes or accessories, or the color of eyes and hair. You get the idea.
- Find something to say to each customer:
  —[Employment badge] "You work at Progressive? I hear it's a great company. We love all our customers who work at Progressive. How can I make your day?"
  —[Hat or shirt with logo] "We have a Buckeye fan! Aren't they doing great?"
  —[Terrific garment or accessory] "That's an awesome tie!" [or belt or whatever]

When you think of things that separate Nordstrom from other stores, it is the details that really make a difference. It is how employees walk around the counter, genuinely thank you and hand you your bags. If they don't have your size, not only do they find it, but they will have it shipped to your house within a few days. They send you personal thank-you cards after you shop. They have quick alterations on site if you need them, and you can return anything, even if you lose your receipt. Are other retailers doing any of these things? Yes, but none of them are doing all of them as consistently as Nordstrom, which makes for a powerful shopping experience.

### Custom Service

By simply asking the question, "What's the occasion?" at the time a reservation is made, you can trigger a multitude of responses: We are celebrating a promotion, a graduation, an engagement, an anniversary, a reunion. When the customer arrives, the greeter presents him with a special-occasion greeting card from the team.

If you are one of the organizations that holds preshift huddles, it is easy to ensure that every staff member encountering that customer congratulates him. One of our team members took this a step further when a couple came in for pedicures. She prepared a sign above their station that read, "Celebrating 25 Years." It's amazing how effective this simple system can be.

What's the occasion can be asked by any greeter, on the phone when scheduling an appointment or when someone walks into a location by the hostess/greeter. This is a great way to personalize the customer's experience. In nearly every situation, there is an occasion for someone doing something. Many times it will be significant and other times it might just be because they wanted to. But either way it opens up the opportunity to get some customizable customer intelligence that can be used later in their experience that will certainly leave a lasting impression of how well your company personalized it and made them feel.

Another easy Secret Service system that every consumer business should use—and so few do—is to thank a customer by name when he or she uses a credit card or check. Most consumers pay with a card or check, and this technique is so easy. It should be a nonnegotiable standard for every employee, every time!

### Recognizing Your Customers

Many types of businesses—such as offices, hotels, restaurants, and salons—can use the reservation system to develop another strong Secret Service system to identify a VIP or a special occasion. Here's how we do it at John Robert's Spa (Figure 8.6).

## JOHN ROBERT'S TEAM HUDDLE
### Today is Wednesday, June 27th
4 weeks: July 25th; 6 weeks: August 8th; 8 weeks: August 22nd

Birthdays: Laura T. 6/25
Anniversaries: Denise K. 6/28

Jeans Day Thursday, July 5th for Project Daymaker!!! $5!!

**Above and Beyond Story:** Sany drew diagrams on a head sheet for her client one night because she is moving to Hong Kong.

### Concierge Info:

| VIP's | Special Occasions |
|---|---|
| 1. _____ | 1. _____ |
| 2. _____ | 2. _____ |
| 3. _____ | 3. _____ |
| 4. _____ | 4. _____ |
| 5. _____ | 5. _____ |
| 6. _____ | 6. _____ |
| 7. _____ | 7. _____ |
| 8. _____ | |
| 9. _____ | **New Clients** |
| 10. _____ | 1. _____ |
| 11. _____ | 2. _____ |
| 12. _____ | 3. _____ |
| 13. _____ | 4. _____ |
| 14. _____ | 5. _____ |
| 15. _____ | 6. _____ |
| 16. _____ | 7. _____ |
| 17. _____ | 8. _____ |
| 18. _____ | 9. _____ |
| 19. _____ | 10. _____ |
| 20. _____ | 11. _____ |

Multiple Appointments

1. _____
2. _____
3. _____
4. _____
5. _____
6. _____
7. _____
8. _____

**FIGURE 8.6**   John Robert's Spa Daily Guest Report

Acquiring this information is easy. Any time our reservationists find out about a special occasion, they enter a popup note in the customer file, notify the salon manager, and make sure that note is included in that day's preshift huddle.

As part of this process, at the end of each evening, the closing manager runs a report that gives us all the information about tomorrow's appointments: new guests, VIPs, people with three or more appointments, and special-occasion guests. This information is put into our preshift huddle and gets shared with our teams.

## Starbucks Difference

I guess it is safe to say that Starbucks is not just a fad; it is certainly part of our society today. If you think about its simplicity, a quick-service café that sells a commodity, coffee and breakfast treats, it is baffling how Starbucks has differentiated itself so dramatically from hundreds of similar concepts. The Starbucks model proves, more than anything else, how important superior customer service can be as a value proposition.

How has Starbucks come to dominate the retail coffee industry and also emerged as an icon in millions of people's daily lives? Is it their product? Not at all; many people prefer other brands but remain loyal Starbucks customers. Is it the location? No, because although Starbucks generally has great locations, so do many of their competitors. Is it their facilities or equipment? No, those have also been duplicated by competitors. What the competition can't seem to duplicate is the way Starbucks captures the emotional capital of their customers, by what I call the "Starbucks difference." At nearly every Starbucks, you can expect the same ambience and atmosphere, the same product quality, and most important, the same way of engaging the customer. Starbucks associates are trained to greet customers in a very friendly and courteous way, with a smile, to remember regulars and treat them as such. They find a way to incorporate the customer's name into the order; they even greet regulars by their drink order instead of their name, and people love it. Those few things create the "Starbucks difference" and have produced a long-term cult following unlike anything I have ever seen. While this is a very simple strategy, very few companies come close to doing any of this.

## Starbucks Mania

Starbucks understands the part they play in our society and what they really sell. As Starbucks' President, Howard Schultz, pointed out in his book, *Pour Your Heart into It*, Starbucks is today's "third place" for people, a place away from work and home where they can safely connect with others in the community. It has been said that Starbucks could stop selling coffee and just charge people admission to use their place to meet.[3] I know that wherever my family vacations, one of the first things we do is to locate the nearest Starbucks and make it a ritual to visit daily. And my local Starbucks, in Aurora, Ohio, is like the town meeting hall. Any time I go there, I am guaranteed to see several people I know.

Customers become so engaged with Starbucks that they will straighten up the condiment station or hand the barista a milk thermos that needs refilling; they actually help Starbucks deliver service to its customers! A Starbucks cup has become a status symbol, like a designer label or the make of car we drive.

Starbucks has made even ordering your drink an experience. First, they don't say no to customization, I literally have notes in my cell phone of how my wife likes her coffee, because it is like a long formula impossible to remember—venti iced coffee with sugar-free caramel, nonfat milk, and a shot of espresso!

## Whose Experience Is It?

It is the customer's experience that the customer is paying for, not our employees' experience. Unfortunately, too many front-line employees forget that and ruin a customer's experience by making it apparent that they are having a bad day or overshare about personal problems.

Several years ago, I took an amazing class at the Disney Institute in Orlando Florida: "Disney's Approach to People Management." It was an incredible learning experience, from the classroom to the field trips. On one field trip we got to go underground at Magic Kingdom, where the Cast Members punch in, take breaks, and eat lunch. There was Snow White herself, on break, complaining to her fellow Cast Members about some guy she was dating. A few moments later, her break ended, and I saw her walk up some stairs and back onto the Magic Kingdom grounds, where a dozen little children greeted her. She turned back into a beautiful princess, smiling and signing autograph albums. It was cool to see how she changed instantly from a regular young woman to the Snow White that the children were there to see. It's not our experience we are selling, it is our customer's experience. Make sure to sell your customer's experiences.

Another situation that can ruin the customer's experience is employees having unprofessional conversations in front of the customer or with the customer. One of our salons invented a way to self-police this situation. Whenever an employee's conversation strays into the unprofessional area, a coworker asks that employee, "Have you seen Beth's new haircut?" Because the salon doesn't have an employee named Beth, it is a polite way to make the employee aware that she may want to change the topic of conversation. This technique has become very popular and we now use it companywide.

# Secret Service Case Study: The Melting Pot Restaurants

## The Opportunity

The Melting Pot Restaurants, an upscale franchise headquartered in Tampa, with over 110 locations all over the United States, were challenged to be able to successfully handle their rapid growth. Nearly all chains are challenged with differentiating themselves from other crowded players in their industry and the ability to create processes that dramatically reduce variation from location to location. "While we were an exceptional restaurant in all aspects, nothing set us dramatically apart from our competition," says Kendra M. Sartor, Vice President of Brand Development, The Melting Pot Restaurants. They hired The DiJulius Group to help create the ultimate dining experience and live up to their mission:

> To provide our guests a chance to *escape, create memories*, and *pursue their dreams.*

It was obvious that one of the strengths of The Melting Pot was helping guests enjoy special occasions. In order for the chain to truly brand themselves as a wonderful dining experience, they needed to do three things: (1) not just be known as the rare special occasion place; with all the stress in our lives today, the restaurant's experience could and should be an increasingly regular necessity to escape versus the rare special occasion place; (2) get buy-in from their 100+ franchisees and employees; and (3) create realistic, nonnegotiable experiential standards that could easily be standardized in all their locations.

The President of The Melting Pot, Bob Johnston, has a passion for service I have seen in very few people. From the beginning of this project, he was adamant about making sure their mission and vision had a life of its own, "getting young employees to focus on exceptional service is a challenge.

Ironically, we discovered that our team members identified with our guests better when we focused on understanding the reasons the guest chooses to celebrate with us rather than focusing on just service. In other words, they were much more inclined to go the extra mile for the guest when they know what was at stake for the guest," says Johnston.

## The Action

The first thing I did was present a customized Secret Service keynote speech at their annual franchisees' reunion, which I call the "arouse and inspire." By sharing simple Secret Service ideas that demonstrate easy ways to engage customers and create loyalty, it typically arouses the managers to say, "We could do that, why aren't we doing things like that." Then we followed up with the Customer Experience Cycle Workshop (explained in detail in Chapter 9), which allowed the franchisees a chance to help create the ultimate dining experience, versus the corporate headquarters dictating these initiatives. Then for the next 12 months, behind the scenes, The DiJulius Group worked with The Melting Pot's Secret Service project team that was comprised of several key franchisees and corporate support staff. During the process, the mission evolved and from it was created a strong Service Brand Promise, known as "Perfect Night Out." In order to consistently do that, a powerful Secret Service system needed to be created to allow all Melting Pot employees the ability to engage guests more often and personalize their experience. Out of all those meetings, long hours, and a lot of hard work, we created the Secret Service Guest Card.

"We adopted a culture focused on providing our guests the Perfect Night Out, empowered our teams to make decisions, not just at the unit level, but at the table level, and created an emotional bond with our guests by going above and beyond to exceed their expectations," says Sartor.

### Secret Service Guest Card
The Melting Pot introduced this new system early in 2007. While providing an exceptional memorable experience has always been The Melting Pot's point of difference, the Secret Service Guest Card (SSGC) has elevated them to another level and has allowed them to achieve their mission: To provide the Perfect Night Out.

The SSGC (Figure 8.7) is Secret Service at its best: free, simple and easy to execute, and, at the same time, leaves guests scratching their heads and wondering, "How did they do that?" Here is a breakdown of SSGC at each stage of the guest experience cycle:

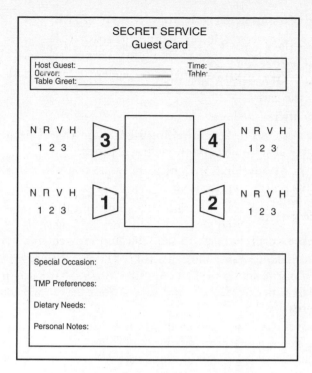

**FIGURE 8.7** Secret Service Guest Card

## Reservations

- The reservationist simply asks each guest calling in, "what's the occasion?" And then tracks that information in their software so they can personalize their dining experience.

## Setting the stage

- When a hostess arrives for her shift, she immediately starts a SSGC for each guest who has made reservations, filling out only the name the reservations are in (Host Name) and time.
- The hostess checks the customer database, reviews the information entered for guests who are returning, if they are celebrating any special occasions, and records pertinent personal information. For example, Mr. Jones owns a local dry cleaning company, likes Merlot wine, and prefers to be seated at table 24.
- Last, she sorts the cards by reservation time.

### Greeting guests upon arrival

- During the 6 o'clock hour, she has at hand all the reservations expected in that hour.
- When a party arrives, she immediately finds their SSGC and welcomes the party.
- She identifies the host.
- She is alert to overhear anything significant that is happening with the party that would call for congratulations.
- If she hears anything of significance, she records it in the special-occasion section on the SSGC.

### Seating the guests

- Hostess escorts the party to the table and seats them.
- While handing out menus, she asks, "Is this anyone's first experience at our restaurant?" She tells first-timers, "You are in for an incredible new experience!" and says, "Your server will be with you momentarily."
- She leaves the table and records where the host of the party is sitting, where the new guests are sitting, and so on.
- She then gives the SSGC to the server.

### Server greets guests

- Server reviews the SSGC before approaching the table.
- On arriving at the table, he immediately welcomes the host and gives him the wine menu.
- Server tells the new guests, "I understand it is the first time for both of you. You are in for a great experience!"
- During his visits to the table, he listens for and records any pertinent information shared at the table, such as special occasion or special dietary needs.
- Server gives the SSGC to the manager on duty.

### Manager's table visit

- Manager reviews the SSGC before approaching the table.
- Manager greets the party, distinguishes between the host and new guests, and personalizes everyone's experience.
- Manager notes and records any pertinent information shared at the table.
- Manager gives the SSGC back to the hostess.

## Closing

- Hostess updates all information from the SSGC into the database in order to personalize the guests' next dining experience. Most of the information on the SSGC is obvious. What might not be is the following:

  N = New Guest, R = Returning Guest, V = VIP Guest, and H = Host.

  1, 2, and 3 indicate a guest's morale upon arrival, as noted by the hostess or server, with "1" being high and "3" being low. If guests are marked "3," it becomes the job of everyone who comes into contact with them to try to get them to a "1" before their experience is over.

  The large "3" means position 3 at that table.

Figure 8.8 is an example of what the Secret Service Guest Card might look like after the guests depart.

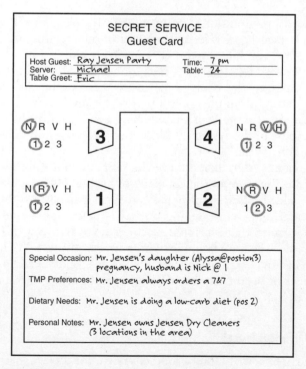

**FIGURE 8.8**   Completed Secret Service Guest Card

The beauty of this system is that it fits the description of Secret Service to a "T." Hidden systems obtain customer intelligence and through visual triggers, allow other staff members (server and manager) the ability to personalize the customer's experience, and anticipate their needs. It also avoids repetitive questions that customers find annoying (i.e., "The hostess, server, and manager all asked if this was our first time here.") Customers should be scratching their heads, saying, "How did they do that and how did they know that?" It elevates everyone's game. It allows the hostesses to be detectives and requires them to ask engaging questions versus a sterile transaction.

At the end of the night, there is also a checks and balances to see where the system is breaking down. If there were 50 reservations tonight, but only 25 Secret Service Guest Cards filled out, the hostess didn't do her job. If a server had 10 tables, however, and four of the cards have no information filled in, the server didn't do his or her job. The general manager can see how many table visits were done by the manager on duty by the comments filled in. And finally, it can be verified if the hostess updated all the guests' information in the database at the end of the evening.

## The Results

"We completely revised our training materials, using the 'Perfect Night Out' Guest Experience Cycle as the center of our learning initiatives. We also put into place simple systems that made providing a new 'high touch' level of service easy for the team," says Johnston. "Almost immediately, we noticed a change in the things our guests were telling us. We received complement letters from our guests before; however, now they contained an emotional tone that tells us that we have connected to them in a whole new way. Because of the systems we have put into place, we know our guest better than ever. What's more, there is a greater sense of a 'heroic cause' within our team. We are doing more than serving our guest, we are helping them enjoy life more in the company of people they care about."

Sartor added, "Letters of praise have quadrupled into the Franchise Support Center and we are seeing positive guest counts and sales in an economic downturn that is crippling others in the industry. It [Secret Service] has become the foundation on which we do business. We have discovered that in dealings with our guests, employees, vendors and our families, when we focus on secret service, all of our relationships prove more fruitful and rewarding."

## Mandarin Oriental Hotel

The Mandarin Oriental Hotel group is known for its legendary service. It operates 21 five-star properties worldwide (17 more are under development). They pay attention to details. It is not uncommon that on arrival the hotel associates greet you by name and ask how your trip was from . . . and they say the city you were traveling from. With recent revenue growth of 22 percent, Wolfgang Hultner, chief executive of Mandarin Americas says, "This business is very simple, no Service, no profit!"[4]

The hotel has guests fill out an outline form indicating time of arrival and other particulars, so the staff can customize their service. From setting the room's thermostat preset to your preferred temperature, a color touch screen on the telephone displaying the weather forecast for your home zip code, to a flat-panel HDTV featuring a personalized text-message display, they even have an antenna system running up the building's core to provide better cell phone coverage for their guests.

The Mandarin leverages technology behind the scenes to help its staff deliver personalized service and rebound from snafus. For instance, if room service fails to deliver, an all-points bulletin gets sent out over the hotels rapid-response communication system, firing text messages, and within minutes the hotel manager is making it right with the guest. Over 1,500 special request alerts are sent each day in Mandarin's U.S. hotels via its rapid-response communication system.

When it drops the ball, the Mandarin's service recovery style is to overcompensate, sometimes heroically. As was the case one time in San Francisco when an associate misplaced a guest's luggage. To remedy the situation, they flew a bellman to Los Angeles to reunite the luggage with that guest.

Mandarin Hotels live by their 11 legendary quality experiences, whereby the properties and associates are held accountable for the service levels they deliver. Mandarin ranks each hotel's service monthly and annually. The year-end ranking contributes to the size of employee bonuses.

## Peripheral Vision

But what does engagement really mean? It is a new buzzword that you hear a lot, but how do you teach it? "It is teaching our employees how to balance their duties with being truly warm and friendly. Anybody can deliver food to a room or set up a banquet room, we need to engage a guest as we pass them in the hallways, when we deliver room service, as they walk by us on a ladder changing a lightbulb. We need to have peripheral vision," explains John Rolfs, General Manager of The Ritz-Carlton.

This is where The Ritz-Carlton is at its best, training its employees to see opportunities to engage the guest. It is not uncommon for an engineer to get off his ladder and help a guest with luggage to their room. Or a housekeeper, who notices a cigarette box on the dresser, to put an ashtray on the guest's balcony. Or when a housekeeper noticed that the book a guest was reading had the pages bent, she got him a bookmark and placed it in the book with a note that said, "I thought this bookmark would help keep your book in better condition." Or the time a guest called to make reservations and mentioned that all he wanted to do was watch football games that day in his room. When he arrived, he found a detailed schedule of all the scheduled games and what channels they were on, and several football magazines—all because an operator was paying attention on the phone.

"This all starts with a leader's vision that initiates and energizes the staff to live that vision," says Rolfs. One of the best ways The Ritz-Carlton does that is through their daily lineups. Everyday 30,000 staff members of The Ritz-Carlton line up prior to their shifts to hear stories similar to these and be inspired to seek out similar opportunities to engage the guest and make them feel so good, they come back.

## SuperService

The success of Superquinn grocery store, 17 locations in Dublin, Ireland, can be traced to what the owner Feargal Quinn calls the "boomerang principle"; doing everything to keep customers coming back, which often means looking past short-term expenses to long-term customer loyalty.[5]

Here is how Superquinn does not let the boomerang principle be a fancy buzzword: They have a concierge on the premises who recommends restaurants or helps organize parties; a greeter who looks after shopping carts, offers coffee or soup to shoppers, and is responsible for recognizing and directing new customers. Superquinn also provides an umbrella service for unprepared shoppers who get caught in a sudden downpour, package carryout to customers' cars, and a delivery service to customers' homes. Every Superquinn store is equipped with a playhouse area, staffed by trained child care specialist, where Superquinn customers can leave their children to play, free of charge, while they shop.[6]

Superquinn also has a Superclub program, which is a loyalty program. It is not like all the rest; its uniqueness is in how Superquinn uses the loyalty program to create services that are valued by customers. For instance, customers can get reward points on their cards for pointing out problems in the stores, such as wobbly shopping carts, or an out-of-date product. This has turned their entire customer base into quality control agents, while having fun at the same time. The Superclub card also makes it possible for Superquinn to understand its customers. The card clearly identifies customers as members of a particular household, which allows them to collect the purchase history of the entire household. When the customer checks out with the Superclub card, his or her name is displayed on the cashier's screen, allowing the cashier to address the customer by name.

## Hyatt Rolls out New Wake-Up Call Service

Hyatt Hotels and Resorts introduced customized service allowing friends and family to record personalized wake-up call greetings for traveling loved ones, known as the New Hyatt Wake-Up Call. The service is designed to help frequent business travelers maintain connection with others while on the road and personalize their stay with the sound of a familiar voice in the morning. All wake-up calls are sent directly to members' cell phones. "The New Hyatt Wake-Up Call is the latest in a series of new products and services that demonstrate our commitment to business travelers," explains Michael Hickey, general manager at Hyatt Regency Cambridge.[7]

# Notes

1. B. Joseph Pine and James H. Gilmore, *The Experience Economy: Work Is Theater & Every Business a Stage* (Boston, MA: Harvard Business School Press, 1999).
2. The Disney Institute and Michael D. Eisner, "Be Our Guest" (Disney Institute Leadership Series), *Disney Editions*, May 1, 2001.
3. Joseph Michelli, *The Starbucks Experience* (New York: McGraw-Hill, 2006).
4. Bill Breen, "Mardarin Oriental Hotel Group," *Fast Company*, issue 108 (September 2006), www.fastcompany.com/magazine/108/open_customers-hotel.html.
5. Feargal Quinn, *Crowning the Customer* (St. Johnsbury, VT: Raphel Marketing, 2001).
6. Superquinn, Customer Services, www.superquinn.ie/Multi/default.asp?itemId =305; Superquinn, "Leadership Tools for Maintaining Corporate Values, Goals and Ideology," May 13, 2003, www.superquinn.ie/multi/default.asp?id =17&itemId=124&multiitemId=126&searched=1&section=Press+Room.
7. Hyatt, "Wake-Up Call Service: Guests Register for Limited-Edition Wake-Up Call by Supermodel Christie Brinkley to Benefit the Make-a-Wish Foundation," http://cambridge.hyatt.com/hyatt/hotels/news-details.jsp;jsessionid =W4BTRLJOFVBHJTQSNWDVAFWOCJWYOUP4?newsId=5142904.

# 9

# Commandment V: Training to Provide a World-Class Customer Experience

*Systems and processes that remove variation and provide a consistent customer experience*

---

*Give a man a fish and he'll feed his family for today, teach him how to fish and he'll feed them for a lifetime.*
—Unknown

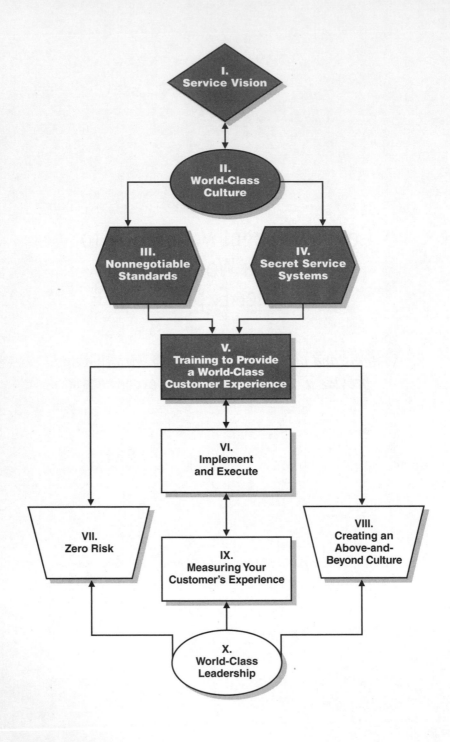

World-class service organizations have an incredible training program for all new and existing employees consists of soft-skill training that increases their service aptitude, giving them the knowledge and tools to provide a world-class customer experience.

If you have successfully achieved the first four commandments, now is the tough work. You have turned standards into systems, but who knows about them? It is critical to ensure every new employee gets trained on these systems, otherwise the next generation of employees will dilute your Service Vision.

A common misconception is that the only way to get better people is to pay more than everyone else. There are many great examples of world-class companies who do not necessarily pay better than their competitors. In fact, employees at Disney are hired from the same labor pool every other organization uses and are paid the going rates. The real reason why their people are so good at customer service is how well they are transformed into Walt Disney Cast Members, which occurs in their training.

> Customer loyalty is won or lost at the front lines of each individual location.

This is the most important chapter of this book. Customer loyalty is won or lost at the front lines of each individual location, however, what determines the consistency of delivering the experience is the quality of the systems and training that are supported by a company's corporate resources. Just like in sports, the contest, match, or game, is decided long before the actual event takes place, it is won in the practice room and by the preparation leading up to the event.

Let's revisit the 10 sins to being a World-Class customer service organization:

1. **Lack of service aptitude.**
2. **Decline in people skills.**
3. Inability in connecting employees' jobs and their importance to the success of company.
4. Poor hiring standards.
5. **Lack of experiential training.**
6. **Not letting employees have input on systems.**

7. Failure to implement and execute consistently.
8. Lack of a strong employee culture.
9. Lack of measurements and accountability.
10. Focus on artificial growth.

Your company can avoid four (those in bold) of these 10 barriers by *properly* training all your employees, both new and existing ones. Superior customer service companies that have great training programs deal with barriers 1, 2, 5, and 6.

Inadequate training is definitely the biggest underlying reason for the inconsistency and scarcity of great customer service. Companies skimp on training because it costs money, but, as shown in Chapter 1, companies that invest in customer service, which means investing in training their new employees, reap great financial benefits.

If, after you read this book, the only thing you do differently is to dramatically improve your training, that alone will probably raise you to an entirely new level of customer service.

## Hard-To-Soft Training Ratio

If you had to choose only one answer between the product you sell or the customer experience you provide, which would be why your customers buy from you?

If the product (or service) you sell is weighted more than the experience, you may be in danger because product is the easiest thing to duplicate, and companies that distinguish themselves only by their product are extremely vulnerable to their competition.

If the customer's experience is the primary reason your customers buy from you, that is good, but you still may have a problem. Take a look at the initial training your employees receive, and calculate how much of it is hard training, dedicated to product (technical and operational skills; job duties) versus soft skills (such as customer service, relationship building, role-playing, service recovery, experiential training).

When companies do the math, most, even those that admit customer service is crucial, are shocked to discover that technical and operational education constitute the lion's share of a company's training time and budget. The average hard-to-soft training ratio is typically 90/10 or worse.

Remember: Front-line employees come to you with virtually no world-class experiences and with a very low service aptitude (see Chapter 2).

Soft-skill training is the only way to raise front-line employees' service aptitude to world-class level.

Companies that deliver superior customer service devote as much as 25 percent to 50 percent of their training hours and budgets to soft training. It makes total sense. If providing a great customer experience is a major component in retaining customers, shouldn't customer service be a major component of your company's training?

## Shadow Training Is a Shadow of What You Need

Most companies' training programs vary considerably, but too many look like this: During the first few days, the new employee is taken through company policies and watches some training videos. After that, the new employee shadows an experienced employee and learns the technical and operational portions of the job. However many experienced employees have not been trained how to teach new employees or have the type of behavior you want emulated.

Ask yourself if your current training for all your new employees achieves the following:

- Instill abundance of pride in the company and its service legacy.
- Instill a sense of purpose in the significance of doing one's job well.
- Increase the new employees' service aptitude.
- Enroll them emotionally and intellectually in the value of delivering a superior level of service to customers.
- Enable them to understand the customer's perspective.
- Identify the nonnegotiable standards that *must* be delivered every time.
- Increase awareness of all the service defects.
- Increase awareness of all the above-and-beyond opportunities that most front-line employees miss.
- Cover company policy and what employees are and are not allowed to do.
- Identify to what extent employees can go to make things right with a customer.
- Include a measurement component that certifies when the employee is technically *and* experientially ready to start performing each part of the job.

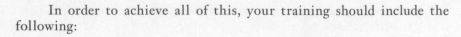

In order to achieve all of this, your training should include the following:

☐ 1. A company orientation that covers company policy and the company's history.
☐ 2. The functional components of the specific job.
☐ 3. The operational procedures of the job.
☐ 4. All technical training, including product knowledge, use of equipment/tools, software and other technology, and scope of services.
☐ 5. Experiential training on soft skills, especially how to create relationships and personalize encounters, how to prevent customers from feeling like transactions, and customer recovery techniques.
☐ 6. On-the-job shadowing.
☐ 7. Testing and certification, including extensive testing on experiential skills.

At the end of training for new employees at John Robert's Spa, they take the Employee Service Aptitude Test (E-SAT) and must also know the entire Guest Experience Cycle. We expect our new employees to do much more than recognize the right answer; they have to be able to recall and summarize the elements and skills learned in experiential training.

With regards to the "components of a customer's experience" (Chapter 7), most businesses focus exclusively on functional, technical, and operational skills—yet the even-more vital experiential skills, however, typically get little if any attention.

Assuming your company is doing an excellent job of training in the first three components, I will focus entirely on what most companies lack and what is the strength of The DiJulius Group: experiential excellence.

## Customer Experience Promise

That is why it is imperative for companies to ensure that every employee—new and existing—truly understands what their organization's Customer Experience Promise is. The Customer Experience Promise is what the organization is supposed to deliver to their customers, consistently, at every stage of their interaction. Every employee needs to understand the importance of each point of contact, what to avoid, what are your company's nonnegotiable standards that every customer must receive and what are the potential opportunities to really "wow" them. Organizations need to make sure their Customer Experience Promise is structured in such a way that all employees learn, understand and execute it.

## Customer Experience Cycle Workshop

This workshop is the best exercise for companies that want to create world-class Secret Service systems. When The DiJulius Group is hired to work with a company, we start with facilitating the Customer Experience Cycle workshop (we sometimes call it the Guest, Client, or Patient Experience Cycle).

We have done this workshop with hundreds of companies, including The Ritz-Carlton, Lexus, Nordstrom, Cameron Mitchell Restaurants, Melting Pot Restaurants, Hallmark Gold Crown Stores, Nemacolin Resort, Panera Bread, Sport Clips, Cheesecake Factory Restaurants, Wingstop Restaurants, and Progressive Insurance. And today, at many companies, this workshop is the foundation of customer service training for both their new and existing employees.

### *Map the Customer's Experience Journey*
Identify all the significant points of interaction—called "stages"—that your customers may have with your company.

Figure 9.1 is a restaurant's Guest Experience Cycle and Figure 9.2 is a financial service company's Client Experience Cycle.

The following is the Client Experience Cycle for The DiJulius Group, which provides customer service presentations, workshops, and consulting for companies:

1. Prebooking process—lead generation.
2. Sales lead—selection process.
3. Hired.
4. Preevent.
5. Event.
6. Postevent.
7. Maintaining the relationship.

Many businesses have multiple customer experience cycles. For example, there might be a cycle for sales, one for technical support, and one for service. You need to map the stages for every different department/component of your business and do the Customer Experience Cycle workshop for each cycle.

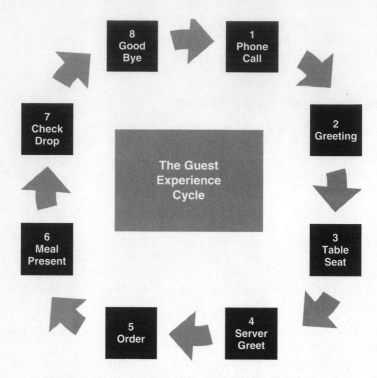

**FIGURE 9.1** Restaurant—Guest Experience Cycle

Once you have mapped out your customer experience stages, you need to get your employees involved in helping create what those stages should look like. You then break each stage down into four individual components:

- *Service Defects:* All the things that can ruin the customer's experience at this stage.
- *Operational Standards:* All the tasks or jobs for each stage.
- *Experiential Standards:* The actions that will create an exceptional experience and a raving fan.
- *Above-and-Beyond Opportunities:* Common situations that we want our front-line employees to recognize and be prepared for in order to make a customer's day.

The objective of this exercise is to focus more on the experiential actions and less on operational actions that each department can deliver at

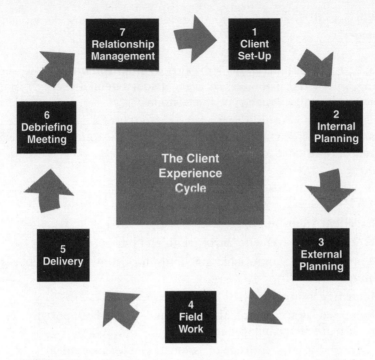

**FIGURE 9.2** Financial Services—Client Experience Cycle

each stage of the customer interaction because the experiential actions are uniquely critical in order to deliver an unforgettable experience.

Before going through this exercise, many front-line employees assume that if the meal is good or if the order is correct, then the customer will be happy. Employees need to be fully aware of all the ways a customer experience can be ruined. In the process of listing all the service defects at each stage, employees come to realize that the quality of the food or accuracy of the order may have the least to do with whether a customer returns.

Break your employees up into smaller groups and have each group work on the components of each stage, listing the Service Defects, Operational Standards, Experiential Standards, and Above-and-Beyond Opportunities.

This workshop is a creative think tank on how the entire organization can consistently deliver an unforgettable experience. This allows you to get everyone's feedback, ideas, and buy-in to ways the organization can deliver a better customer experience.

We ask all participants to focus on the following components of each stage:

- Specific experiential standards that distinguish among new, returning, and VIP customers, so every associate/employee will immediately recognize which type the customer is.
- Techniques to profile customer's personal information so it can be used and shared throughout the location to customize the experience and to document for future return visits.

Benefits from this workshop include:

- Excellent team-building exercise.
- Front-line involvement, enrollment, and buy-in.
- A model of nonnegotiable standards for front-line employees and units to follow.
- Increased awareness of all Service Defects.
- Increased awareness of all Above-and-Beyond Opportunities that most front-line employee miss.
- Increased service aptitude of associates and management.
- Awareness of the information that becomes the basis for the systems and processes that remove the wide variation of experiences the companies tend to deliver. This information allows companies to create training materials, tests, and the next generation of customer service standards.

## Systems and Processes That Remove Variation in the Customer's Experience

Many businesses struggle with the ability to deliver a consistently superior customer experience. Employees need to understand the condition of customers. Not all customers should be treated equal. As it was pointed out in Chapter 8, there is a huge difference between first-time and returning customers. Take for example a customer versus a potential customer calling in, which most businesses call a "sales lead." At The DiJulius Group, the person handling incoming calls and answering questions has to be aware of each type and how to handle each differently. We call this stage "Prebooking process/lead generation."

We train the person to know how to deal with:

- Someone who heard about John DiJulius, but has never heard him speak.
- Someone who saw John present and wants to hire him.
- A past client of John's.
- Private company having an event.
- Speaker bureau.
- Meeting planner.

The Customer Experience Cycle workshop helps the company create processes for each scenario.

Many of the world-class customer service companies that we have worked with have used this exercise as the cornerstone of their customer service training. The following examples show some of the kinds of training materials you can create from this exercise.

Figure 9.3 shows some sample pages from the John Robert's Spa Guest Experiential Cycle Training Manual, which new employees are required to study when they are hired.

Figure 9.4 shows the corresponding pages from our Guest Experiential Cycle Test Manual that new employees are required to pass before they can start working with guests.

## Enterprise Rent-A-Car

In the early 1990s, Enterprise Rent-A-Car was experiencing dramatic growth, "we were seriously compromising our commitment to customer service," says CEO Andy Taylor. Enterprise developed a corporate training program around the "Cycle of Service," which was the moment of truth when customers interact directly with Enterprise employees. The program included practical tips on what to say, how to establish rapport, and how to ensure that customers have a pleasant experience, all while their needs are taken care of promptly and efficiently. Training materials included standards for service details such as the maximum number of telephone rings permitted before answering the phone, mention of both employee's name and the customer's name during the call, a thank-you at the end, and greeting the customers with a handshake and a smile.[1]

Enterprise's renewed customer service focus has certainly paid off. Fred Reichheld, best-selling author, cited Enterprise as a model of how to generate customer loyalty.[2] "I have to say that learning to measure and manage customer service was not easy. We only had a vague idea of how

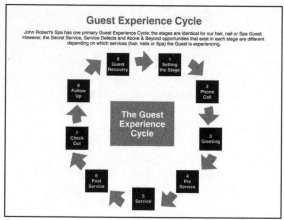

# Guest Experience Cycle

## Training Manual

John Robert's
JR
SPA

---

## Terminology

**Secret Service:** Hidden systems that deliver unforgettable customer service. Consistent, non-negotiable acts that every team member must deliver to every Guest, every time. *Secret Service* acts are customized to meet the needs of our New, Returning, Spa, or VIP Guests.

**Non-negotiable:** Team Members can not pick and choose if *Secret Service* acts are delivered, regardless of the circumstances.

**Guest Experience Cycle (GEC):** All the points of contact a guest will encounter, during each stage of their experience, within each department.

**Stages:** The individual points of contact within the Guest Experience Cycle; i.e. phone call, greeting, check out, etc.

**Above & Beyond:** Random acts of heroism providing legendary service to the Guest.

**Service Defects:** Obstacles and challenges, that occur, at every stage of the GEC, that can ruin the Guest's experience.

**Guest:** Individual who comes in to experience (purchase) our services and products

**The Answer's Yes...** Now what's the question?

---

## Guest Experience Cycle

John Robert's Spa has one primary Guest Experience Cycle; the stages are identical for our hair, nail or Spa Guest. However, the Secret Service, Service Defects and Above & Beyond opportunities that exist in each stage are different depending on which services (hair, nails or Spa) the Guest is experiencing.

The Guest Experience Cycle

1 Setting the Stage
2 Phone Call
3 Greeting
4 Pre Service
5 Service
6 Post Service
7 Check Out
8 Follow Up
9 Guest Recovery

**FIGURE 9.3**  Sample pages from the John Robert's Spa Training Manual

## Guest Experience Cycle

John Robert's Spa has one primary Guest Experience Cycle; the stages are identical for our hair, nail
or Spa Guest. However, the Secret Service, Service Defects and Above & Beyond opportunities that exist
in each stage are different depending on which services (hair, nails or Spa) the Guest is experiencing.

1. _____
2. _____
3. _____
4. _____
5. _____
6. _____
7. _____
8. _____
9. _____
10. _____

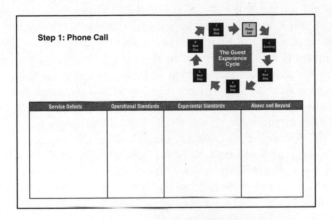

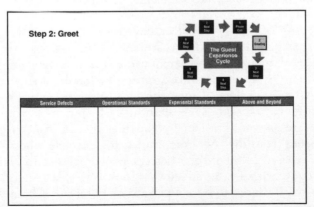

**FIGURE 9.4** Sample pages from the John Robert's Spa Guest Experiential
Cycle Test Manual

**193**

difficult it would be. Of course, we didn't anticipate how great the rewards would be for our customers and our people. We were out of balance, with too much emphasis on the financial numbers and not enough on pleasing our customers. We have come a long way toward achieving a more consistent service performance," says Taylor.[3]

## Million Dollar Keynote Presentation

Every day each employee of The DiJulius Group has to find ways to walk the talk and set the example for being a world-class organization. One of the exercises I do internally with my team is the Million Dollar Keynote Presentation. I ask my team, "If we charged one million dollars for a keynote presentation, what would it look like? When someone calls to inquire about our services, what does a million dollar greeting look like? Would we be patient and take our time, offer to send them a DVD of one of our presentations? Leading up to the event, should they ever have to call us and ask us for anything or would we anticipate all their needs before they even were aware of them (e.g., marketing materials to promote the event, headshot, bio, a/v needs)?" We could possibly help customize the marketing of their event, since we have all the information they need (speaker bio, presentation content, etc.). We go through the entire process, each stage and see how we could possibly justify a million dollar keynote presentation. Then when it is all said and done, we realize that none of our new ideas actually cost us anything, so what if we delivered a million dollar keynote experience, but charged a lot less? Wouldn't that make our current keynote fee seem like a bargain? Wouldn't that make price irrelevant?

As a result of that exercise, we have created some new experiential standards that help exceed our customers' expectations. For instance, during most of my keynote presentations for private companies, unknown to them, I record my entire speech by having a tiny recorder on my lapel. After I am done, I give the CEO my presentation on a USB stick as a gift. He can choose to share it with employees who may have missed the presentation, or some companies like to make it part of the new employees' training. At some events, for example when I spoke for Goodyear Tires to 2,200 of their dealers at a conference in Dallas, I provided Goodyear with a value added that they were able to pass on to their top customers. I offered to have a private early morning breakfast, question and answer session with Goodyear's top 20 dealers. Goodyear's top customers got to have a 90-minute breakfast, asking whatever questions they wanted to.

# Only Companies That "Get it"—Want It

As bad as customer service is today, it is ironic that the vast majority of the organizations that hire me to consult with them on customer experience are the companies who are level 4, well above average or level 5, already world-class (see Chapter 4). Which is precisely why they are there; they are driven, committed, and relentless to raising the bar. A perfect example is The Cheesecake Factory, who has a reputation for being one of the best customer service organizations in their industry. The Cheesecake Factory's Service Vision is:

> To create an environment where absolute guest satisfaction is our highest priority.

Many companies have statements that sound really good on paper, however, few actually put the systems in place to back it up as well as The Cheesecake Factory does.

## Understanding Guest Happiness

The Cheesecake Factory trains their employees to be sensitive to their guest's moods. In order to do that, they need to first recognize the level of the guest's happiness upon their arrival. Employees are taught to realize how many things factor into a guest's mood, such as they may be having a serious business lunch, or they were delayed in traffic. All can have an impact on their dining experience.

The Cheesecake Factory uses a Guest Happiness Rating that provides a quick, simple way to communicate the mood their guests are in (Figure 9.5). This helps the employees communicate with team members and managers to ensure every guest leaves a 9 or 10, thus one step closer to the Cheesecake Factory's vision of "absolute guest satisfaction."

David Overton, CEO, defines service mindedness:

> We are dedicated to unparalleled hospitality and genuine care of our guests. The reason we exist as a company is to provide absolute guest satisfaction. We recognize that we are all linked together in the service process—that each of us plays a distinct and vital role in delivering our company's promise of caring service. The entire company
>
> *(continued)*

must actively participate and constantly seek service opportunities. A mindset of "being of service" must flow throughout our organization. We have a responsibility to support and serve one another, because ultimately we are all serving our guests.

Whenever you find a superior customer experience organization, you will always find they have a great training program. The Cheesecake Factory was featured in *Workforce Management* magazine and recognized as an industry leader for their training and development systems. Some of the training staff members go through to ensure they maintain the high guest experience standards includes:

- Upon hire, all staff members attend a full-day orientation, which covers company service culture, expectations, and performance standards.
- They take an open-book quiz.
- Training consists of on-the-job, role-playing, games, worksheets, hands-on demonstrations, and video training.
- Trainees also complete assigned readings and written exercises.

---

**Using Happiness Ratings**

We use "happiness" ratings to discreetly communicate guest satisfaction to other staff and the management team, to provide service that will enhance our guests' dining experience.

Follow these steps to communicate guest happiness for tables in your station and dining room:

STEP 1:  Assign a number on a scale from 1 to 10 that assesses our guests' happiness:

    1 = Very Unhappy          10 = Total Guest Enjoyment
                                           (Very Happy!)

STEP 2:  A rating of "7" or lower indicates displeasure or unhappiness.

STEP 3:  If the guest is a "7" or lower, communicate with a manager to determine what steps you can take to improve the guest experience.

STEP 4:  If the guest is a "7" or lower, the manager will also visit the table to get more information, which will be shared with staff so that they can work together to meet guests' needs.

RESULT:  Our goal is that no one should leave the restaurant below a 9.

---

**FIGURE 9.5**  The Cheesecake Factory Guest Happiness Rating Card

- Staff members are expected to successfully complete their certification, passing with a score of 90 percent or better.
- They also have to take a "high stakes" test and score at least a 90 percent.

With today's fast-paced lifestyle where both parents are frequently working, Americans are dining out more than ever. The Cheesecake Factory understands that guests have become more discriminating and have higher expectations than ever before. The Cheesecake Factory trains their employees that good service is unacceptable; "Exceptional Service" is the only option. The Cheesecake Factory wants their minimum service standards to be what their competitors consider above-and-beyond.

## World-Class Training

Let's look at some things The Ritz-Carlton Hotels, a two-time winner of the Malcolm Baldrige National Quality Award, does to train its new employees:

- Every new employee goes through two days of new employee orientation, covering their service values training.
- 21 days of training certification, where they work side by side with a trainer, who is relaying the importance of the "why" and recognizing credo moments (The Ritz's 20 basic principles).
- Employees are trained on problem resolution training and their empowerment process.

When asked what the most difficult aspect is of delivering superior service that businesses have today, Jim McManemon, general manager of The Ritz-Carlton Sarasota, said, "Consistency! Staff members might have been trained on it, they know it, but actually doing it every time can be difficult and is the real challenge."

## What Does Great Service Look Like?

"It is not about what we perceive great service to be, but really knowing and understanding what great service looks like to our customer is the first key to meeting and exceeding their expectations on a regular basis," says John Maguire, Chief Operating Officer of Panera Bread. "The second key is training each employee so they are crystal clear on what it takes to provide what has become known as the Panera experience." This means being:

1. Friendly and attentive.
2. Knowledgeable and helpful by answering questions.
3. Speedy.
4. Accurate.

While friendly, attentive, and knowledgeable seem like what the majority of companies want their employees to be, Panera takes it much deeper by providing training that ensures employees know how to create the "Panera Warmth" that customers have grown accustomed to and count on when they visit "their Panera."

The three Es to creating the "Panera Warmth" are:

1. *Engage:* Greet, welcome, smile, make eye contact, and remember.
2. *Explore:* Anticipate customer needs based on if they are new (i.e., guidance on understanding the menu), returning (telling them their order before they tell you), or need special assistance (i.e., help carrying a large to-go order out to their car).
3. *Exceed:* Know customers' expectations, different customers have different expectations (i.e., new customer versus vs. Panera Club regulars).

Maguire explains, "When we execute this level of service and provide this type of experience, our customer loyalty is incredible. Our core customers are extremely loyal.

"We have regular customers (Panera Club), who have created lifelong relationships with other regular customers and as a result, join groups, go on trips, and connect regularly at 'their Panera.' Customers approach me all the time and say, 'What have you done to my Panera?' They take ownership in their local Panera."

Panera Bread educates their managers to focus on what is known as PPC (People, Pegs, and Cost Balancing):

## P—People

- Who you select
- What you do to develop them
- How you keep them

## P—Pegs

- P: Product (quality and availability)
- E: Environment (cleanliness, energy, atmosphere, music, WiFi)
- GS: Great Service

## C—Cost Balancing

- Financially responsible

"By focusing on PPC, sales and profit take care of themselves," says Maguire. "Those profits sustain the growth of our concept and our people, which ultimately provide possibilities."

These philosophies are the key reasons why Panera Bread has had the #1 ranking on J.D. Power & Associates' Annual Restaurant Satisfaction Survey. The *Wall Street Journal* reported Panera Bread scored the highest level of customer loyalty among quick-casual restaurants. In 2006, Panera Bread was recognized as the top performer in the restaurant category for 1-, 5-, and 10-year returns to shareholders, reported by the *Wall Street Journal*'s Shareholder Scorecard.

## World-Class Benchmarks

Having studied numerous world-class service organizations, the following is typical training they put their employees through:

- New employees receive one full day of orientation that not only covers policies and procedures, but more importantly covers the legacy and history of the company.
- New employees receive one full day customer service (a.k.a. Secret Service Boot Camp) and Customer Experience Cycle Workshop.
- New employees get tested on the service defects, standards, and above-and-beyond opportunities of the stages of our customer's experience.
- New employees take a Service Aptitude Test.
- New employees go through technical/operational training (technical, product knowledge, job specific).
- Existing employees go through re-orientation, at the very least, every other year with new employees.
- Existing employees go through Secret Service Boot Camp, at the very least, every other year with new employees.

### Employee Service Aptitude Test

One of the best tools for measuring if an employee's service aptitude is high enough to start interacting with a company's customer is the Employee Service Aptitude Test (E-SAT, Figure 9.6), created by The DiJulius Group. The E-SAT is a customized test that asks 50 to 75 multiple-choice questions of the most common situations that may arise between the employee and their customer, ranging from nonnegotiable standards, service recovery, above-and-beyond opportunities, to uncomfortable and awkward

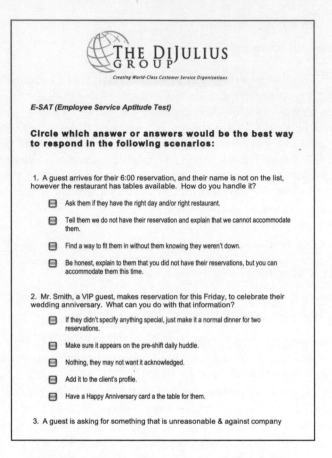

**FIGURE 9.6** Employee Service Aptitude Test

situations that are not uncommon. We suggest the E-SAT be given before and after the new employee goes through their initial training to monitor how their service aptitude has increased. At John Robert's Spa, a new employee cannot start working in their department, training for their actual position, or interacting with our guests without scoring 100 percent on their E-SAT.

We also create SAT for experienced employees, which instead of having 3 wrong answers and 1 right, may have 2 wrong answers and 4 correct; we want them to tell us the order in which we want them to try to solve the situation. For example, answer "D" might be the best, however "D" is not always possible, if it is not, then "A" would be the next best resolution, then "E" and so on.

Here are some sample E-SAT questions for a server at a high-end restaurant:

> Circle the answer or answers that are closest to how you would respond in the following scenarios:

1. A guest arrives for her 6:00 reservation, and her name is not on the list, however the restaurant has tables available. How do you handle it?
   a. Ask her if she has the right day and/or right restaurant.
   b. Tell her you do not have her reservation and explain that you cannot accommodate her.
   c. Find a way to fit her in without her knowing she wasn't down.
   d. Be honest, explain to her that you did not have her reservation, but you can accommodate her this time.

2. Mr. Smith, a VIP guest, makes a reservation for this Friday to celebrate his wedding anniversary. What can you do with that information?
   a. If he didn't specify anything special, just make it a normal dinner reservation for two.
   b. Make sure it appears on the preshift daily huddle.
   c. Nothing, he may not want it acknowledged.
   d. Add it to the client's profile.
   e. Have a Happy Anniversary card at the table for him.

3. A guest is asking for something that is unreasonable and against company policy, what do you do?
   a. Tell her you will find out if it's allowed and see if she brings it up again.
   b. Tell her no.
   c. The answer is always yes, even if the request is against our policy.
   d. Get the manager.
   e. Tell her what you can do (alternatives) for her without saying no.

4. A guest has not touched his meal:
   a. If he doesn't complain, then don't bring it up.
   b. Find out if it's the restaurant's fault.
   c. See if there is something different the guest would like and put a rush on it.

5. A guest asks you, the server, if you think his steak is overcooked:

a.  You look at it and tell him your honest opinion.
b.  You get the opinions of at least three other people.
c.  You find out specifically what the guest's version of medium rare is and have a new steak prepared.
d.  You have the chef come out and explain that the guest's steak is in fact medium rare.

Visit www.thedijuliusgroup.com/esat for more about Service Aptitude Tests.

# A Smile Is Rare Today

A smile is one of the most underrated customer service tools a business can have. Businesses neglect its importance and the necessity of training new employees about it. A smile is more the exception today rather than the norm. Test it; just observe people and see how many smile when they say hello—strangers or even people you know. Watch your own employees interact with customers and coworkers, and count the number of times people smile when they make initial contact with people. They will probably smile less than 50 percent of the time (Figure 9.7).

For many people, a smile is not a natural response. Businesses need to train people to smile. As I said earlier, younger generations do not have the inherent people skills that previous generations were forced to have, so we can no longer take for granted the simple courtesies that used to be common. You should require all employees to role-play a smile to accompany all our daily greetings (hello, you're welcome, how are you, thank you, goodbye, have a great day). Repeat, repeat, repeat, until the words automatically and intuitively produce a smile, every time.

The smile role-play is a great smile training technique to use when you have new employees going through soft-skill training. Select two employees at a time to role-play interacting with customers, with one employee as the customer and the other as the employee. The employee playing the customer is also required to smile. You pick specific common situations that will be part of the employee's daily work and have them interact for 2 to 3 minutes. The rest of the new employees are the judges and track the number of times each person smiled at the "smiling cue words." At first, employees expect this to be a breeze, until they realize that even when focusing on smiling, there are many times they need to consciously remind themselves to smile in all the appropriate situations.

➤ Hello!

➤ Welcome to. . .

➤ Thank you for calling.

➤ How are you?

➤ Thank you!

➤ We appreciate your business.

➤ Goodbye.

➤ We hope to see you soon.

➤ Is there anything else we can do for you?

➤ Have a great day!

➤ Certainly

➤ My pleasure

➤ Absolutely

**FIGURE 9.7** Smile Cue Words

This applies to people working on phones; they should smile at the same places in the conversation as if they were speaking face-to-face. This role-play becomes fun and very competitive. Some of the employees at John Robert's Spa have told us that smiling became a habit not only at work but also in their everyday lives, that they heard positive comments from family and friends, and that they were convinced that smiles brought them better treatment and better service.

Eventually, with extensive and consistent training, a smile can become an automatic response. But just role-playing is not enough; it has to be managed like anything else. You can't stress it enough because a smile, rare as it is today, is one of the strongest customer service tools you can have.

## A Smile Is Part of the Uniform

A policy we have at John Robert's Spa is that a smile is part of the uniform. From time to time, our managers have sent people home for being out of uniform. At restaurants, I suggested posting mirrors at telephones, drive-thru intercoms, and drive-thru windows. Customers can hear a smile, and mirrors force employees to be cognizant of their facial expressions and how they are being perceived. I also suggested that all these businesses provide "color of people's eyes" training. During the initial training on interacting with customers, the trainer needs to ask at random, "What is the color of the last customer's eyes?" When you do this several times an hour, it forces new employees not to become task-focused but to remain customer-focused. New employees get overwhelmed with procedures, which can make customers feel like they're part of an assembly line. It is a lot easier to come across as sincere and genuine when you look people in the eye and say, "My pleasure," and "Thank you." Remember that a smile includes teeth!

Another great policy is the 10-feet greet, which I think Wal-Mart created. This should be a policy for both customers and coworkers. Any time an employee comes within 10 feet of any customer or coworker, the employee is to smile and give a sincere acknowledgment, even if the employee has already greeted that customer or coworker several times.

# Notes

1. Andy Taylor, "Top Box: Rediscovering Customer Satisfaction," *Business Horizons*, September–October 2003.
2. See note 1.
3. See note 1.

# 10

# Commandment VI: Implementation and Execution

## *How to go from ideas on paper to consistently executed concepts*

---

*Becoming world-class is not an event. . . . It is a cultural evolution.*

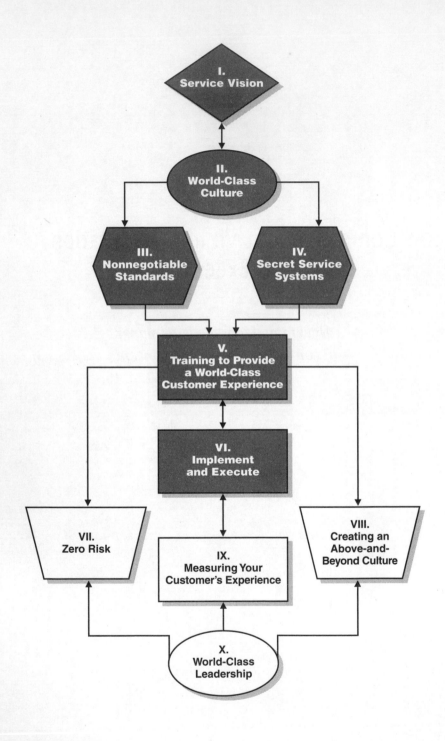

World-class service organizations have a solid process allows the realistic implementation of the customer service initiatives and systems that are executed consistently by front-line employees.

Without execution, systems in manuals are nothing more than ideas on paper. This is where most companies fail, the execution of these systems. The implementation and accountability of these standards and systems are every manager's responsibility.

## Consistency and Continuity

The two most important words in the success of implementing systems are *consistency* and *continuity*. Nearly every company has more ideas than it knows what to do with. Here's a scenario familiar in every company: Some executives attend a fantastic seminar, get dozens of great ideas, and return to work all fired up and eager to start executing all those ideas. A month later, not even one idea is being executed even 10 percent of the time. The managers are either preoccupied with a crisis or have moved on to a new focus.

Have you ever attended a seminar so great that six months later it had dramatically changed the way your company does business? Probably not!

The real problem is that more ideas are the last thing companies need. Managers are not short on ideas; they are short on an implementation strategy that will result in those ideas being successfully implemented. This chapter will enable you to implement those great ideas. Better yet, it will raise the standard for your organization—and for your competition.

After being deluged a number of times with great ideas, employees realize they don't need to panic or actually start doing what their managers tell them. If employees just wait long enough, these newest ideas will also pass. This syndrome has been called *Flavor of the Month*, or as Heather Thitoff, Training Director at Cameron Mitchell Restaurant calls it, POTY (Program of the Year).

There are two big rules for implementation:

*Rule 1:* Select a path, train on it, and stick with it. Have training continuity and use one concept that all your future themes will support.

*Rule 2:* Implement slowly and properly, which above all means that you never try to introduce too many ideas at one time. This enables you to implement your ideas successfully.

## Rule 1: Select a Path, Train on It, and Stick with It

I can't tell you how often I hear the same thing from many of the companies I speak or consult for: "A few years ago, our theme was 'Fish' (from the great book on *Pike's Fish Market* by Lundin, Paul, and Christensen, New York: Hyperion, 2000). Last year our theme was 'Raving Fans' (from the book of the same name by Blanchard and Bowles, New York: William Morrow, 1993). And this year our theme is your book, *What's the Secret?*"

It's the POTY. It's no wonder nothing sticks! No systems are created. There's no enrollment or buy-in by employees. There's no continuity from one generation of employees to the next, because they joined under a different theme, and it has very little correlation with your training program.

There is nothing wrong with using any of those books and concepts as themes. They are all fantastic. What I am saying is, "Pick a path." The world-class customer service companies focus on one concept and build their training program around it. They create their own internal terminology as it relates to customer service (see Table 10.1). Over the years, every new employee goes through the same training, learns the same underlying concept and theme, reads the same book, and hears the same message.

In *Good to Great*, part of Jim Collins' formula for success is that people need to hear a few messages constantly.[1] That doesn't mean the training doesn't evolve—every year, your current training should make last year's training program pale by comparison. But you have a consistent foundation on which everyone has been trained. And it can't just be new employees who go through intensive training; existing employees need to be retrained and reenergized on at least an annual basis. Beyond that training, the world-class customer service companies advertise superior customer service to their employees on a daily, weekly, monthly, and quarterly basis; everything from preshift huddles (see Chapter 12) to departmental meetings to re-orientation. If I could sum up this process in one word, it would be continuity: continuity of theme and continuity of training.

When you have developed your terminology, make it an integral part of the training you give your employees. Table 10.1 is a sample of John Robert's Spa terminology on which we train all employees.

## Rule 2: Implement Slowly and Properly

Let's assume you have just successfully completed the Customer Experience Cycle Workshop (Chapter 10). You should now have the "buzz"—everyone who attended the workshop is pumped up, and you have numerous sheets filled with ideas for each stage of your customer interaction. The workshop was a home run, your team got the concept and the message, they

**TABLE 10.1** John Robert's Spa Service Terminology

---

*Above-and-Beyond:* Random acts of heroism providing legendary service to the guest. The answer's "Yes" . . . now what's the question? Never use the word "No." Find a way to make it happen. If you absolutely can't make it happen, provide an alternative but never respond with the answer, "No."

*Customer service* = Reality – Expectations.

*Fashion-Escape-Rejuvenation (FER):* People come to us for these experiences: Fashion expertise, to escape the stress in their world, and rejuvenation, so they can be the best at what they do (at home, at work, or in the community).

*Guest:* An individual who comes in to experience (purchase) our services and products.

*Guest experience cycle (GEC):* All the points of contact within each department that a guest will encounter during each stage of his or her experience.

*Making price irrelevant:* The experience our guests receive is so great that our prices feel like a bargain.

*Nonnegotiable:* Secret Service acts that team members absolutely must deliver, regardless of the circumstances.

*Our Service Vision:* To enhance the quality of lives around us.

*Secret Service:* The ability to obtain a great deal of information and to then utilize that knowledge, using invisible cues, to personalize the customer's experience and to deliver on unexpressed needs and desires. The result is that customers ask, "How did they do that?" and "How did they know that?"

*Service defect:* An obstacle or challenge that can occur at any stage of the GEC that can ruin the guest's experience.

*Stage:* An individual point of contact within the guest experience cycle, such as a phone call, greeting, or checkout.

*Team member:* A person who works at John Robert's Spa (an employee).

*A trip to Paris:* We are people's 60-minute vacation from a stressful world.

*VIP:* Guests who consistently receive our services and send us referrals, thereby earning special privileges and constant recognition of their status and loyalty.

*What does John Robert's sell?* We sell an experience: Fashion, Escape, Rejuvenation. We do not sell services (e.g., haircuts or manicures) or beauty products.

*Zero risk:* An opportunity to be a hero and to convert a service risk into an exceptional experience. Team member(s) do whatever it takes to make a defect right. The guest may complain about the service defect, but will rave about how well the team handled it.

---

shared and debated ideas, and they are now totally pumped to go back to work and start being world-class to their customers.

Stop! This is when the train wreck so often happens. The workshop was easy; the hard part is implementation. Yes, you are excited about the buy-in to being world-class. Yes, you want to maintain the enthusiasm and the momentum. But now you must crawl before you can walk or even think about running.

A company cannot rush the implementation process. A "worst practice" is to allow managers to roll out the implementation on their own or to introduce 12 new concepts next week. If you do either of these things, in about 45 days all those great ideas from the workshop will be a distant memory because not one of them will have stuck. The only result will be a loss of credibility with your employees and with your customers. Employees will feel that all their work at the workshop was just a bunch of rah-rah and hot air, because nothing ever came of it. This will result in your employees feeling like the workshop and all their efforts were a waste of time. Customers will be disappointed by the inconsistency between your promises and their experiences.

Having said all that, we devote the rest of this chapter to the steps necessary for a proper implementation process. When you have completed the Customer Experience Cycle Workshop, you should have four sheets of ideas for each stage of customer interaction: one sheet for Service Defects, one for Operational Standards, one for Experiential Standards, and one for Above-and-Beyond Opportunities.

### Secret Service Project Team's 20 Steps to a Successful Implementation

1. Create a (Secret Service) project team, who will champion converting the "buzz" into world-class reality. The size and makeup of the project team will vary, depending on the size and nature of your organization. Typically, a workable size is 6 to 12 persons, who represent operations and training, chiefly persons at senior management and department-head levels, with some representation of front-line staff.

2. Transfer all the ideas to a stage template (Figure 10.1) so it can be better organized.

3. As a group, review every item in all four sections of each stage (Service Defects, Operational Standards, Experiential Standards, and Above-and-Beyond Opportunities) to be sure that all items (on all lists) are well stated, approved by the team, and in the stage where they belong. To do this, code each item as follows:

   $\wp$ = Statement is 100 percent correct and acceptable.

   S = It needs to be more specific.

Stage ______________________

THE DIJULIUS GROUP
Creating World-Class Customer Service Organizations

| Service Defects | Operational Standards | Experiential Standards | Above and Beyond |
|---|---|---|---|
| | | | |

The Dijulius Group www.thedijuliusgroup.com 216.839.1430

**FIGURE 10.1** Stage Template

? = Its meaning is unclear.
X = We disagree with it or dislike it.
E = This should be under Experiential.
O = This should be under Operational.
A = This should be under Above-and-Beyond Opportunities.

4. Add any ideas overlooked during the workshop. As you go through each stage, you will think of more ideas. Add and code them.
5. Fix the items that don't have a check mark. Now that the project team has calibrated the ideas and is in agreement on them, clean up your communication and make sure that every item is detailed, specific, and stated in positive language. If, for example, you said you want a "friendly greet," that terminology is unacceptable because it is too vague and open to misinterpretation. Define exactly what a friendly greet looks like. Finally, move items that were in the wrong stage to the right one. As you fix each item, put a ℘ next to it, indicating that it is 100 percent correct and acceptable.
6. Scan your lists once more. Before you proceed to the next step, every item should have a ℘.
7. This step applies only to your lists of Service Defects and Above-and-Beyond Opportunities. You could easily have 20 items for each

category and each stage. Trim your lists of Service Defects and Above-and-Beyond Opportunities. For training purposes and memory retention, it is best to limit them to the most common and important items per category. When you finish this stage, you should have only six to eight Service Defects and six to eight Above-and-Beyond Opportunities in each stage. You are now done with Service Defects and Above-and-Beyond Opportunities. The rest of your work involves the nonnegotiable standards in each stage.

8. Classify your Operational and Experiential Standards, assessing how consistently your organization delivers each service initiative. Classify and sort the ideas:

1 = We already execute this 85 percent or more of the time.

2 = We say we do it, but we really don't do it at least 85 percent of the time.

3 = This is a new idea that we need to implement.

4 = This is a new idea that we like, but this is not the time to tackle it.

It is imperative that your team be honest in assessing how consistent your organization is in delivering your existing service initiatives. Most likely you will have some stages without a single 1. In general, your total list of 1s will be very short. Don't be alarmed; this is normal. This is why your organization has committed to going through this customer service transformation. It means that your team has made an honest assessment of where your organization is.

If you rate items as a 1 when they are really a 2, you will be undermining your chances of success. It is very important that you resist the urge to become embarrassed or to panic and to go back and fudge your assessment by turning some 2s into 1s. I repeat: It is perfectly normal to have very few 1s. CEOs need to know this up front so they don't blow a gasket.

9. Review your 1s and 2s and eliminate any that are not cost-effective, have no real impact on customer satisfaction, or are difficult to do consistently. In most cases, the degree of difficulty is the reason for inconsistent execution. It is always better to do less and do it well than to tackle more and fall short (see the Guillotine Filtering System that follows).

10. Because it is of utmost importance that your classifications are accurate, the next step is to conduct an internal audit on 1 items and confirm that your organization is delivering consistently on each of the items you listed as a 1 (85 percent+). Whatever audits you use, you need to do them now. You need to know that your core service is being executed at least 85 percent of the time before you start introducing new ideas and concepts.

11. While your organization is conducting an audit to verify consistency of delivery on your list of 1s, your project team needs to focus on the list of 2s and 3s (new ideas that you need to find a way to implement). Determine which items on these lists are high-priority, meaning that the items meet your criteria of "low cost and easy to do and important to the customer." Be picky when you make your high-priority list. Remember: Do less, achieve more.

12. Once you have made your list of the high-priority items you want as part of your customer service standards, you need to put them through your own filter to ensure that they are realistic, that they are low-cost, easy to do, and important to your customers. This process will help you succeed because when you have completed this step, you will have eliminated from 10 to 50 percent of your ideas and will have tweaked the remaining ones to be more effective. (The DiJulius Group uses what we call a Guillotine Filtering System.)

13. Prioritize to determine the order in which you will implement your new Nonnegotiable standards. As you begin this step, you will have an excellent final list of high-priority standards that you want to implement and consistently execute 85 percent or more of the time in 85 percent of your departments/locations. I suggest you frontload your list with a mix of standards that address your biggest weaknesses, that offer experiential opportunities for maximum impact, and with very simple standards (low-hanging fruit) so that your management and front-line employees can see rapid and dramatic results aiding future buy-in.

14. Create a Standards Rollout Calendar that introduces a maximum of three standards every 120 days. These standards may include existing standards that your company has always said it does but that are not being delivered consistently. This limit of three standards is extremely important. Two to three standards every 120 days may seem slow, but do not attempt to exceed this limit. You cannot fast-track standards. If you have successfully assured that you are in fact doing your original list of 1s at least 85 percent of the time, then you can introduce two or three new standards every 120 days. This way your managers can implement the flow of coaching, measuring, and accountability required for the successful execution of these new standards. (See Table 10.2.)

15. Communicate up front. Communicate the new launch of 2 to 3 standards 30 days prior to when they will be "live," that is, when you expect your people to consistently deliver these new standards to your customers. Communicate at meetings, via paychecks, preshift huddles, and so on.

**TABLE 10.2** Standards Rollout Calendar

| Phase | Date | Stage |
|---|---|---|
| Phase 1 | 1/1–1/31 | Verify your 85/85 list: you are executing 85 percent or more of the time in 85 percent of your locations. There is no learning curve, just ensure you are in fact delivering on these over the next 30 days. |
| Phase 2a | 2/1–2/28 | Daily awareness of the first two to three standards that will be live as of March 1. |
| Phase 2b | 3/1–5/31 | Roll out two to three (existing or new) standards to be executed. Have them tracked, managed, rewarded, and celebrated. |
| Phase 3a | 6/1–6/30 | Daily awareness of the first two to three standards that will be live as of July 1. |
| Phase 3b | 7/1–9/30 | Roll out two to three (existing or new) standards to be executed. Have them tracked, managed, rewarded, and celebrated. |
| Phase 4a | 1/1–1/31* | Daily awareness of the first two to three standards that will be live February 1. |
| Phase 4b | 2/1–4/30 | Roll out two to three (existing or new) standards to be executed. Have them tracked, managed, rewarded, and celebrated. |

*Most businesses have a busy season (in the retail sector, our busiest season is the fourth quarter, October through December). Do not introduce any new standards during your busiest season; instead, focus on existing standards and delivering the ultimate customer experience.

16. Plan and set up systems for measurement. Decide how the new standards will be measured, and put systems in place to verify that they are getting done, such as spot-checks and mystery shoppers.

17. Plan how you will recognize success. Figure out ways to celebrate and create awareness of customer response to the new standards. Remember: What gets recognized gets repeated. Also determine what the ramifications will be if the standards are not executed consistently.

18. Create a training manual for your Customer Experience Cycle. The manual should contain the Service Defects, Operational Standards, Experiential Standards, and Above-and-Beyond Opportunities of each stage listed (see Figures 10.2 and 10.3).

19. Decide how you will use your manual to train both new and existing employees, how you will conduct testing and certification, and so on.

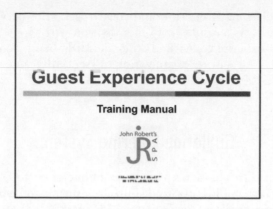

**FIGURE 10.2**   Customer Experience Cycle Manual

For example, you could create a mandatory boot camp on customer experience standards and require that all new team members go through it. As part of this boot camp, you would hand out the nonnegotiable standards workbook and have team members study it and be tested on it, with testing adapted to the functions of each department. This way you make sure that everyone retains the information and that everyone is doing what needs to be done.

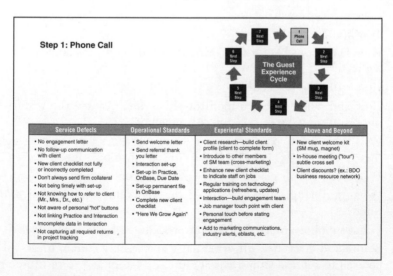

**FIGURE 10.3**   Customer Experience Cycle Sample Stage

20. Congratulations. Your slow and steady pace allowed you to control the process. As a result, in 15 months, you will have a fresh and new customer experience, with all the standards being consistently executed by your entire organization. Essentially, you will have just raised the standard for your competition.

## Guillotine Filtering System

At The DiJulius Group, we use this series of questions to filter out which ideas fit the criteria of low cost and simple to execute and which ideas may be too complex to roll out at this time. The new standards created from the Customer Experience Cycle workshop should get put through the following list of questions to measure how implementable and realistic these potential standards are:

1. How cost-effective is it?
2. How will you educate the staff about what it is, how to do it, and how it benefits everyone?
3. How will you remind your team continuously until it is executed 100 percent of the time?
4. Who (what departments) is responsible for providing this standard?
5. How will it be provided or executed?
6. When? How often?
7. To whom?
8. Who is responsible for managing it (ensuring it gets done and tracking it)?
9. How will it be tracked?
10. How and when will you monitor this system to see the results and the response from guests and team members?
11. Will there be a consequence for team members who do not execute this system? If yes, what will the consequence be?
12. What will be our gauge to know if it is successful?
13. What scripting must be created for it? Who will script it and by when?
14. What supplies are needed? What procedures for inventory?
15. Before and after kick-off, what daily and weekly communication will be used to remind employees about this system and to reinforce it?
16. How will new staff be trained on it?

## Manage the Experience

It is imperative that every manager is uncompromising about the execution of your standards. Your standards have to be truly nonnegotiable. Your employees have to know that they cannot pick and choose, that every standard has to be delivered to every customer. That is why it is very important not to have a dozen standards for every stage of interaction. Keep it realistic to achieve.

As soon as employees start to think no one is really paying attention, or cares, the standards go from nonnegotiable to optional. To avoid this, managers have to routinely do audits of the standards and recognize when they are being executed and immediately coach when they aren't. You can have the greatest customer experience on paper, but it is the leadership's responsibility to make sure every employee is well aware of the importance of the execution.

**Annually**

- Existing employees go through the customer experience cycle and retake that test.
- Secret Service Project Team updates the components of the customer experience cycle (Service Defects, Nonnegotiable Standards, Above-and-Beyond Opportunities).
- Eliminate or retweak any standards that are stale, more costly or complex than expected, or that fail to deliver the anticipated impact.

## Notes

1. Jim Collins, *Good to Great: Why Some Companies Make the Leap . . . and Others Don't* (New York: HarperCollins, 2001).

# 11

# Commandment VII: Zero Risk

*Anticipating your service defects and having
protocols in place to make it right*

---

*We knock the ball out of the park as well as anyone, but there
are times we can drop the easy pop-ups.*
— Trey Matheu, Director of Operations,
Nemacolin Woodlands Resort

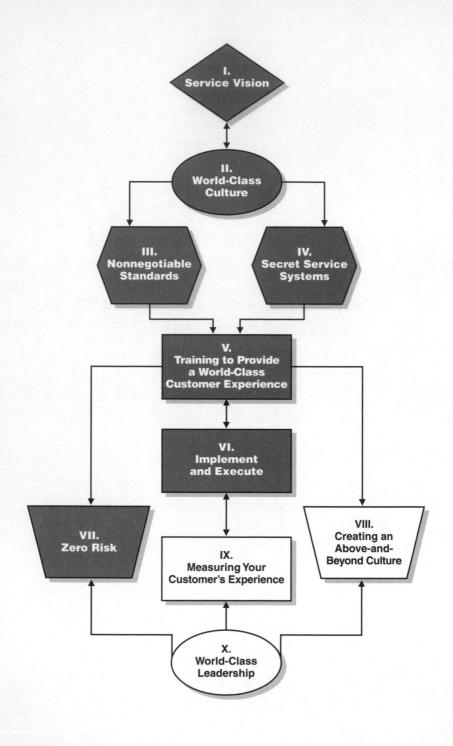

If you have successfully tackled the first six commandments, that means your company is living your Service Vision, training employees to execute the incredibly simple, yet power Secret Service systems you created, and your customers are loving it. Until something unexpected goes wrong and the customer is inconvenienced. Now what? No one said it was always going to work like clockwork. To be honest, perfect world circumstances are rare, and the exception: you can count on human error, call offs, customers being late, technology breakdowns, service interruptions, out of stock items, and undependable vendors. Is your company prepared? Is your frontline employee trained and ready? If these things are normal daily occurrences, then tell me why most employees act like a deer in headlights, when they do occur?

Zero Risk: having all your employees fully aware of the potential common service defects that can arise at each stage of the customer experience cycle and trained and empowered to provide great service recovery when defects do arise, so your company is known to be zero risk to deal with.

Everyone's service aptitude appears strong when things are going smoothly, but employees' and the company's true service aptitude is revealed when things don't go as planned and service defects arise.

What does zero risk look like? As a customer, you have a sense of security when you deal with a company that if something goes wrong, they will make it right. Thus, that business is zero risk to deal with.

Zero risk addresses an intimidating array of issues that can produce unhappy customers: service defects, lack of concern about the customer's experience, and incidents or emergencies that aren't your fault. Zero risk is essential in order to create a Wow! experience and make the customer yours for life. If and when you become zero risk, you will indeed be in very exclusive company.

How many zero risk companies do you deal with? The following scenario happens every day: You are unhappy with your experience as a customer. You express your displeasure to a front-line employee, who sometimes, but not the majority of times, may say, "Sorry," but that's it. The employee isn't allowed, required, or trained to fix the problem. You can tell that nobody at this company cares whether you are disappointed, and you realize it is a waste of time and energy to do anything about it. Because of this, you stop telling the company about your displeasure, and even worse (for the company), you stop coming back. That is the opposite of zero risk.

Service is so bad today, that if it's not horrible, we are relieved.

Today, we expect very little from companies. We feel it is a waste of time to complain because companies will be defensive and will not take responsibility for the problem. By now you probably have heard the urban legend about a customer who returned tires to a Nordstrom store and Nordstrom refunded the money even though Nordstrom has never sold tires. It doesn't really matter if this story is true; what does matter is that Nordstrom has almost mythic status for its "no-hassle" customer service.

## Don't Ask If You Don't Want to Know

Many companies have their front-line employees ask, "How was everything today?" but no one teaches them how to respond. It is a canned question that they are supposed to ask. I was checking out of a hotel and the front desk employee asked the customer in front of me, "How was your stay?" The guest said, "I had no hot water in my shower." The front desk person's response was, "Oh, ah, sorry about that, I will make sure maintenance gets right on that." A lot of good that does the customer now, after he is checking out. If you are going to ask, then be ready to rectify the situation. It could be as simple as; "I apologize for that Mr. Smith. For your inconvenience, I am going to credit you the movie you rented in your room last night, would that be okay?"

While they may complain about the service defect, they will rave at how well we handled it.

I admit that at John Robert's Spa, we drop the ball as much as any other company. However, we train our employees to know how to pick up the ball and make things right. We know the most common areas where problems will arise, and have set up protocols to make those problems right. We teach every new team member how and when to use these protocols. In other words, we empower all our team members to fix these problems, on the spot, by themselves. Our goal is to make sure all guests leave satisfied.

## Fine or Okay Is Unacceptable

Why do we drop the ball so much? There are two main reasons. First, we see about 5,000 guests a week, so even if we do it right 99 percent of the time, which I know we don't, then we will upset at least 50 people each week. Second, we aggressively identify guests who are less than thrilled with their experience. We train our guest-care personnel to ask a guest, "How was your experience today?" when the guest is checking out. If the guest answers, "It was okay," or "Fine," that is unacceptable. I know a lot of businesses would be happy with "Fine" or glad that the guest didn't complain. I say that "Fine" is unacceptable. I would hate it if anything I did was "Fine." "Fine" really means, "Let me pay and get out of here so I can tell people how disappointed I am with this experience."

When a guest says, "Fine," our team member asks, "What about your experience wasn't excellent?" Typical answers are, "My stylist ran 25 minutes late," or "I felt rushed," or "This look isn't exactly what I wanted." Now we have an opportunity to fix the problem and, more importantly, to prevent customers from leaving disappointed and possibly engaging in "brand terrorism," which is to tell everyone they know about their horrible experience with your company (brand).

> Know how to serve in terms of the customer. They don't care about your situation; they only care about their situation.

### A Complaint Is a Gift

A CEO once told me, "A complaint is a gift. A complaining customer is willing to tell you for free what's wrong with your business, that we would normally pay a consultant a lot of money to tell us."

> Worry about the customers who don't complain, because they're not coming back. After a negative experience is reversed, the satisfied customer will tell everyone about the positive encounter and the company's fairness. My experience is that the customer who brings up an issue not only wants to right a wrong but is also, many times, subconsciously looking for a reason to continue to do business with the organization.[1]
>
> —*Michael Feuer, co-founder of OfficeMax*

In addition to having protocols in place to make things right immediately, companies also need communication tools that immediately allow all employees, managers, and front-line staff to capture a customer's complaint. In this way, upper management can determine if the issue was resolved and can follow up with that customer to ensure they are now 100% satisfied. By documenting customer challenges, management can identify the company's most common service defects and put systems in place to reduce the chances that these defects will occur again in the future. The Guest Challenge Form (Figure 11.1) is used by team members at John Robert's Spa, who are expected to fill it out any time a customer challenge arises.

To be zero risk, a company must be well aware of all the potential service defects that can arise and that can detract from a customer's experience. This is just as important as employees knowing all the service standards that should be executed to create the experience, and knowing the above-and-beyond opportunities.

Most front-line employees have a total misconception of what dictates the level of a customer's experience. The typical employee mindset is that the customer will be happy if the order is accurate and delivered on time, or if the meal is warm and tastes good. That is totally untrue! When you do the Customer Experience Cycle exercise (Chapter 9), and discover all the service defects that are possible at every stage of the customer's interaction, you realize how many things there are that can ruin the customer's experience.

New employees starting with us assume that the service stage, stage 4 of the John Robert's Spa guest experience cycle (Figure 11.2), which can be either the haircut, manicure, facial, or massage, is the stage most important to the guest's experience. However, the service stage has little to do with successful guest retention, because anyone who pays $50 to $110 for a haircut expects it to be excellent. The guest needs to get more in order to justify traveling past several less expensive salons to come to us. Nobody books a $700 room at The Ritz-Carlton just for a clean room and a comfortable bed.

All employees need to be aware of the most common service defects that can and do occur at each stage of interaction. Awareness of service defects will make the staff more sensitive to the customer's experience, more likely to try to reduce those service defects from happening, and more prepared to handle those defects when they do arise. World-class service companies not only train their employees on service defects but also test their employees on their knowledge of those defects. If front-line employees are not properly trained, you are playing Russian roulette with your customers; some will respond well because of a higher Employee Service Aptitude or E-SAT (Chapter 9) and that is how they are, but most won't have a clue how to handle a customer complaint.

John Robert's
JR
S P A

## <u>GUEST CHALLENGE</u>

Guest Name:_____Telephone Number_____

Date of occurrence:_____Notified Employee_____

Employee ('s) involved_____

Situation:_____

_____

_____

_____

_____

Employee's response:_____

_____

_____

_____

_____

_____

Contact from Company by:_____ Date:_____

Resolution offered/agreed:_____

_____

_____

_____

_____

<u>FOLLOW UP:</u>
DATE CONTACTED:_____ BY WHOM:_____

DATE RETURNED:_____ MANAGER'S SIGNATURE:_____

**FIGURE 11.1**   **John Robert's Spa Guest Challenge Form**

The Ritz-Carlton in Sarasota, Florida, has both a Hall of Fame board that displays stories and letters from exceptionally satisfied guests and a Hall of Shame board that displays the service defects that went wrong (i.e., a guest's unsatisfactory comments). "Our employees need to be equally aware of what ruined a guest's experience so we are all sensitive

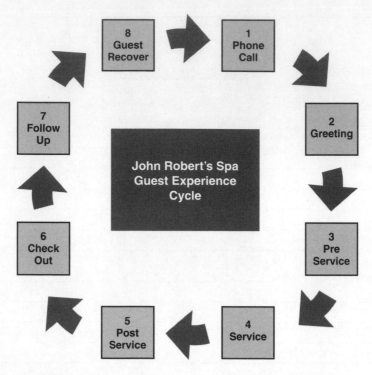

**FIGURE 11.2** John Robert's Spa Guest Experience Cycle

enough to avoid those mistakes in the future," says Jim McManemon, General Manager of The Ritz-Carlton.

As I said, it is critically important to have protocols in place in order to fix service defects and reduce the casualties. Whether your customers are the public or other businesses, you probably can identify hundreds of potential service defects. Fortunately, the vast majority of defects will be in just a few categories, which will make it relatively easy to create protocols to address those few problems when they occur. At John Robert's Spa, for example, almost everything that can go wrong falls into one of just four categories:

1. An appointment mistake.
2. A delay in being served.
3. Unhappiness with service (i.e., haircut, manicure).
4. An employee's lack of professionalism.

We do our best to reduce the likelihood that these types of situations will happen, however, we know we cannot come close to eliminating these problems. So we have protocols in place to address them immediately so they don't spin out of control and create brand terrorists. An integral part of our process for training new employees is teaching them how to be zero risk, by recognizing and anticipating potential service defects and having the protocol resolutions to fix them. We train, role-play, and test on zero risk. Our Employee Service Aptitude Test—E-SAT (Chapter 9) contains many zero risk scenarios.

## Own the Problem, Own the Customer

Here's a great example of a zero risk protocol, for a guest who arrives for an appointment that is not on our books. We may have the guest scheduled for a different day. It doesn't matter. In fact, we expect our front-line employees to avoid the typical mistake of letting the guest know that we didn't have her down for an appointment. We teach our team members to handle it—we say "to resolve it"—this way:

> If you own the problem, you own the customer. If you lose the problem, you lose the customer.[2]
>
> —*Jeffrey Gitomer*, Customer Satisfaction Is Worthless, Customer Loyalty Is Priceless

### Mistaken-Appointment Resolution

1. Act as if we were expecting her and find a way to get her in with the service provider she expects, and with little or no inconvenience to the guest.

2. If that isn't possible, for example if her service provider is unavailable, be honest and say there was a miscommunication. It is very important not to say or imply whose fault it is. Try to accommodate the guest's appointment with a provider who is available. If the guest appears to be totally satisfied with this arrangement, nothing else needs to be done.

3. If the guest does not wish to see any other service provider, try to get the guest in for an appointment with that provider as soon as possible and at a time convenient for the guest. Make it right for the guest

by giving her something additional for her inconvenience, such as a gift card.

4. If the guest is extremely upset because she was really inconvenienced—for example, she left work early, got a baby sitter, or drove across town—then make a future service totally complimentary.

I was extremely proud to receive the letter in Figure 11.3 from a guest. It told me that our training is paying off and that my front-line employees understand one of my favorite *Secret Service*-isms:

While they may complain about the service defect, they will rave about how well we handled it.

---

Dear John,

I have been impressed with your spa for many years. Your customer service sets you far above not only other salons but also above most businesses in any industry.

On March 18, I arrived at your Mayfield location for a half-hour massage and pedicure. I was greeted and while I was being checked in, it became apparent that there was a problem. My appointment was not in the computer. I was being helped by Nicole Montecalvo. She explained the problem and offered me an appointment later in the day. I was not available at that time, and I was disappointed and frustrated. I said I would make an appointment at a later date. However, Nicole would not accept that for a solution. She found a time that was convenient for me, and because of my inconvenience, she upgraded my half-hour massage to a full hour at no additional charge. I was amazed by her persistence to solve the problem. Not once was I asked if I had the wrong date or time. Blame was not placed; rather, the customer was satisfied! Nicole's customer service is outstanding! I look forward to returning to your salon and spreading praise for your facilities!

Thank you for caring about the customer and teaching your employees to care,

Julie

---

**FIGURE 11.3  A Successful Service Recovery at John Robert's Spa**

It shouldn't surprise you that Nicole Montecalvo has been promoted several times throughout our organization and that today she is in senior management.

## It Is Not Our Fault but It Is Still Our Problem

After an exhilarating day at Disney, your family is leaving Magic Kingdom Park. It is 8:30 PM and you are in the parking lot. All of you are exhausted and impatient to get back to your room to shower and hit the sack.

You look at your spouse and ask, "Where did we park?"

She looks at you and says, "You're kidding—right?" Neither of you remembers where you parked. So how hard can it be to find your car? Like 20,000 other people, you came here in a rented white minivan. There are miles and miles of white minivans in the parking lot. Your only option appears to be to wait until the park closes at 11 PM and see what white minivans are left.

Whose fault is this: Disney's, yours, or your spouse's? Should Disney be responsible for reminding you where you parked? Disney, however, is aware that the average family visiting today traveled four hours, they arrived in a white minivan, and before the driver put the car in park, the kids opened the door and were running for the entrance. The parents are too concerned about catching up with their kids to stop and think about where they parked. Disney already knows that tonight a number of families will return exhausted to the parking lot, not remember where they parked, and just want to get back to the hotel.

What does Disney do? They anticipate a major service defect. And they solve it, even though it isn't their fault. They have people drive around the parking lots in golf carts in search of families that look lost.

A Disney Cast Member pulls up to your family and says, "Did you forget where you parked?"

You nod and say, "We're driving a white minivan. Does that help?"

"Do you remember when you arrived? A ballpark time will do."

"About 11:15 to 11:30 AM."

The Disney Cast Member checks his clipboard and says, "Between 11 AM and noon we were parking in the Goofy section. Jump in! I will take you to that section, and we can find your car with your remote key." And it's done.

Was it Disney's fault that you lost your car? Absolutely not. Is it their problem? Absolutely yes because Disney knows that every day several people will lose their cars and potentially be stranded for hours, a situation that could totally ruin the memory of their Disney experience.

This is a great example of what being zero risk is all about. Being zero risk applies regardless of whether your company is at fault. World-class service companies create protocols to proactively handle their most common service defects, and they train their employees how to extinguish small flames long before they turn into a raging fire. Even if a defect is not your fault, your customer will associate the issue with doing business with you. This is a critical issue for all businesses, at all levels, because when these situations arise, in the vast majority of instances, the employee immediately and instinctively becomes defensive and responds, "It's not our fault." Managers and front-line employees alike are shocked that the customer expects the company to be responsible and make it right. Here are more examples of situations that are not necessarily the company's fault but that are its problem.

## Sorry, but Your Credit Card Was Declined

While I was working with The Melting Pot restaurants helping them become zero risk, I discovered that one common service defect that occurs often is that a guest's credit card gets declined. Ouch! Who wants to tell Mr. Vice President, when he is entertaining two of his best clients, that his credit card was declined? Yes, he's the one who maxed out his credit card. Is it world-class service to risk embarrassing him by pointing this out in front of his guests and asking for a different card? No! It's not necessary. To avoid this exact situation from happening, The Melting Pot Restaurants' Secret Service project team, made up of their top franchisees and corporate executives created the courtesy card shown in Figure 11.4.

The server returns to the table with the check presenter, and the customer opens it, expecting to sign the receipt. On reading the little courtesy note, he can discreetly insert another form of payment, and nobody is the wiser. Brilliant and a customer is retained! If you spend the time on your most common service defects, you can create effective zero risk systems that can go that extra mile for the customer.

## Owning Shipping Problems

CUSTOMER: I am trying to find out what happened to the order that I placed?

COMPANY: We shipped your order on time. Here's your UPS tracking number. You can call them and find out what happened.

Is it acceptable that you shipped the order exactly as the customer wanted (i.e., next day air)? Yes. Can anyone expect you to control the shipping industry? No! Is this your problem? Yes! Zero risk, world-class service companies take ownership of shipping fiascos. They contact the shipper and locate the package for the customer. If a customer is desperate,

Thank you for dining with us
this evening. Unfortunately, we
were unable to obtain
authorization for payment with
this credit card. I will be back
momentarily to process an
alternate form of payment or
you may seek assistance from
the Hospitality Specialist
at the front door. We apologize
for any inconvenience.

**FIGURE 11.4**    The Melting Pot Restaurant's Courtesy Card

they may even reship the order and work out the details later. Take for instance the *New York Times* article, shared in Chapter 1, about the customer service representative of Amazon.com, who sent out a $500 replacement PlayStation, to the customer who said they never received it, even though it was signed for by someone at his apartment building. Not only did Amazon not charge him for the replacement, but they didn't even charge him for the shipping.[3]

## Your Room Is Not Ready

We have had the pleasure of vacationing several times at the Marriott's Ko Olina Beach Club in Oahu, Hawaii. Its General Manager, Chad Jensen, runs a world-class resort. One time at check-in, our room was not ready when promised. Without our saying anything, the associate at the front desk said, "We apologize for this inconvenience. I am putting a $35 credit on your room account; feel free to enjoy lunch on us or some drinks in our lounge while we get your room ready." Who can complain with service like that? The next time we visited Ko Olina Beach Club, we were disappointed that our room was ready for us! That is truly zero risk: we go back to Ko Olina Beach Club because of the comfort and security of knowing that we will get great service, and if for some reason we don't, they will make it right.

### You Can Go Online for That Information

Wanting to purchase the new latest and greatest iPhone when it came out, I went into a wireless store where it was being sold and asked a lot of questions about its features. The sales clerk didn't know the answers and just responded, "I'm not sure," and "I don't know about that." When I asked how I could get this information, she responded, "You can go online. There are a lot of forums where consumers discuss these issues." Two lessons that all businesses need to learn are (1) know your product, and (2) don't make the customer do your job! Needless to say, I didn't purchase the phone.

## Management Service Recovery Training

It is difficult to expect your front-line employees to handle service recovery when they have poor role models. Service Management Group (SMG), headquartered in Kansas City, Missouri, who measures the customer experience for multi-unit businesses, found some startling information when tracking customer complaints for one restaurant client. SMG coded all of the complaint comments into categories and expected to find that most problems would be related to either the food or the service, and that was true. But the unexpected discovery was that the restaurant managers were the main cause of the very worst problems. These were the situations in which a guest complained about the food or the service, so the manager came to the table. But the manager made the original problem worse by being defensive or unwilling to solve the problem. One-third of worst problems—the ones where customers called into the company's headquarters to complain—were about the manager's failure to resolve the original complaint!

As a result, this restaurant company gave their managers the authority to take whatever action was needed to solve customer problems. They also used customer voice comments to provide manager training on how customers react to poor problem resolution. Finally, they held workshops to share best practices in service recovery and to role-play the typical scenarios managers face.

A study conducted by SMG discovered only 35 percent of customers who had problems were highly satisfied with how they were resolved (Figure 11.5).

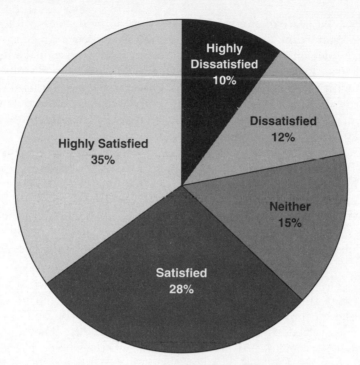

**FIGURE 11.5** Satisfaction Impact from Service Recovery (Service Management Group Client Data). *Note:* Most customers are not highly satisfied with problem resolution. Only 35 percent of customers were highly satisfied with service recovery.

## How Accessible Are You?

It is incomprehensible to me how many corporate offices and senior management teams are totally inaccessible. They are hiding from the public, and it's no wonder. In the past year, I had issues with Northwest Airlines (NWA), which lost my luggage. After a comedy of no-response, I demanded to be put in touch with a human being at Northwest's corporate offices. The NWA representative said, "That is not possible. Nobody can call our corporate offices. I can give you an address where you can mail your complaint." These experiences seem to be all too common. I have had similar experiences with utility companies.

Here's a refreshing approach. When you shop for a car at Motorcars Honda/Toyota in Cleveland Heights, Ohio, you will notice a red phone in the middle of the showroom with a sign that reads: "Hotline to Owner Chuck Gile."

Customers know that if any issues arise, they have the power to talk to the top executive in the organization. Now that is zero risk to me. That provides great peace of mind and a zero risk of doing business with a company like Motorcars. On top of that, the red phone sends a message to all employees, demonstrating the lengths Motorcars will go to make the customer happy. Everyone at Motorcars knows to please the customers because they are the ones who have the power. Has anyone ever used the red phone to call Chuck Gile? A salesman said, "Are you kidding? If we see anyone make a move toward that phone, we make a flying interception and fix the situation before he can call Chuck!"

Another great example of an owner who remains accessible is Mark Cuban, the billionaire owner of the NBA Dallas Mavericks. Cuban discusses his customer service philosophy in his blog "Connecting to your customers" (November 7, 2006).[4] In it, Cuban shares one of his favorite quotes: "Treat your customers as if they own you . . . because they do. You have to re-earn your customers business every day."

Cuban also points out his unique perspective on being accessible:

> It's interesting to watch different CEOs of different companies and how they deal with the issue of making customers happy. You can tell the ones that don't trust their products or services. They protect themselves from any possible interactions, whether direct, phone, or email, by having secretaries filter everything, and they respond with form letters or assistants, if at all.
>
> I don't know how they do it. I make my email available to everyone and anyone. Not only that, and more importantly, I make sure that all the customer service emails get forwarded to me. If someone is complaining, I want to know what about, and I want to get it fixed quickly. The best focus groups are your customers telling you what they think. No company is perfect, but the CEO who doesn't listen to direct feedback from customers will not take the company as far as it can go.

How refreshing! And what a great role model Cuban is for all senior management. Get out from behind your desk and talk to some customers.

> While the customer is not always right, NEVER make them wrong.

Proving that it was your customer's fault can be detrimental to your business. One of my best learning experiences came when I was working with a manufacturer. The purchaser, an employee of a company that was a very good customer of the manufacturer, contacted his inside sales representative at the manufacturer and told her that she sent them the wrong product. The purchaser explained that he desperately needed the correct product ASAP. The inside sales representative told the purchaser that she had sent exactly what he ordered. When the purchaser insisted that he didn't order the wrong product, the sales rep faxed him the original order form that he had sent, thus proving the purchaser did in fact order the wrong product. The sales rep also informed the purchaser, that due to his mistake, if he needed a different product, he would have to pay for the next-day air shipping, as well as be responsible for paying a standard 15% restocking fee. Obviously this was not the sales rep's fault, she sent exactly what the customer ordered and proved that. Obviously the customer learned his lesson, apologized for accusing his sales rep of sending the wrong product and admitted to his boss that it was his fault and that he was the one responsible for the 15% restocking fee, right? Wrong!

Even though it was clearly the purchaser's mistake, his company never ordered from that manufacturer again. Why? Because what he did tell his boss was how horrible the service he kept receiving from that manufacturer was, and his boss instructed him to find a new supplier.

> While you may feel like your client is demanding, your competition won't.

My wife encountered this type of situation when she wanted Lasik eye surgery, an expensive elective procedure that improves vision to nearly 20/20. She had several consultations at different practices and chose the one she liked the best. The surgery involved several pre-op visits, one of which was a 15-minute appointment with the doctor, whom she had never met. My wife scheduled it for 4:45 PM, which was his last appointment of the day. I drove her there, and we walked in at 4:50. The receptionist told us the doctor had left already because we were late. He didn't even give us five minutes leeway. My wife went elsewhere for the surgery and we ended up being the ones who taught that doctor a $3,500 lesson.

At John Robert's Spa, we make it hard for our service providers to turn away late customers. We say, "Feel free to turn that late customer away, provided you can guarantee that, in all the years she has been coming to you, you have never kept her waiting because you were running late." That's a very unlikely scenario.

## Oversharing

All companies are guilty of their front-line employees oversharing with the customer. When problems arise, your only job, as an employee, is to make things right immediately. The customer does not need to know how and why it happened or even that it almost happened. The customer just wants the experience he was expecting. Have you ever been on a flight where the pilot suddenly announced on the intercom, "Holy cow, we almost crashed!" None of us needs to know that. Unless we are going down, it is best to keep those things to yourself.

### *Oversharing II*

I was in Nashville speaking for cj Advertising, a world-class service organization in the advertising industry. Mark Scrivner, Director of Operations, picked me up from the airport and brought me to the hotel. As we checked in, the hotel front-desk associate could not find my reservation. Mark gave her the confirmation number and she then said, "Oh, here it is, unfortunately we had you down checking in last night, checking out today." Mark said, "Are you sure? That isn't the way we scheduled it." The associate said, "I am positive, let me see if I can give him a room for tonight." While she was able to find me a room for that evening, the question that remains is: Did I need to know all that? In this instance, I never needed to be made aware that there even was a problem in the first place. When she found my reservations and saw that there was a mistake made, she could have easily checked and saw that there was availability that night, and placed me in that room. Oversharing makes the host company look bad, like they screwed up.

## Calling an Audible

One of the best people I have ever seen provide world-class service in all types of situations is Tommy DeWitt, Lead Butler at Falling Rock of Nemacolin Resort. DeWitt is at his best during service recovery. While giving a tour of the hotel to a couple, who was celebrating their anniversary, the wife became upset with her husband for not being romantic enough to plan anything special during their stay at Nemacolin.

That is when Tommy jumped into service recovery mode. The tour of the hotel took a little longer than usual, and by the time he had completed the tour and took the couple to their room, they found flowers in the room, rose petals all over the bed, and chocolate-covered strawberries and a bottle of champagne, with an "I Love You" note attached. The wife turned to her husband and apologized for underestimating his romance. The husband thanked DeWitt for not only saving him but making him look great.

## See? It's Not My Fault!

I was holding a Secret Service Workshop at a beautiful hotel where my company had made all the hotel reservations for attendees. In the lobby, I bumped into David Akers, an attendee and a friend of mine. When he told me the front desk could not find him on the check-in list, I realized we had not made a reservation for him because I did not see him on my list of attendees.

I immediately said, "Let me take care of it," and went to the check-in desk, with David following right behind me. I was greeted by the front desk manager, who was aware of the situation.

He immediately said, "We do not have Mr. Akers on the list your company sent us."

Not wanting David to realize my people had screwed up, I responded, "Do you have any more rooms?"

"Yes, but see, here is the list of attendees that your office sent me," and he held up the list for both David and me to see, "and Mr. Akers is not on the list."

"Great," I tried again. "Since you have available rooms, can we just book him a room?"

"Certainly," said the manager, proud that he had finally made it clear that it wasn't his fault and that it was The DiJulius Group who was responsible—for bringing several hundred people to his hotel.

The proper thing would have been to book David into a room first. Then after he left, the manager and I could figure out what went wrong. It is never appropriate to discuss these matters in front of the customer.

## Unconditional Guarantees

You hear about guarantees all the time, but how many companies offer a guarantee similar to the one made by Graniterock, a company in Watsonville, California, that provides the construction industry with materials and products. Graniterock truly stands behind its products and services. As Jim Collins pointed out in his book, *Good to Great*, Graniterock's Bruce Woolpert put his company's money where its service is.[5] Woolpert calls it "short pay," meaning that he gives Graniterock's customer full discretionary power to determine how much to pay on an invoice based on the level of satisfaction. No permission is needed from the company, nor does the customer have to return the product. The customer sends a check for what he feels is fair. What is Woolpert's rationale for this aggressively customer-friendly policy?

You can get a lot of information from customer surveys, but there are always ways of explaining away the data. With short pay, you absolutely have to pay attention to the data. You often don't know that a customer is upset until you lose that customer entirely. Short pay acts as an early warning system that forces us to adjust quickly, long before we would lose that customer.

Graniterock has inspired us to institute that policy at The DiJulius Group. For any speaking or consulting work, our invoice clearly states:

> ## UNCONDITIONAL GUARANTEE:
> Please pay what you think is fair!

I can live with someone paying less because we will find out why the client was unhappy, and it is significantly better for him to share that displeasure with us rather than to pay the fee and never let us know the things the client was unhappy with. Not only would that client not hire us again, but I am sure they would do pretty good brand terrorism. This policy also ensures that we bring our "A" game to every client we work with, knowing that the client has that power to pay what he thinks is fair. To date I have made this offer to over 300 clients. Just two did not; they actually paid more. Fortunately, this focus has permitted us to do zero advertising, as 100 percent of our new business is by referrals from our existing clients. Our experience confirms the point that you don't need a sales and marketing department when you are wowing your customer base.

## Problem Solved = Loyalty

One upset customer can actually be converted to a more loyal customer than any customer you never make upset. Research by Service Management Group has revealed that customers who are highly satisfied with problem resolution are more likely to return than those customers who reported no problem (Figure 11.6).

Believe it or not, I actually like it when things go wrong, because it is an opportunity to blow our customer's mind. At The DiJulius Group, there have been situations when a customer orders a DVD and never received it or it doesn't play. Whenever our customers are inconvenienced, we immediately send out a new DVD and typically add some additional product for free to their order, thanking them for their patience. Another time a company hired me to do an all-day workshop with their entire organization. They had brought over 300 people in from different

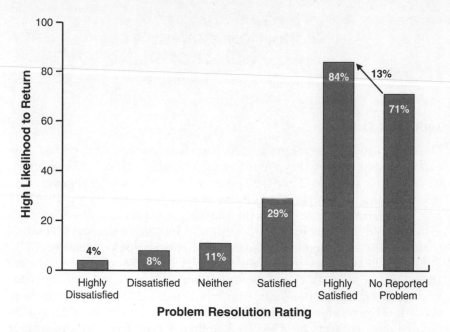

**FIGURE 11.6**  Loyalty Impact from Service Recovery (Service Management Group Client Data). *Note:* **Customers with problems can become very loyal. Customers who are satisfied with problem resolution are more likely to return than those with no reported problems.**

locations throughout the United States. When I arrived that morning, I found that the 300 Secret Service books they had ordered had never arrived, even though we had sent them out well in advance. The CEO had wanted to surprise all his employees with a book and keep the momentum going after my workshop.

Obviously this wasn't our fault, however, I realized this was our problem. Not only were they not going to get the books that day, but I couldn't do a book signing for them as we had discussed and when the books finally did arrive, they would have to ship each unsigned book out to their various locations where these 300+ employees worked. How did we make it right? Easy, my assistant Kristen Jackson got on a plane with over 300 books and personally delivered them a few hours later, before the workshop was over. The CEO was blown away and in his closing remarks, shared with everyone that The DiJulius Group truly walks the talk and told everyone about how well we handled it. When it came time for that CEO to pay, I wasn't too worried when he read the notice on this invoice:

UNCONDITIONAL GUARANTEE
Please pay what you think if fair.

## Southwest Airlines

Over the past 20 years, Southwest Airlines has demonstrated, through exceptional service, how they are the most profitable airline in the industry, when the rest struggle. They turn potential customer service disasters into opportunities to blow their passengers away. If you travel frequently, there is a good chance you have had the unpleasant experience of sitting on a plane, idle on a runway for a few hours (or in JetBlue's case, over 10 hours), with very little communication from the flight crew on your status.

A total customer service disaster, right? On Southwest, in similar situations, pilots walk the aisles, answering questions and offering constant updates. Flight attendants, who "really seemed like they cared," keep up with the news on connecting flights. And within a couple of days of arriving home, travelers have received apology letters from Southwest that include free round-trip ticket vouchers.

This is standard procedure for Southwest Airlines, which almost six years ago created a new high-level job that oversees all proactive customer communications with customers. Fred Taylor coordinates information that's sent to all front-line reps in the event of major flight disruptions.[6] He's also charged with sending out letters, and in many cases flight vouchers, to customers inconvenienced, even those beyond Southwest's control. "It's not something we had to do," says Taylor. "It's just something we feel our customers deserve."

# Service Recovery Quiz

Let's test both your service aptitude and service recovery skills. Picture this: A retailer's worst nightmare; your store is jammed with shoppers just before the holidays—a good thing, a real good thing, unless your computers suddenly crash none of your cash registers will function for an extended period of time. Ouch! You have just incurred a considerable loss in revenue for the day and potentially long term, due to the fact that, because of circumstances out of your control, you have just inconvenienced hundreds of your customers. Before reading any further, ask yourself what you would do in that situation. Decide how would you handle this on the spot, needing to make an immediate decision. Would you temporarily close? Would you ask your customers to patiently wait, knowing that is will be several hours before you get your registers working again? Let's see how your resolution compares to the following.

## A World-Class Service Recovery

Ted Donoghue, the Assistant Manager of Whole Foods supermarket at Bishops Corner in West Hartford, made a snap decision: All customers passing through the registers would get their food for free until the computers were working again. Shocked? Does your resolution pale in comparison? I doubt any other chain store would have done the same thing, but this is Whole Foods, where customer satisfaction is not just a saying but a practice.[7]

"It didn't seem right to punish the customers by making them wait," Manager Kimberly Hall said. There was no storewide announcement of the problem, or its consequence. Cashiers simply told customers there was a computer glitch, bagged their groceries, wished them a happy holiday and a safe drive, and sent them on their way.

## Title Nine Sports

Title Nine Sports, a Colorado-based retailer, which specializes in women's activewear, has a flexible return policy. Even after three years if you aren't happy, they will take it back. That is the service culture at Title Nine Sports. "During a week of our customer service training, one of the most important things is learning that you have to do what it takes to make it right so it doesn't escalate. We do what it takes, which is a very different approach from other call centers that give very distinct scripts for their telephone representatives to follow. We say rules make us nervous," says Rebecca Wara, Head of Brand Marketing and Creative at Title Nine.[8]

# Silence Is Not Always Golden

No news is bad news, when it comes to your customers. A recommended strategy is to create vehicles for your customers to be heard. Customers who complain are the best; they give you the opportunity to fix things before they go to your competitor. Complaints give you information that would cost tens of thousands of dollars from a consultant or research firm. Set up a process that makes it easy and simple for customers to share their experiences, both good and bad.

## How Can Your Company Become Zero Risk?

Look at your most common customer challenges, the ones that are not your fault but that you can predict will happen every week. Typical problems are a customer being unprepared or desperate. Your front-line employees are your best source for this exercise. Have them consider challenges that are not caused by your company and then have them figure out the best alternatives that will make your company the hero. Customer service does not have to be hard. When you foresee problems and prepare for them, customer service can actually be easy and rewarding. Make a customer's day tomorrow by anticipating his needs before he is even aware of them.

# Notes

1. Michael Feuer, "Window of Opportunity: Worry about the Customers Who Don't Complain, Because They're Not Coming Back," *Smart Business Akron/Canton*, March 2007.

2. Jeffrey Gitomer, *Customer Satisfaction is Worthless, Customer Loyalty is Priceless: How to Make Them Love You, Keep Them Coming Back, and Tell Everyone They Know* (Austin, TX: Bard Press, 1998).

3. Joe Nocera, "Put Buyers First? What a Concept," *New York Times*, January 5, 2008.

4. Mark Cuban, "Connecting to Your Customers," *Mark Cuban weblog*, November 7, 2006, www.blogmaverick.com/2006/11/07/success-and-motivation-connecting-to-your-customers/.

5. Jim Collins, *Good to Great: Why Some Companies Make the Leap . . . and Others Don't* (New York: HarperCollins, 2001).

6. Jena McGregor, "Customer Service Champs: *BusinessWeek*'s First-Ever Ranking of 25 Clients," *BusinessWeek*, March 5, 2007, www.businessweek.com/magazine/content/07_10/b4024001.htm.

7. George Gombassy, "Whole Foods Shows You Can Get Something for Nothing," December 21, 2007, www.courant.com/business/hc-watchdog1221.artdec21,0,4569213.column?coll=hc_business_util.

8. Bill Breen, "Mandarin Oriental Hotel Group," *Fast Company*, no. 108 (September 2006), www.fastcompany.com/magazine/108/open_customers-hotel.html.

# 12

# Commandment VIII: Creating an Above-and-Beyond Culture

*Constant awareness and branding of how to be a hero*

---

*Many times, when a customer complains about the price, it isn't because they are cheap or not willing to pay it, it is because the experience didn't warrant it.*

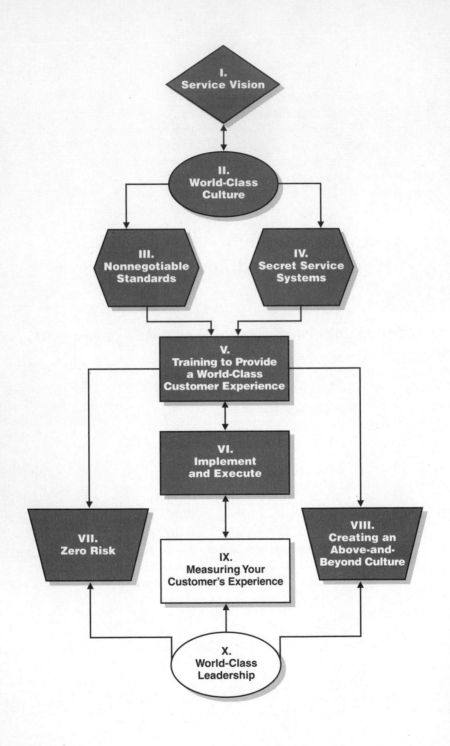

World-class service organizations create an awareness of the most common opportunities that employees can really deliver heroic service for the customer, which creates an above-and-beyond culture.

Are your employees empowered and inspired to exceed customer expectations? Do you have mechanisms in place to collect and re-distribute above-and-beyond stories to constantly remind your employees of the Service Vision?

Many times, when a customer complains about the price, it isn't because they are cheap or not willing to pay it, it is because the experience didn't warrant it.

## Creating Loyal Customers

In 2005, John Robert's Spa took a hard look at our VIP guests and what made them so loyal. We are lucky to have well over 100,000 guests in our database, but only the top 2,000 guests are labeled VIP (Silver, Gold, Platinum). One day, while reviewing the lists of VIP guests, we realized that in many cases we had dropped the ball with them, in some cases drastically or repeatedly. We wanted to figure out what we did that resulted in many of these people being so loyal and forgiving, so that we could do it with more of our guests.

To accomplish this, we arranged focus groups with our top VIP guests. We asked them point-blank, "Why are you so loyal to John Robert's Spa?" We received basically two answers: About 20 percent said something similar to, "I have been coming to John Robert's Spa for many years now, and it always is upbeat and friendly, and I can always count on getting a great haircut, and I get plenty of compliments from family and friends." Everything you possibly would want to hear from your clients.

The other 80 percent of our VIPs told us a specific story about how someone at John Robert's Spa went above-and-beyond for them. One guest told about the time she called to cancel her day of pampering. Our guest-care person could tell she was upset and asked if everything was okay. The customer responded, "No, my husband and I are opening a café, and we are 90 days late and thousands of dollars over budget. He purchased this day of pampering for me at your spa because he knows how much I enjoy it. I have had it on my calendar, counting down the days until today. I just locked my keys in my car, and I think I am having a nervous breakdown." Our employee said, "I see that you live just

15 minutes away. I would be happy to come pick you up, so you don't have to lose your day of pampering."

Another VIP told us a story about the time she walked into one of our salons for her 1 PM manicure appointment. The receptionist said, "We have been trying to contact you all morning because the nail technician who was to do your manicure went home sick." The VIP responded, "You had better find me someone who can do my nails because I have an important meeting this afternoon and my nails look horrible. I don't care who it is, but you had better get someone." A few minutes later the receptionist returned and said, "I apologize. Unfortunately we have no one available to do your nails, but we called the salon a few doors away. They have an opening now, so we booked and paid for a manicure with them."

More than 80 percent of our VIP guests had specific above-and-beyond stories to tell. After these focus groups, we realized that we are not good enough to give a dozen flawless experiences in a row to make someone loyal. Nor do we want to wait until a customer has had a dozen appointments with us. I would rather have one of our team members shock the customer by going above-and-beyond during one of her first few visits with us. That way the customer will be more loyal and, if and when we do drop the ball, more forgiving.

## Above and Beyond Is a Matter of Service Aptitude

I have always said, "Don't just tell me about how a Nordstrom salesperson made a quick trip to a competitor to purchase the pair of shoes you wanted because Nordstrom was out of them. Tell me how I can get all my employees to think and act that way." Does their behavior depend on whether the management is present, or does it depend on which employee you get, or if that employee is having a good day? While I like to think we have always had an "above-and-beyond" culture at John Robert's Spa, not all of our employees were providing that kind of experience. When we asked, "Why don't you go above and beyond more often?" the typical response was, "The opportunity never presents itself."

Now, the truth of the matter is that everyone gets the same number of above-and-beyond opportunities; the only difference is some employees see the opportunity and act on it, while others fail to see it. We had to proactively create an above-and-beyond culture. When we did that, we started to see a dramatic increase in the incidence of above-and-beyond stories and in the percentage of service-minded team members who were making those stories happen.

## Five Steps to Creating an Above-and-Beyond Culture

1. Empower employees with autonomy and confidence that they can aggressively go above and beyond without being second-guessed by management.
2. Train employees to be able to consistently recognize above-and-beyond opportunities that occur.
3. Inspire them on how to think outside the box and go above-and-beyond for the customer.
4. Acquire and document all above-and-beyond stories that happen in your organization.
5. Advertise and recognize those stories and employees throughout your entire organization.

Here is the crazy thing: You only have to do three of the five steps. Steps 4 and 5 actually take care of steps 2 and 3. When you put systems in place to catch all the above-and-beyond stories (step 4) and then continuously celebrate and advertise them to everyone in your organization (step 5), you start teaching your employees where all the opportunities exist (step 2), and how to deliver above-and-beyond service (step 3). The more that happens, the more that gets recirculated and it can become self-perpetuating, as long as you keep documenting and celebrating.

The above-and-beyond culture starts with documenting every above-and-beyond story that you hear from someone in your company. You can't just hope you find out about these stories; you have to solicit them. First, at every John Robert's Spa location, our close day report, which gets sent to our corporate office, includes these stories (Figure 12.1). It's not at all unusual for one location to forward several great new above-and-beyond opportunities in a single day. We also ask our customers. We have signs where guests check out that read, "Tell us if any of our team members were a hero for you. If so, please fill out an above-and-beyond card, and you will be entered to win a day of pampering." We encourage our employees to submit stories about themselves and each other.

All the stories we collect from guests, employees, and managers get added to our above-and-beyond document, that today has over 2,000 stories in total. We then recirculate the top stories in orientation, in customer service training, and in our employee newsletters. Every day we end each preshift huddle with a recent above-and-beyond story, hoping to inspire our team members to recognize similar opportunities that may present themselves. We also adopted a concept from Cameron Mitchell Restaurants; every time a guest sends us an e-mail, letter, or voicemail with a positive story about an experience, we prominently display that item, with the team member's name, so all team members can see it.

## Close Day Report

| | | |
|---|---|---|
| Closing Manager | | Carla/Chrissy |
| Date | | 12/4/07 |
| Total Sales | | $14,175.76 |
| Total Gift Certificate and Series Sales | | $ 1,482.51 |
| Average Retail per ticket | | $ 4.52 |

**Drawer Balances:**

| Drawer 1 Staff | Carla | Over/Under | $ 2.15 |
|---|---|---|---|
| Drawer 2 Staff | Chrissy | Over/Under | $(1.57) |
| Drawer 4 Staff | Joyce | Over/Under | $ 3.36 |

**Team Challenges:**

➢ Everything went smooth today

**Above-and-Beyond Stories**

➢ A lady came in with her young son, after we closed and all the designers had gone home, she said her son tried to cut his own hair and really messed it up and she was really desperate for someone to fix it, because it looked like he had cut it himself. I called Angie who does not work here anymore, on the chance she might want to help out. I didn't even have to ask twice and she said she would come up here to do it. The mom was SO thankful and the boy had a huge smile on his face when he left. This better go in the huddle!!!

➢ Aisha gave up her lunch to accommodate a guest of a spa party who decided at the last minute that she wanted a manicure.

➢ Mary stayed late after she rearranged her schedule so she could do a haircut and highlight on a guest who was incorrectly booked.

**Guest Challenges:**

➢ A guest came in for a requested blow-dry style today with Christina and her appt. was not on the book. Christina was totally booked; we apologized and offered to have Amy perform the service. The guest was fine with that. For her inconvenience we gave her a manicure with Jenna.

**Attendance:**

**FIGURE 12.1** Close Day Report

And finally, at our annual awards event, we give out the Secret Service Award, an award determined by employee vote, to the team member who performed the best above-and-beyond story of the year. This honor meets two objectives. First, it's a great way to recognize the individual for outstanding heroic service, and second, we are educating our employees about all the different opportunities for them to deliver world-class service, since all employees review all the top above-and-beyond stories to cast their vote.

## The Answer's Yes . . . What's the Question?

I hate the word no. I truly do. I can't believe how many people, in a vast number of companies, use it. It should be stricken from the English vocabulary. Well, that may be a bit severe, but it certainly should be stricken in any company focused on customer service. While staying in a prominent hotel in Las Vegas, I ordered room service. When asked if I wanted fries or coleslaw as my side, I asked if I could have a side of fruit. The person's response was a quick and unfriendly, "No! Do you want fries or coleslaw?" I said, "What do you mean, no? I see a fruit dish on your menu." And she responded, "Well, I would have to charge you." I wasn't asking for it for free. How easy would it be to say, "Certainly, while you cannot substitute the fruit for your side dish, I can add it to your order."

Cameron Mitchell Restaurants not only has removed the word no from the vocabulary of its 2,000 associates; it also has a great service brand promise: "Yes is the answer . . . what's the question?" This is not just lip service. Nearly everyone in this company walks this talk. This company has created such a strong above-and-beyond legacy that nearly all its employees try to outdo each other daily with unconventional ways they can exceed their guests' expectations.

Cameron Mitchell himself created a brilliant metaphor on which the company's service philosophy is founded. It is known as the "Milkshake." Legend has it that several years ago Mitchell and his family were customers at a restaurant, and his son asked if he could have a milkshake. The server said, "No." There's that word again. Mitchell knew the restaurant had ice cream, milk, and a blender, and he couldn't understand why someone wouldn't accommodate a guest on such a simple thing. So the milkshake became an icon to remind everyone at Cameron Mitchell Restaurants about finding a way to say yes. Having three young boys myself, I can't tell you how many times this exact scenario has happened to me. Similarly, more than a few times we have been in a restaurant where one of my sons didn't like anything on the kid's menu and asked if he could have a grilled cheese sandwich. Again, nearly every time the answer was no. Once I asked the waiter, "Do you mean to tell me that your restaurant doesn't have bread and cheese that someone could throw on a stove?" and the waiter responded, "Yeah, but I wouldn't even know how to ring it up." I responded, "I don't care if you charge me the price of a steak. You don't want my kid upset because he can empty this restaurant faster than a fire can!"

The milkshake has grown into a life of its own at Cameron Mitchell Restaurants. The company does an incredible job of creating constant awareness of what the milkshake represents. They start every company meeting with a "milkshake toast," and they give a Milkshake Award to the associates who best demonstrate the spirit of their Service Brand Promise, "Yes is the answer . . . what's the question." In any of their locations, you are likely to see several associates wearing milkshake pins and milkshake icons on posters and pictures. Outback Steakhouse's original Service Brand Promise was similar: "No Rules, Just Right."

Learning from Cameron Mitchell Restaurants, we have adopted the same philosophy at John Robert's Spa. The word no is like a foul four-letter word. The point of this philosophy is that too many employees and companies say no way too quickly without thinking how easy it would be to grant the customer's wish. Many times it is blamed on company policy. Many times it can be just laziness on the part of the front-line employee or the manager.

## Focus on What You Can Do, Not What You Can't Do

At John Robert's Spa, we have secret shoppers try to get our employees to say no. We train our employees how to not say no in situations where they cannot say yes. We can't always say yes, but the word no should never be used. If a guest wants something that isn't possible, instead of telling the guest what we can't do, we tell her what we can do. For instance, if a guest arrives extremely late for an appointment and asks if we can still take her, our guest-care team is trained to respond, "While we cannot perform a full pedicure, we can do an express pedicure." Or we may offer an alternative service provider. The customer may say no, but at least we are not the ones saying no.

In implementing this, first consider all the common situations that may arise that are difficult for you to say yes to a customer, and then work on creative alternatives in response to each. You are training your employees to make your customers feel that their request was granted, similar to my side-of-fruit dilemma. The second exercise is to create a metaphor or icon similar to the milkshake and then to advertise it constantly to your entire organization on a daily basis in many ways, including recognition, signage, and awards. Empower everyone in your company to do whatever it takes to deliver genuine hospitality.

Donna Rynda, a professional trainer in the hospitality industry, emphasizes the importance of hearing what the guest is really asking for, instead of hearing just the words. As an example, she tells how she checked into a hotel late one evening and asked if room service was still available. The associate at the front desk said, "No." Was she really asking about room service? In a sense, yes. But if the associate had really been listening, he would have realized she was saying, "It's late and I'm hungry. What are my food options?" And he would have been able to respond with an answer that satisfied her, such as, "The kitchen is closed, but we have vending machines. And there are restaurants that will deliver to our hotel. May I order something for you?"

## C.E.-NO

You might have seen the humorous Capital One credit card commercials with star David Spade working the phones of a typical credit card company, saying "no" to every question, in every possible language. The final question the customer asks him is, "Who's in charge over there?" and Spade replies, "That would be our C.E.-NO." Do you have any "C.E.-NOs" working for you, saying no to your customers?

### Remove No from Your Vocabulary
I am a VIP customer for a dry-cleaning and tailoring company because I travel so much and wear many suits and sports jackets, all of which need to be cleaned and tailored. One day I walked in with a pair of pants that needed tailoring and asked the owner if I could use the bathroom. She pointed to a sign on the wall:

> OUR BATHROOMS ARE NOT FOR OUR CUSTOMERS

I was shocked! She proceeded to take my measurements for my pants and asked me when I would like to pick them up.

I said, "Whenever they are done, just have them delivered to my office."

She said, "No, we don't deliver tailoring."

"But you have been picking up and delivering dry cleaning to my company twice a week!"

"Yes, but we don't deliver tailoring."

I cannot imagine what her logic was for refusing to include my tailoring on their next stop at my company. I can tell you I found a new dry cleaner and tailor who will deliver my tailoring.

### "No" Service
While walking through John Robert's Spa call center one day, I overheard one of our personnel say no to a guest on the phone.

After she hung up, I said, "Why did you just say no to a guest?"

"She is leaving us and going to a nearby competitor, and she wanted her color formula so she can have the other salon do her hair color."

I said, "So, call her back, give her the color formula, and then give her the phone number and extension of our hairdresser who has been doing her hair. In the event her new salon has any problems converting the color, they can call, and we can help them."

We don't own the guest or her color formula, and by saying yes, maybe the guest will have second thoughts about leaving us; however, if nothing else, she won't do brand terrorism on John Robert's Spa to everyone she knows.

### "No" Reason

I had to bring my new vehicle back to the dealer for service one morning. They were a good 30 minutes away from my house, and they estimated it would take about an hour to fix. On my way to the dealership, I realized that I actually had an errand to run about 10 minutes down the street from the dealership. I knew that I would not have any time after my vehicle was fixed to run the errand, so I thought that it would be perfect if I could run the errand while my car got fixed. So when I arrived at the service department at the dealership, I asked the service manager if I could borrow a car for 20 minutes to run down the street while I waited. He said, "No, we have no loaner cars." I said, "I know, but I just need a car for literally 20 minutes, isn't there any way you can give me one of these cars?" He responded, "No, we have no loaner cars." Now they have over 300 cars on their lot.

So I walked out of the service door and around to the front of the building into the dealership where I was greeted by a new car salesman, "How can I help you?" I said, "I want to test-drive one of your cars." The salesman said, "No problem." And then he and I left the dealership for a test drive, and about 10 minutes later, my errand was done, and we returned to the dealership.

### Find Your Milkshake Metaphor

I help many companies come up with their icon and metaphor, similar to the milkshake, specific to their culture. The first thing a company has to do is to find its best above-and-beyond stories and then choose the most significant one that will serve as the example to inspire similar behavior. Once a company has this story, the next thing they do is to create the symbol, logo, or picture that represents their best story. Eventually words will be unnecessary; when employees see that picture, they will instantly be reminded of the culture they work in and the legacy they have to uphold.

When I helped The Melting Pot Restaurant come up with its milkshake metaphor, it wasn't an easy process because The Melting Pot had so many amazing above-and-beyond stories. The company felt that many of these stories were relatively insignificant, but many other businesses would consider these stories to be outrageously above and beyond.

The Melting Pot Secret Service Project team came up with "POW," for Pot-on-Wheels, which was the result of a story that came up about their Minneapolis, Minnesota, location. There was a couple dining in their restaurant one evening. Although the couple was having a great time, they had to leave before enjoying their favorite part of the meal, the chocolate fondue. The woman was pregnant and had started having contractions earlier and now realized they were close enough together to necessitate leaving the restaurant and going straight to the hospital. In most cases, a restaurant would warmly wish them well and that would be it. However, the managers and employees of this Melting Pot wanted to go above and beyond the call of duty. They wrapped up some chocolate fondue along with some dippers and delivered it to the hospital so that the couple could enjoy their chocolate fondue when they felt up to it. It had a big impact on this couple. POW is a metaphor for delivering the Perfect Night Out to our guests through immaculate inviting surroundings, happy team members, exceptional food and drink, and genuine hospitality.

The Melting Pot is one of the best organizations at creating above-and-beyond awareness throughout their 110+ locations. After the creation of the "POW" award, I was a keynote speaker at their annual franchisee convention. I got to see an award show for their finalists for the coveted POW Award, which is the highest honor a location can win for above-and-beyond service. Each finalist was videotaped telling their story and the impact it had on both the guest and their staff. By the time the winner was announced, there was not a dry eye in the building. It felt like a "Pay it Forward" movement.

Besides their annual convention, The Melting Pot brands their legendary stories on a regular basis through posting them on their Intranet, as well as in their Pot Luck Press (Figure 12.2). They have a companywide newsletter that goes out quarterly that features the most recent POW submissions and letters and e-mails from guests sharing their Perfect Night Out experiences (Figure 12.3).

### Secret Service Detective

For a long time, we struggled with demonstrating to our call center what the staff could do to become an integral part of the guest's experience. The solution came from a woman we hired to work in our call center. Upon arrival, Martha Wright started to alert different locations to be ready for certain guests coming in. She would call a location to tell them to have a congratulations card ready for a guest celebrating her graduation from college or she would notify another location to be prepared for a couple having

**FIGURE 12.2**   Pot Luck Press

a spa day and celebrating an anniversary. Martha started doing this several times a week. I asked her how she found out so much about what was going on in our guests' lives.

She replied, "They give me cues. For instance, any time a woman schedules an updo hairstyle or makeup, something big is going on. Any time someone wants multiple spa services, typically she is celebrating something or it is a gift. So I just ask them, 'What's the occasion?' and they tell me. Then I call the salon and notify them so they can make their experience special that day."

**FIGURE 12.3    Perfect Night Out Stories**

She just asks them. That's it. How simple! We at John Robert's Spa recognized the value Martha's abilities could provide and immediately had her teach the rest of our call center personnel to be able to pick up on these cues and ask, "What's the occasion?" We gave them tracking sheets to fill out when they recognized a special occasion (Figure 12.4). The tracking sheets are then forwarded to the salon manager and entered into the preshift huddle in order to alert the team members of these special-occasion guests.

Upon the guest's arrival, the hostess will greet her with a card for this special occasion. Throughout the guest's visit, several of our team members may congratulate her in hopes of making it a truly world-class

Martha
May 9-12
**Special Occasion Log**

| Guest's Name | Date of Appointment | Salon | Services | Occasion | Action taken |
|---|---|---|---|---|---|
| Judy Thomas | 5/9 | Mayfield | Stone.mas.1 | The Birthday girl (mom) | |
| Kristen Thomas | 5/9 | " | mas.1 | Celebearing with her mom This is a surprise | |
| Marcy Fuerst | 5/9 | Chagrin Falls | mani/ped | The Birthday Girl! | |
| Cindy Asher | 5/12 | Mayfield | updo | going to a birthday party | |
| Greg Feketik | 5/12 | " | mas.1 | husband & wife day out Relaxing | |
| Kathy Feketik | 5/12 | " | mas.1 | wife & husband " " " | |
| Bethany Staats | 5/11 | Mayfield | preg mas.1 | Cara & Rebecca visiting for her baby shower | |
| Cara Rich | 5/11 | Mayfield | mas.1 | Visiting Bethany for baby shower | |
| Rebecca Rich | 5/11 | " | fac.1 | " " " " " | |
| Julie Davis | 5/12 | Mayfield | fac/mas (man) | Mom & daughters day out | |
| Julian Davis | 5/12 | " | fac/mas (man) | " " " " " | |
| Sara Davis | 5/12 | " | fac/mas (man) | " " " " " | |
| Linsey Davis | 5/12 | " | fac/mas (man) | " " " " " 14 | |
| Nancy Dolezal | 5/8 | Mayfield | ped | She Treating Elaine to a day out | |
| Elaine Nicholson | 5/8 | " | ped | Her husband was caller she Taking a day of Relaxing | |
| Marty Bird | 5/10 | " | spa day | Celebrating her 50th Birthday! | |

**FIGURE 12.4** Special Occasion Log

experience. We recognize anywhere from 20 to 50 such occasions in a week. That doesn't seem like a lot out of 4,000 appointments, but before this, we hadn't recognized 20 special occasions in our entire first 12 years of business.

## First Impressions versus Final Impressions

It has been said that a first impression plays a significant role in customer retention. However, I believe the final impression is just as critical. I have seen and experienced hundreds of companies that put a great deal of emphasis on the front end of the customer's experience and severely miss their mark on the back end.

Consulting and speaking on customer service has afforded me an opportunity to experience many luxuries that I probably wouldn't have been able to enjoy otherwise.

One of my favorite places, that I have been fortunate to work with a great deal, is Nemacolin Woodlands Resort, in Farmington, Pennsylvania. This is truly a world-class customer service organization. On their property they have a new hotel, Falling Rock, a five-diamond hotel. During peak season, a suite can cost $500 to $800 per night. While Nemacolin is redefining the word *experience* with their award-winning architecture, PGA golf course, shooting academy, spa, and Hummer driving school, it is their front-line associates and their attention to detail that makes Falling Rock such a superior customer service organization. Especially their valet, doorman, and butlers.

For example, when you depart, the Nemacolin experience isn't over. The valet team may deliver your car clean and spotless, with a cold can of your favorite soda in your cup holder. (How did they do that? They paid attention to what you ordered in the restaurant or used from the mini-bar in your room.) On future visits, the butler may customize your mini-bar based on what you took from it your last time. If you like Peanut M&M's, you may have six in your mini bar this time versus six different kinds of candy. On your dashboard when you leave, you might find a MapQuest printout of directions to your next destination. On some occasions, with your permission, they fill the gas tank for you (and charge it to your room). They have been known to organize the inside of your car; they might even find a CD you thought you lost. (I have three boys and a Suburban, so I won't go near the third row.)

So picture this: You are leaving Falling Rock in a clean car, sipping your favorite cold soft drink, following your MapQuest directions, and listening to that CD you lost three months ago. You call your spouse or business associate and start raving about this place and all the amazing things you experienced.

The real value here is that Falling Rock left you with such an incredible last impression that you will forget that you got a room with a double bed instead of the king you ordered or they may not have had your dinner reservations. But with such an incredible close, the only thing you remember is how this place delivered such an unforgettable experience.

What final impression are you leaving with your customer? Will your customer brag about you? Or will she remember only the things you did wrong?

## Anticipating and Delivering on Your Customer's Needs

My Nemacolin experience inspired me to evaluate what we do at my salons and spas, to increase the emphasis of delivering Secret Service at the close in order to strengthen the last impression we give our guests. A perfect opportunity to deliver Secret Service at the close is during the week of Mother's Day. We usually have a long line of men waiting to purchase a day of pampering. Typically, after they purchase a gift certificate, they have to run to another store to get a Mother's Day card to go with it. Not any more; now our guest-care team (receptionists) pull out a stack of Mother's Day cards and invite the men to choose one at no charge. While we may spend a couple of dollars for a card, that day of pampering can run from $300 to $500.

What's the real value? Hopefully, the next anniversary, Valentine's Day, or the next time they are in the doghouse, they will think of John Robert's Spa before they think of the local florist.

Another opportunity to deliver Secret Service came when someone realized that every Friday and Saturday we have about 50 women booked for hair styling and makeup because they are in a wedding or attending one. From my personal experience, every time my wife and I drive to a wedding, we have to stop at a drugstore for a wedding card. So John Robert's Spa started keeping an inventory of wedding cards.

When a woman comes to checkout for an updo hairstyle or makeup services, we ask, "By chance are you going to a wedding?"

She typically replies, "Yes."

"Do you have a wedding card yet?"

"No, thanks for reminding me. I need to do that on my way home."

Then the guest-care person pulls out a dozen wedding cards. "Would any of these work for you?"

The guest is usually blown away, especially when she learns there is no charge for the card.

The more your organization creates emotional capital with your brand, and the better you are at doing it, the more forgiving your customers will be when negative situations arise and the less likely your customers will be to shop your competition.

## Become a Storytelling Company

If you want to have an above-and-beyond culture, you have to be a storytelling company. World-class customer service companies are great at storytelling. They retell their best story over and over again in order to inspire current employees and to educate the next generation of employees to act similarly. "This is who we are, this is our culture; we make it happen."

I personally witnessed the power of storytelling in a preshift huddle at John Robert's Spa. We ended the huddle with a story about a guest who was checking out after a pedicure, still wearing disposable slippers. She couldn't wait for her toes to dry because she had to be somewhere. The receptionist checking her out noticed that it was raining hard, asked the guest for her car keys, brought her car to the front door, got an umbrella, and walked the guest out to her car. It was a great story. Later that day, a manager told me how another guest came to checkout in disposable slippers and another receptionist immediately looked outside, saw there was not a cloud in the sky, and was actually disappointed that she couldn't do the same thing. When you constantly retell your above-and-beyond stories, your employees start to recognize opportunities that they never would have previously.

## Branding Your Above-and-Beyond Stories

An outstanding job of building above-and-beyond awareness is done by Cameron Mitchell Restaurants. In their corporate offices and employee break rooms, and at company events, you always see several above-and-beyond stories from their customers, 11 × 14 and mounted on foam board, which include a letter from a guest and the employee's picture (Figure 12.5).

Above-and-beyond signage motivates employees to constantly seek ways to WOW customers. It's no wonder Cameron Mitchell is known for customer service. The Director of Training, Heather Thitoff, who has one of the sharpest customer service minds I have had the pleasure to work with, says, "We celebrate a great example of our culture monthly when we make posters that are distributed to every restaurant in our company recognizing an associate. Associates are selected from a variety of sources: a guest e-mail, a guest letter, or even another associate. We know our culture is strong and continues to thrive because it is a topic of every meeting, and we continue to cultivate it. We want more than just words; we want to make an impact by recognizing our culture in action whenever an associate is living our culture with a guest or another associate."

This type of above-and-beyond branding creates a healthy competitive culture, where employees try to outdo each other by constantly doing something significant for their customers. It should be no surprise that The Ritz-Carlton Hotels (a world-class organization) go to great lengths in order to recognize and brand their employees who demonstrate superior legendary service. They have the following programs:

- Hall of Fame that displays great stories—this could be a letter from a guest or a manager's recognition.
- Lightning Strikes—A daily award recognizing superior service given by one of their employees.

We're Making
Raving Fans

Dear Cameron,

We hosted a rehearsal dinner at Martini Short North and I would like to compliment you on the sensational service we received.

Bill was always so helpful and gracious (even though I must have called him at least a thousand times!)

We had family that came from as far away as Ireland, and (I'm gonna brag a little) my nephew, who is the publisher for *Rolling Stone Mag*, said he was impressed with the service!!!! (and he has been to some pretty super parties!

Laura was remarkable!! She is a real gem. I am a flight attendant, and because of my job have been able to go to many fine establishments! I want to congratulate you on your sensational staff. All of the servers were wonderful, but I was particularly impressed with Laura.

I would, and will, recommend Martini to anyone that has a special occasion to celebrate in Columbus. Once again, Bill and Laura...kudos, and thank you!

Penny Castelli

*Martini*
ITALIAN BISTRO

Bill Anderson, General Manager, and Laura, Server, Martini Italian Bistro Short North

**FIGURE 12.5** Customer Service Recognition Letters

- Five-Star Employees—Recognizes the top five employees who delivered exemplary service this past quarter. They hold a dinner for these five-star employees, their spouses, and the person who nominated them.

- At the end of the year, they recognize the top five of the quarterly five-star employees and those top five-star employees win a week's paid vacation and an all-expense-paid trip at any Ritz-Carlton property.

As Jim McManemon, General Manager at The Ritz-Carlton, points out, "that recognition really connects the emotional capital of the employee with the company and the benefit of providing that type of service to our guests."

## Train and Test for Above-and-Beyond Opportunities

It is critical that all employees are trained and tested on the different ways they can go above-and-beyond for customers. Most front-line employees have no clue about even 5 percent of the opportunities to really wow a customer. Because of this, almost all opportunities will go right over the head of employees who haven't been properly trained to see them.

When that happens, a company misses the chance to build emotional capital with that customer. We don't want above-and-beyond acts to happen by chance; if possible, we want a high percentage of the opportunities to be executed. Our newly hired employees receive their John Robert's *Customer Experience Cycle Training Manual*, which includes the service defects, standards, and above-and-beyond opportunities for each stage of interaction (Chapter 9). In each stage, such as a phone call, we insert approximately six above-and-beyond opportunities. Because we have documented all our known above-and-beyond actions over the years, we can easily plug in the ones that are easily achievable and that present themselves frequently. Next, during Secret Service Boot Camp, employees take the Customer Experience Cycle Test, where they have to list the most notable above-and-beyond opportunities for each stage, ensuring that employees will be more likely to recognize those opportunities if and when they arise.

After being hired, each new employee receives the *Guest Experience Manual* that includes above-and-beyond opportunities that exist at each stage of interaction with our guest. The new employees are required to learn these above-and-beyond opportunities and then are tested on them to ensure they won't miss an opportunity when it presents itself.

## Is It a Standard or an Above and Beyond?

Here's how we decide whether an action should be considered a standard or whether it should be an above and beyond. If we can realistically do it consistently (at least 85 percent of the time), we make it a standard. If we can't and we can only do it when resources allow, then it is an above-and-beyond. For instance, we can't possibly print MapQuest directions for every customer; however, when we find out that a guest needs directions and we have the resources, staff, and technology available to do it, we will. Similarly, we don't have valet service, so if it's raining hard, we can't possibly walk every guest to her car or pull her car up to the door, but we will do it as often as we can. Even if we do that for just five customers, that is probably 99 percent better than those customers experience with any other business that doesn't have valet service.

## A Swing and a Miss

While above-and-beyond opportunities may be obvious to many people in management, they may not be obvious to your front-line employees, who are the ones who touch your customers the most often. That is why the training and testing of above-and-beyond opportunities is critical to cultivating that type of culture. For instance, one Saturday afternoon, while playing football in the backyard with my sons, I thought, "Now would be a perfect time to go check out the newly released Suburban." I had been driving one for many years and had heard that the new model had many bells and whistles that mine did not. So I drove to the local car dealership. When I walked into the showroom, the first thing I encountered was service defect #1: five or six car salesmen standing around the front counter talking college football. They stopped talking and looked at me. I was wearing a t-shirt, grass-stained shorts, and a baseball cap. I am convinced that each one looked me up and down and said, "You take him, I don't want him." The important thing is what the standard should be: Get rid of all those salesmen milling around the reception area, and put a very friendly greeter at the entrance who can assign the right salesperson to the customer.

A young man in his twenties got me, and we went out for a test drive. Instead of telling me about all the bells and whistles on the new car or about the great service that comes with the vehicle and the dealership, he proceeded to say how he'd had one too many drinks the night before: service defect #2. The standard should be to talk only about what the customer wants to talk about.

About five minutes into the test drive, my wife called to say she was at the grocery store, half a mile from the dealership, and she needed me to come pick her up because she had bought so many groceries they wouldn't fit into her car. I hung up and told the salesman that we needed to end the test drive because I had to go save my wife. His response was, "That stinks! I hope you can come back after you are done." After I left, I got aggravated because it might be another three weeks before I could go car shopping again. I thought, "Why didn't that salesman offer to go pick up my wife in the new Suburban?" I would have had to buy it. As long as it was just me, I could make a rational decision; get my wife involved, and let her see how nice the new car is, how the back door automatically opens at the push of a button, how a camera shows you everything behind the vehicle when you put it in reverse, and I would have had to purchase that vehicle. This is low-hanging fruit. This is a fastball right down the middle of the plate. A salesman could and should have been trained to recognize it and knock it out of the park. Instead he was oblivious, and he lost a great opportunity to close on a sale.

## People Crave What They Have Experienced and Enjoyed

You can't miss what you never have had. High-end car dealerships are great at understanding this. When you need a loaner, they provide you with an upgraded, newer version, so that when your car is ready, you no longer want it back. For the longest time, I made fun of flying first class, thinking, "Why would anyone pay two to three times more for a flight that doesn't get you there any sooner or safer?" Then one time I was upgraded and got the experience. I sat in a comfortable chair. It wasn't possible for the guy next to me to drool on me as he slept, which had happened on my previous flight. I had leg room, a preflight drink, a hot towel, a digestible meal, hot chocolate chip cookies and milk, and, my favorite, mini salt and pepper shakers. After this experience, I could never go back to coach. Flying first class became a necessity on any flight that had it. Let's not even talk about the difference between first class and coach on overseas flights; I may be the only person who is disappointed when the flight ends.

I had a similar experience at The Ritz-Carlton Hotel. Every so often my wife and I went to a Ritz-Carlton for a weekend getaway, and we always have a very nice experience. Then I started speaking for different Ritz properties. One time when I brought my wife along, as a courtesy the general manager put us on the concierge's floor, which has bigger rooms, more amenities, drinks, and a full-service buffet. After that, any time we stayed at a Ritz-Carlton, it had to be on the concierge's floor; the regular rooms were no longer good enough.

Besides making customers more loyal, an above-and-beyond culture can also be a great sales tool. The businesses that find a way to expose their customers to new services and products will find they have hooked a good percentage of customers on those exact services and products.

# Customer Service Revolution

Maybe there is a light at the end of the tunnel in this decade-long customer service crisis. Recently, I have found great customer service stories in some of the most unlikely places.

Like every other speaker in the world, I love to take shots at the airlines, but a Continental gate agent named Mike Trapp is forcing me to tell a different story. I was about to leave the Cleveland airport for Alexandria, Louisiana, when I realized that I had left my laptop in my office. Now my entire world is on my laptop. Without it, I cannot do my presentation. I called my assistant and asked her to bring it out to me, but she had at least a 45-minute drive and we were 45 minutes from departure. I asked a gate agent if there was any way they could radio someone to meet her because I knew that if I went out of security, I would never make it back through. Like most airline employees, she said, "There's nothing we can do."

Trapp overheard us and said, "Let me know when she's close." When my assistant called to tell me she was pulling up to the curb, I went over to Mr. Trapp. He was boarding passengers, but he immediately got the other gate agent to work his spot while he ran out before I could tell him what kind of car my assistant drives or what she looks like. A few moments later, he raced back in with my laptop in hand. I was shocked and delighted. I pulled out $20 to give him, but he refused to take it.

He said, "No, thank you." Now that's exceptional service by an airline employee.

Painters from College Works Painting headquarters in Southern California are trained to notice above-and-beyond opportunities while they are painting people's homes, such as a loose mailbox or a basketball hoop hanging on three bolts instead of all four. If a painter recognizes this, he tightens the mailbox or adds a bolt to the hoop and leaves a note for the owner.

## Do Your Employees Have to Ask Permission?

The top world-class service organizations empower their front-line employees with a great deal of autonomy, whether it is anticipating a customer's needs or because it is necessary during their service recovery. Take for example at The Ritz-Carlton Hotels, every employee is empowered up to $2,000 per incident to resolve an issue or delight a guest. At both of my companies, John Robert's Spa and The DiJulius Group, our employees are empowered to use their best judgment in making our customer's day. The only thing they need management's permission for is if they want to say no to a customer.

## Don't Win the Argument But Lose the Customer

Starbucks "Just Say Yes" policy empowered employees to provide the best service possible, even if it required going beyond company rules. "The last thing we want to do is win the argument and lose the customer," says Christine Day, Starbucks' senior vice president of administration in North America.[1]

To demonstrate this, a friend of mine shared with me their recent Starbucks experience.

"One time I was in the drive-through at Starbucks. Although normally I get through quickly, I had been waiting a while, and even thought about pulling out of line. By the time I got to the window to get my coffee, I was frustrated. The Starbucks drive-through attendant immediately greeted me with an apology and thanked me for my patience. She then handed me a card for a free coffee of my choice on my next visit. The card basically said we want your experience to be full not half empty and we are sorry for any inconvenience. I now was happy that I stayed in line, and if I need to, I will be happy to wait again, because they demonstrated how they valued my time, and made it worth my while to come back."

## Daily PreShift Huddles

Every world-class organization I know of has mandatory preshift huddles with the vast majority of its people, and holds them at every level of the organization. This is the best way to communicate clearly and regularly with everyone on vital topics:

- Share new information that all associates should be aware of.
- Communicate information about customers who are VIPs, significant first-timers, or marking a special occasion.
- Reinforce service philosophies.
- Create awareness of any service defects that have occurred and that you want to reduce the possibility of recurring.
- Create awareness of recent above-and-beyond stories in order to encourage more employees to recognize similar opportunities.

# Being a Daymaker

Cindy Manzie, who is a key team member in the John Robert's call center, has been delivering outstanding Secret Service for many years. Instead of just answering phones and booking appointments, she finds numerous ways to be a Daymaker, as attested by this letter from a guest (Figure 12.6).

Dear Mr. DiJulius,

On January 29th, I called your salon to book a last-minute appointment. I spoke with one of your guest care representatives named Cindy Manzie. She must have heard the desperation in my voice and quickly got me in at your Solon Spa for that same day. I commented that I hoped that it would not snow because I hate driving in it. She said, "Well you could just have your significant other pick you up and take you out for dinner because when you leave here you will look beautiful!" I said, "Well my significant other is with his new girlfriend in Florida. You think you would know someone after 27 years of marriage." I was having a weak moment; I couldn't believe I was telling a complete stranger my troubles. Cindy could have just ended the call there, but she didn't. She told me that I was not alone. She gave me information on Parents without Partners; she also gave me her home number. She told me to call her any time, day or night!

I had a good cry. I couldn't believe that someone who didn't even know me could be that caring and kind. I drove to your Solon Spa, where I have gone for many years, and was greeted at the door with a dozen beautiful long stemmed red roses! The card attached said, "You'll never be alone!!" Love, your John Roberts Family. This was amazing. We all hugged and cried. I not only left your salon with roses, but with many more caring friends. (I did look beautiful also.) Cindy went way out of the way for someone she has never met. Her kindness and caring will never be forgotten. I just wanted to take this opportunity to let you know that you have many wonderful friends working with you, and I thank you.

A Very Happy Customer!

**FIGURE 12.6** Above-and-Beyond Letter

With staggered shifts, few companies can get 100 percent attendance at every preshift huddle. However, getting the majority of your team to attend a preshift huddle on a regular basis will dramatically improve the chances that everyone will be on the same page and more enrolled and present for today's customer experiences.

When we introduced preshift huddles at John Robert's Spa, we had a schedule of staggered shifts (Figure 12.7). Even though we scheduled five-minute huddles 15 minutes before our major shifts began, almost half of our employees weren't there to attend the daily huddle.

When we saw that our huddles were making such a positive impact on our business, we changed the way we schedule all employees. That's how powerful this commandment is! Today, nearly everyone works one of two shifts, either 8:30 AM to 2 PM or 2:30 PM to 8 PM. We have two preshift huddles daily, one at 8:15 AM and one at 2:15 PM. Another example of a preshift huddle can be found in Figure 12.8.

John Robert's
JR SPA

John Robert's Team Huddle

**Today is June 27th**
4 weeks     July 25
6 weeks     August 8
8 weeks     August22

**Bright Happenings:**
Angela bought her first house!
Marie found out she's pregnant with twins!

**Above & Beyond:**
Yesterday Cindy received a call that Beth Jones had to cancel her appt with Lisa because her car wouldn't start. Cindy called Suzy who offered to drive to Beth's house and pick her up! Since Beth was Lisa's last client of the day she drove her home and even offered to stop at the store for her!

**Open Appointments:**

Hair _____

Nails _____

Spa _____

Let's help fill each other's book!
Look for big openings!

**Out of Stock Products:**
_____
_____
_____

Yesterday's recap:

Average retail per ticket _____

Service to Retail % _____

Weekly Sales _____

**Events:**

June 29  WIN Women in Networking

June 30  Beachwood Chamber of Commerce

July 4    Closed!

July 7    Team meeting

July 8    Rainbow hospital visit

**Current Promotions:**

Playhouse Square Savings: 20% any spa service with Playhouse ticket stub

Product of the Week: Rosemary Mint 10% off

VIP: 10% off highlights

Aveda makeup: Aveda artist will be on site for makeover appointments this week from 12-8

**Today's New Guests:**

| | | |
|---|---|---|
| 1:00 | Tina | Sarah Smaihle |
| 3:30 | Lisa | Heather Borstin |
| 4:30 | Stacy | Jennifer Quill |
| 6:00 | Jen | David Wagner |

**Today's VIPs:**

| | | | |
|---|---|---|---|
| 12:00 | Suzanne | Martha Mancy | Gold |
| 4:00 | Mary | Kristen Jackson | Silver |
| 5:00 | Lydia | Karen Schmidt | Gold |
| 7:00 | Tracey | Barry Nordpandl | Silver |
| 7:00 | Teresa | Jen Fogliano | Platinum |

**FIGURE 12.7** Sample of the John Robert's Spa—Preshift Huddle

## Ways to Acquire Above-and-Beyond Stories

- Document all the folklore stories that have happened over the years, dating all the way back to the company's inception.
- Solicit stories from your customers and employees.

Molly Woo's

**Daily Associate and Manager Pit Stop**

Day______ Date______

Review of Yesterday's Business

| Lunch: | | Dinner: | | Total: | |
|---|---|---|---|---|---|
| Guest Count | ______ | Guest Count | ______ | Guest Count | ______ |
| a)Sales | $______ | a)Sales | $______ | a)Sales | $______ |
| b)Last Week's Sales | $______ | b)Last Week's Sales | $______ | b)Last Week's Sales | $______ |
| Difference(a minus b) | $______ | Difference(a minus b) | $______ | Difference(a minus b) | $______ |
| Check Average | $______ | Check Average | $______ | | |

Comment Card Results: Cards Returned:L-____ D-____ Food% :D-___ L-___ Service%:L-___ D-___

CNS: Sanitation and Food Saftey

Today Last Week

| | | |
|---|---|---|
| Sales | Lunch: | $______ |
| | Dinner: | $______ |
| | Total | $______ |
| Guest Count | Lunch: | ______ |
| | Dinner: | ______ |
| | Total | ______ |

***RAVING FAN HOSPITALITY*** ***What would you do?***

***NEED TO KNOW INFO***

Culinary Highlights

Today's Chef Feature

Beer / Wine Suggestion

Food Cost / Quality Topic

Daily Tastings

Top Focus:

Mistake!:

CONTEST TRACKER

**FIGURE 12.8** **Sample of Cameron Mitchell Restaurant's Preshift Pit-Stop**

- Make it a part of the manager's close day report (see Figure 12.1).
- Document every story to be shared with the entire organization.

## Ways to Advertise Your Above-and-Beyond Stories

- Share top 10 to 20 stories at new employee orientation.
- Share a new one every day at preshift huddles (see Figures 12.7 and 12.8).

- Put all recent stories in employee newsletters (see Figures 12.2 and 12.3).
- Recognize and celebrate new stories at any company meetings and trainings.
- Create an annual above-and-beyond award.
- Create signage of top above-and-beyond stories (see Figure 12.5).
- Train and test new employees to recognize above-and-beyond opportunities.

# Notes

1. Youngme Moon and John A. Quelch, "Starbucks: Delivering Customer Service," *Harvard Business Review*, July 31, 2003.

# 13

# Commandment IX: Measuring Your Customer's Experience

## What gets measured gets managed

*If you want to see how a company is doing now, look at their current sales, if you want to know how a company will perform in the future, look at their current customer satisfaction scores.*[1]

—Joe Calloway, Author and Speaker

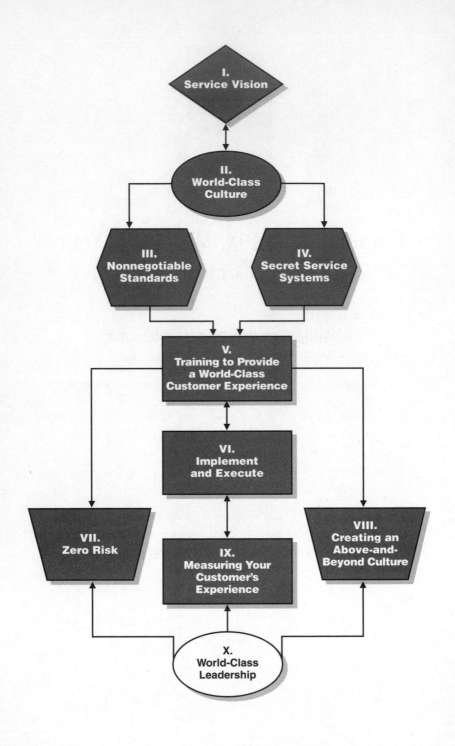

World-class service organizations use a scientific method to measure your customer's experience and satisfaction, providing benchmarks for performance in each location/department.

Your goals must be measurable, tied to a specific metric, that lets you know how satisfied your customers are with you, who is clearly serving customers, who is inconsistent, if you are keeping your Service Vision to your customers, how effective your service recovery is, and how you stack up against your competition.

By now you are aware of the significant obstacles to customer service, the formula for being world-class, the importance of an internal world-class culture, how to recruit and train your employees, how to develop service recovery systems, and ways to create an above-and-beyond culture and legacy for your customers. Another key component that is still needed is a definitive way to measure the customer's experience and level of satisfaction. Without doing this, you will have no idea of how consistent your locations and departments are in delivering customer service. You will not know what your customers value or what produces little or no return on investment. You won't know what problems are lurking and causing customers to defect to your competition until it's too late.

Strong sales can disguise many serious issues. We all know many companies that open with a bang, decide they have a proven model, and grow too rapidly, with the sad result that within a few years they are struggling to reinvent themselves in order to stay afloat. Why? Because once the novelty wears off and your competitors duplicate your product, the consistency of the experience you provide will be the only criterion your customers use to determine your value versus the value of your competition. If you plan to open your business in new markets, regionally or nationally, then the need for measurement becomes even more critical. Too many businesses fail to realize that customers view all of a company's locations as equal—equally good, equally bad, or equally indifferent. To a customer, one bad experience with a brand can be its death sentence.

Measuring the customer experience means you have a definitive red-flag mechanism that you can use to immediately address all its components: who, what, where, when, and how. You can measure what is working and what customers value, you can measure defects in your overall system, and you can pinpoint inconsistencies and lower performing locations.

What keeps a customer loyal and highly satisfied is the experience and value the customer perceives that you offer for the price you charge—not what you the owner and your employees perceive the value and experience to be.

As mentioned in Chapter 1, most companies don't have a clue about how well they are delivering customer service. How can 80 percent of the companies think they are providing superior service, but only 8 percent of their customers agree with them? Who's right? The customer.

## Don't Try This at Home

Measuring customer satisfaction and disseminating the data has become a science, one that growing companies should not try to do themselves. Perhaps the most significant factor in creating a superior customer experience is knowing what your customers want. It sounds simple enough; we think we know our customers and we believe we know what they want. But do we really? When was the last time you asked them the right questions in order to find out what they really want? What did you do with that information? Too often we do not have enough of the right information. Or we have great information but we have no idea what to do with it, and we don't have someone in place or empowered to drive the changes needed within the company.

Understanding how to acquire, measure, and act on the right information can mean the difference between a customer sampling your business occasionally and that customer being extremely loyal and referring others to your business. One common mistake made by companies who try to measure their customer experience themselves, is pre-identifying questions and categories, and thus steering customers in a direction.

To create a reliable measurement system, you must first establish a baseline that you have confidence in. A baseline is an historical benchmark that gives you an idea of what's going on with your customer base: your starting point, what the customer already likes about you, and where your strongest areas of opportunity lie. Use a reputable third-party company to establish your baseline; in this way you will ensure that the information received is valid reliable data. Using a third-party eliminates nearly all the mistakes companies make when they try to measure customer satisfaction themselves.

I called on two of the top experts in customer satisfaction measurement: Service Management Group (SMG), a global customer satisfaction and service improvement company and Direct Opinions, a national survey and research firm. Service Management Group, headquartered in Kansas City, Missouri, is the leader in measuring the customer experience for multi-unit or chain businesses. In 2007, SMG conducted over 28 million customer surveys in 60,000 locations in 43 countries. Working with clients such as Hallmark Cards, Chick-fil-A, and The Cheesecake Factory, I found that each of them use SMG to measure their customer satisfaction. Direct Opinions, headquartered in Beachwood, Ohio, has become one of the leading business-to-business firms in market research and performance measurement studies. It uses telephone surveys to determine customer satisfaction and do market research. Clients include Sherwin-Williams, Google, and Midas.

## Why Measure Customer Satisfaction?

Darlene Campagna, President and Co-Owner of Direct Opinions, points out that most companies object to using a third-party company to formally measure customer satisfaction on the grounds that a company knows what its customers think. Here are some of the common objections, and reasons why they miss the mark:

- *If our customers are dissatisfied, we hear about it.* According to "The Retail Customer Dissatisfaction Study 2006," (1) a study conducted by The Jay H. Baker Retailing Initiative at Wharton and The Verde Group of Toronto, only 6 percent of shoppers who experienced a problem with a retailer contacted the company, but 31 percent shared the experience with friends, family, or colleagues.
- *Our employees keep us up-to-date on our customers.* This argument holds that front-line staff, with their tremendous first-hand knowledge of customers, can provide valuable input in order to determine customer needs and satisfaction.

Direct Opinions says front-line staff will have an extremely biased viewpoint. For example, business-to-business (B2B) sales representatives might well be the cause of their customers' issues, and it is not in their best interest to report it. Campagna has a program designed specifically for inactive or lost customers. "We feel that that's a huge area within companies that people don't like to touch. When you have a customer defect from your business, what typically happens is that those losses are left in the hands of the account manager. If the problem is stemming from that account manager, then the organization may not be getting the full story. We did a study for a major company, and part of our focus was to contact inactive customers. During our interviews and surveys, the information we got back about why they defected was phenomenal. The number one issue was related to their sales representatives. They told us, 'Give me a new sales rep, and I'll come back.' What sales rep would go to their boss and say that?"

Obtaining consistent, reliable feedback is another reason not to rely on internal staff, especially if you have multiple locations or front-line staff with high turnover or inadequate training in customer service. Employee input is still important, but it's not the same as customer input.

Jack Mackey, SMG's Vice President of Sales and Marketing, points out that you also have to identify what will constitute a meaningful measurement within your company because each industry will be different. As a simple example, at the same restaurant the priorities are different for customers dining in and customers placing orders to go. For the latter, the top priority is getting the order correct; this priority falls to the middle for customers who dine in because the error is easily identified and corrected. Your survey should be customized to your business.

Campagna concurs that companies that measure customer satisfaction need to work closely with each client to gain an in-depth understanding of that business, its unique selling points, and the objectives and goals of measurement. The survey instrument and reporting formats should be directly tied to the customer's needs. Survey questions may change based on who is being surveyed and with what purpose. In many cases, prospective customers, first-time customers, regular customers, and VIPs will be asked a different set of questions. Surveying the satisfaction of new customers is quite different from periodically surveying ongoing customers.

Continually track your progress and check for overall satisfaction. Once you have established a baseline and created benchmarks, you can tell fairly quickly if improvements are having a positive effect.

Customer loyalty is won or lost at the front lines of each individual location, but what determines consistency in delivering the experience is a result of your systems and training, and these are the burden of a company's corporate resources. Mackey says, "Behavior that gets rewarded gets repeated. Starbucks customers are loyal because the experience itself is rewarding. They've built up an emotional bank account with you. Customers become loyal because over a period of time they have highly satisfying experiences. Companies spend millions creating and advertising their brands, yet the actual in-store experience is what drives customer perception. And inconsistent experiences can kill a brand. You can say what you want about who you (think you) are, but people believe what they experience."[2]

## The Enemy of "Great" Is "Good Enough"

SMG believes a "good" or "satisfying" experience is not enough. To keep people coming back for more, companies have to do more than just satisfy. Why? Because satisfied customers aren't loyal customers.

## Satisfied Customer Myth

Webster's definition of *satisfied* does not apply to customers. A satisfied customer is an indifferent one. Sales guru, Jeffrey Gitomer said it well in his book *Customer Satisfaction Is Worthless, Customer Loyalty Is Priceless*, where he demonstrates that the old "satisfaction" paradigm is considerably flawed.[3] Managers pound their chests and proudly proclaim, "We have an 88 percent satisfaction rating" (combining levels 4 and 5; Figure 13.1). In reality, only the 50 percent at level 5, the "highly satisfied," represent "customer equity." These customers, also labeled "zone of affection," love you, want to help you, and are more forgiving. Those in level 4, the "satisfied" 38 percent, cannot be counted as equity.

Think about what "satisfied" really means to us as consumers. It means that the company we are doing business with hasn't done anything

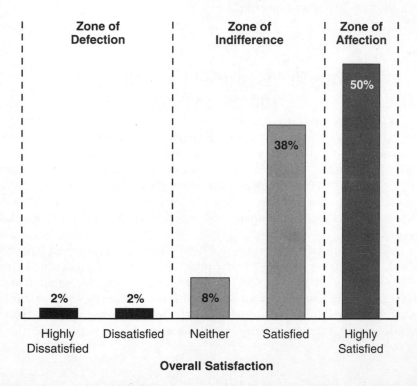

**FIGURE 13.1**   Customer Satisfaction Ratings. *Source: Thomas O. Jones and W. Earl Sasser Jr.,* Why Satisfied Customers Defect, *HBR OnPoint Enhanced ed. (Boston, MA: Harvard Business Review, 2001).*

wrong yet to make us feel the need to go elsewhere; similarly, the company has yet to do anything significant to make us loyal. Therefore, we are indifferent, meaning we are ripe to try a competitor.

Having data about the percentage of dissatisfied, satisfied, and highly satisfied customers is nice to have, but it's not enough. The magic bullet is finding out what things a company is doing to make customers fall into those categories and, more importantly, what it takes to move customers from merely satisfied to highly satisfied.

"The best multi-unit businesses know how to deliver those things, those key drivers of the customer experience," says Mackey. "They focus on improving these key drivers, on improving the customer experience, for a good reason, because a great customer experience is the hardest thing for competitors to copy. It's hard to copy because it's hard to deliver in the first place. To do that, a business, especially a multi-unit business, has to know how its customers feel about the experience they get in each location." This is why the continuous surveying of customers and continuous gathering of data is so important.[4]

## Five Things Learned from Talking to 100 Million People

Data alone can't achieve anything. Experienced and savvy measurement companies, like SMG, can make the data dance. They correlate the results of all those surveys with the company's financial performance. They discover what customers want from the company and what customers actually get from it. Then the measurement companies create systematic ways for the company and its employees to act on that information.[5]

As a result of all the data SMG has collected, analyzed, and disseminated, SMG wrote a white paper titled "Five Things We Learned from Talking to 100 Million People" (Figure 13.2). This document reveals amazing data of the effects satisfaction has on company's performance. As a result, SMG has discovered five principles that apply to multi-unit operators everywhere. In many cases, these principles defy conventional wisdom.

### Principle 1: A Satisfied Customer Is Not a Loyal Customer

A customer says the environment is pleasing, the employees are knowledgeable and helpful, and the product is good quality. Ask that customer,

Five Things We Learned from Talking to 100 Million People

smg

SERVICE MANAGEMENT GROUP

**FIGURE 13.2**   Five Things We Learned from Talking to 100 Million People. Reprinted with permission from Service Management Group.

"Are you satisfied?" and the answer is yes. But ask, "Are you likely to visit again and would you recommend this company to others?" and the answer may surprise you. SMG research has shown that less than half of "satisfied" customers say they're likely to return, and only 30 percent would recommend that business to others (Figure 13.3). "A business that wants to make its customer experience into an engine that drives financial performance must inspire team members to move 'merely satisfied' customers to 'highly satisfied' customers. Satisfaction is the wrong target," says Andy Fromm, SMG President and CEO.

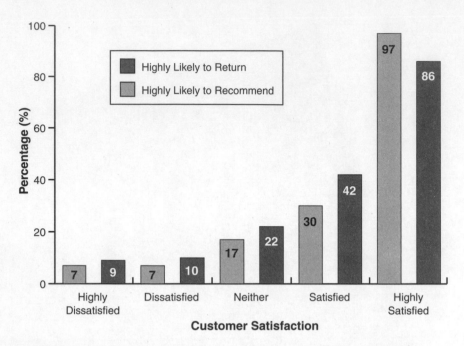

**FIGURE 13.3** Satisfaction Impact on Customer Loyalty (Service Management Group Client Data). *Note:* Satisfied customers are not highly likely to return or recommend.

## Principle 2: Loyal Customers Drive Sales and Profits

What is the value of making your customers happy, as in *really* happy? They come back, and they come back often, and they bring their friends; and sales and profits increase. For proof, here's a comparison of "highly satisfied" and simply "satisfied" customers:

- "Highly satisfied" are twice as likely to return.
- "Highly satisfied" are three times more likely to recommend the business to others.
- Best of all, businesses with more "highly satisfied" customers have higher "comp [same-store] sales" growth. Loyal customers drive top-line growth.

"Companies that deliver great customer experiences will transform browsers into shoppers, transform repeat customers into regulars, and transform regulars into devotees. In the process, they can increase sales

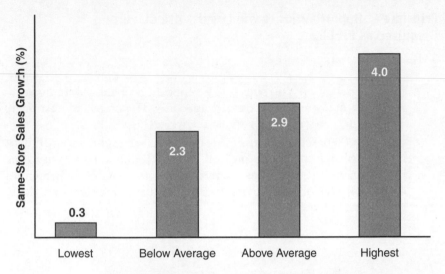

**FIGURE 13.4**   Loyalty Impact on Sales Growth (Service Management Group Client Data). *Note:* Loyal customers drive topline growth. Higher intent-to-recommend scores correlate with higher same-store sales growth.

with only marginal increases in expenses. It's true. Bottom-line improvements are indicated right there in the data," says Mackey (see Figure 13.4).

## Principle 3: Inconsistent Performance Can Kill a Brand— Looking at the Big Picture Can Be Deceiving

A company's overall performance can be positive, but a breakdown by location or department can reveal inconsistencies and weak performers that can eventually threaten the brand's overall reputation. Consumers do not differentiate among locations; they see all locations as one brand. SMG counsels its clients to focus on individual locations, where customer loyalty is won or lost. To improve systemwide, companies need to look at their best performing units, to see what they do differently to make their customers love them, and then to adopt those best practices as Standard Operating Procedures for the entire company. To do that, multi-unit companies need a full set of customer service data gathered at each individual unit.

## Principle 4: Opportunities to Win Loyalty Are Cleverly Disguised as Problems

SMG research found:

- Over 20 percent of customers who reported problems, were dissatisfied with how they were treated and only 35 percent of customers were highly satisfied with service recovery (Figure 13.5).
- However, 84 percent of those customers who are highly satisfied with their problem resolution expressed a high likelihood to return to the business where the problem occurred compared to only 71 percent of customers who did not experience a problem and said they were likely to return (Figure 13.6).

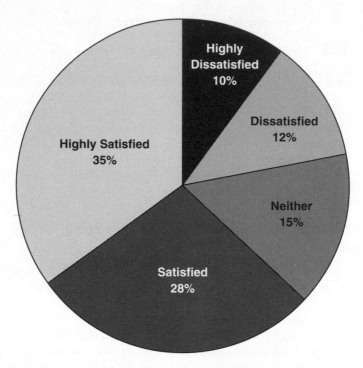

**FIGURE 13.5** Satisfied Customers with Problem Resolution (Service Management Group Client Data). *Note:* Most customers are not highly satisfied with problem resolution. Only 35 percent of customers were highly satisfied with service recovery.

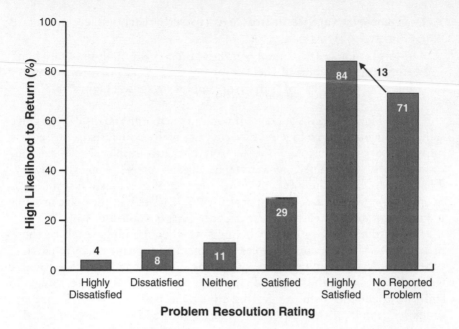

**FIGURE 13.6**   Problem Resolution—Impact on Customer Loyalty
(Service Management Group Client Data). *Note:* Customers with problems
can become very loyal. Customers who are highly satisfied with problem
resolution are more likely to return than those with no reported problem.

Significance: Customers who have had a problem but are highly satisfied with how that problem was handled are actually *more* likely to return
to a business than customers who had no problem at all.

Just being aware of your service defects is not enough. It is necessary
to know how you are dealing with those defects. Handle problems well,
and you can take a customer from "satisfied" yet unhappy to "highly satisfied" and loyal (Chapter 11).

## Principle 5: Brand Loyalty Begins at Home

Loyal employees help create loyal customers. To be a world-class customer
service organization, you must first be world-class to work for. SMG
discovered a very interesting correlation between employee turnover and
customer satisfaction:

- As employee turnover increases, customer satisfaction levels decrease (Figure 13.7).
- A loyal employee is a brand marketer: 86 percent of "highly satisfied" employees recommend their company as a great place to patronize, but only 43 percent of "satisfied" employees do so (Figure 13.8).

Brand loyalty begins at home. If you can't sell it on the inside, you can't sell it on the outside. To find out how they are really doing, smart businesses measure not only customer satisfaction but also employee satisfaction. Fromm says, "Of course, measurement doesn't create employee loyalty. That's what leadership is for: to unite a group of previously disconnected people in a common cause and support them relentlessly in the noble mission of creating a superior customer experience. That is important stuff."

How does SMG go about helping its clients address each of these principles? SMG randomly samples customers by inviting them to participate in a survey and giving them something in exchange for that participation. That something, offered by the business being measured, is significant enough to ensure getting enough responses to compile a representative sample of the full customer base. Survey invitations are usually

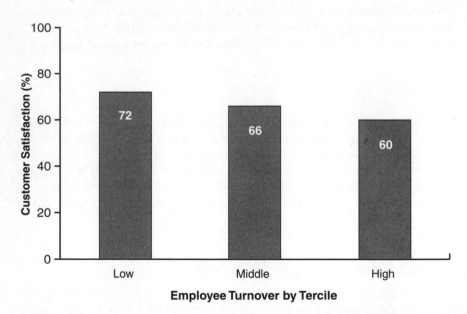

**FIGURE 13.7** Employee Turnover Impact on Customer Satisfaction (Service Management Group Client Data). *Note:* **Higher employee turnover reduces customer satisfaction.**

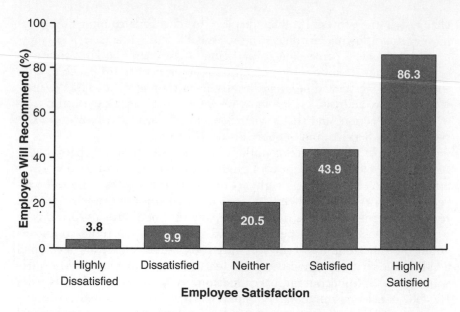

**FIGURE 13.8**  Employee Satisfaction Impact on Customer Referrals by Employees (Service Management Group Client Data). *Note:* Loyal employees recommend their company as a great place to be a customer.

generated electronically at the point of sale, for example, a cash register prints a survey invitation along with every tenth receipt. The survey consists of a combination of closed- and open-ended questions, such as a ranking scale (Highly Dissatisfied to Highly Satisfied) and questions such as, "Tell us what you like most about your experience at this location." SMG analyzes the data and develops actionable recommendations for each client company, down to the unit level, such as prescribing areas to focus on improving the customer experience. SMG shows correlations between a change in the customer experience and changes in same store-sales growth.

## Measurement Can Prevent Costly Mistakes

Here are two examples of how the process of measuring customer satisfaction and feedback helps companies avoid making costly mistakes. Borders bookstore found that wait time was a significant satisfaction factor for their customers. Using customer feedback, the retailer made physical changes in the stores. Product displays by checkout counters were removed, thus allowing customers to see available staffed registers. This improved customers' perception of wait time. "We knew checkout time was important, but we didn't understand its true level of significance to customers until we started hearing directly from shoppers about it. We realized that if we addressed it strongly, we were going to see a natural rise in overall satisfaction, and that's what happened." Says Charlie Moore, Director, Sales, Service, and Support Borders Group.[6]

At a cost of millions of dollars, a major shipping company had a software developer create a tool that would enable all of a company's employees to ship packages right from the desktop. When the test version of the software had been developed, the test process was rolled out for beta testing, and the shipping company retained Direct Opinions to track the success of the beta test and to evaluate customer opinions about the functionality of the software tool. Direct Opinions developed a call guide that explained the basic features and functions of the software in order to encourage participation. When the initial calls were fielded, it became immediately apparent that customers had no intention of installing a software tool on their operating platform that would provide shipping capabilities to all employees. On reviewing the data, the shipping company's senior management team realized the product would not work in a corporate environment. If the shipping company had done research upfront, it could have saved millions of dollars by not creating the product or by producing a product that actually fit customers' needs.

Hallmark Gold Crown stores began working with SMG in 1997 and revamped its customer satisfaction index. "I can see direct results relative to customer satisfaction in the comp store sales at the top line, so to me, that's pretty significant," says Paul Tabaka, formerly Vice President of Stores for Hallmark Retail. "Another way to look at it is that for every point of customer satisfaction I can derive, I pick up a quarter percentage point of comp-store sales. I can provide store-level details and specific customer comments that would derive an actual action plan for that particular store. Then I'd couple that with training material and say, 'Here's what this store's opportunity is and here's what we need to work on.' That's because I can tell you whether customer satisfaction is better or worse on particular days and times.[7] We did not have a good mechanism internally to measure customer satisfaction. Folks can buy our product elsewhere, so unless we differentiated ourselves with service, we did not have a long-term business platform that would be successful for both corporate stores and the independent ownership model going forward."

## Word of Mouth Is Much Louder Today

"One customer's bad experience has an even greater impact on shoppers who were not directly involved as the story spreads and is embellished," says Campagna. Nearly half of those surveyed (48 percent) reported they have avoided a store because of someone else's negative experience. "A traditional retailer (brick-and-mortar), stands to lose nearly 36 current of potential customers for every 100 customers who had a bad experience, according to the study." As staggering as these numbers are, they are almost insignificant when translated to the Internet era. In the age of blogging, the damage that dissatisfied customers can cause today is amazing. For example, consider a negative blog about a high-end vehicle manufacturer's unwillingness to respond to a customer's safety concern. According to the blogger, Emergence Marketing, close to 4,000 people have read the story on this blog alone.[8] In addition, many other sites, including Yahoo news, have picked up the story. Every day, more people find the story when they Google the manufacturer's name.

## Service Recovery

"Loyalty is very fragile," says Mackey. "A customer may have a highly satisfying relationship with your business, and then a manager decides to cut costs by lowering the quality of a product or by cutting back on staffing. The first time customers experience these changes, they may give you another try because they have had such good experiences with you in the past. When they return, if the expectation is not met again, they may begin to consider a competitor. If they visit a third time and again expectations are not met, they will give their business to someone else." So with loyal customers it's tough to see a change in revenue immediately when you make an internal change, because they will give you additional chances to earn back your reputation.

This is another instance where a survey can catch a catastrophe before it happens. How important is loyalty? Gaining a 5 percent increase in customer loyalty can increase profits 25 percent to 85 percent, according to the *Harvard Business Review*.[9] While customers who have had a longer relationship will be more forgiving, first-time customers are less tolerant of an unacceptable experience. If you react and respond to their issues and concerns, they may end up more loyal than before. If you can get a former customer to return, that customer will be more loyal, because in the meantime he has tested your competitors and has probably discovered that you offer more.

Surveying lost customers provides valuable information two ways. First you learn what it takes to win back them back, what's important to them. Properly asked questions provide an understanding of how to turn the situation around. Even more important than winning customers back, you can find out the most common reasons for defection, and you can put systems in place to reduce future customer defections.

## Is Customer Engagement Overrated?

Another factor surveys reveal is the strong statistical relationship between customer satisfaction and market valuation. It's not surprising that data obtained from customer satisfaction surveys can predict growth and stock market performance. What is surprising is that it is also an indicator of Personal Consumption Expenditure (PCE) growth that had previously been thought to have inconsistent indicators. People will indeed spend more when they are highly satisfied with their experience. SMG research for one retailer uncovered that the average tickets for customers who were thoroughly engaged by the associate spent 100 percent more than the customers who were not engaged.[10]

## What Gets Measured Gets Managed

Measuring your customer's experience is not enough. Now you have all the data, reports, and results coming in on a regular basis. How do you ensure this is not just another report that eventually gets stale and elicits less and less response from your people? One way is to tie performance evaluations, incentives, raises, and promotions at each location to that location's satisfaction scores.[11] Surveys show their true value only when you put all this information into action. As important as it is to measure the experience and gather the information, it is equally important to have a system to act on the information. This system gives everyone at every level feedback on the survey and details on each location's performance. And of course employees should be recognized and rewarded accordingly. Hallmark uses SMG data to reward employees at its corporate stores and has seen turnover drop. Bonuses for store managers are tied to comp-store sales and customer satisfaction scores. The top managers are taken on a reward trip for their performance.

Make sure that a team or individual is identified in advance and is given the responsibility for change within the organization and the authority to create a plan and put structure in place to make that change happen. Otherwise, you may as well not bother to do the survey at all.

SMG knows how time sensitive it is to get the customer feedback in to the managers and employees who actually face the customers and deliver the service. "We customize a web-based Performance Dashboard that managers can see 24/7. We'll develop a customer experience P&L that those managers can share with employees every reporting period," says Mackey. Getting the managers the information is not enough, helping them take action on the right things to improve the experience is the most important part. "We analyze the customer survey responses at each individual location and for specific transactions. We figure out statistically which improvements would matter most to the customers and we prescribe just two areas for focus at each store or restaurant. Then it's pretty easy to see if those scores are improving or not," explains Mackey.

## The Ultimate Question

Fred Reichheld, author of *The Ultimate Question*, has the simplest approach to measuring customer satisfaction: Ask one question.[12] Research proves that companies that focus on and generate loyal customers have 2.5 times the growth rate, industry after industry. The key is giving managers the metrics and muscle to garner the same attention to loyalty as one might give to productivity, quality, speed, and so on. The key metric is the Net Promoter Score (NPS), which is calculated by just asking the customer one question "Would you enthusiastically recommend our company to a friend?" Reichheld is specific about using a 10 point scale versus the 5 point. The only other question you ever need to ask the customer is: "If you didn't give us an eight or better, may we call you to discuss it?" That's it—forget all the other questions you're asking customers (on your standard customer satisfaction survey).[13]

## Sport Clips

Sport Clips uses a survey system that enables each customer to call in his responses about his experience at Sport Clips, or to log onto a web site and enter comments online. "We get thousands of surveys back each week from our 465 stores that enable us to measure and evaluate the degree to which we are meeting and exceeding our clients' expectations," says Gordon Logan, CEO of Sport Clips. "We have several questions about our execution of the various steps in our Five-Point Play and the customers' overall experience. We ask if they plan to return and if they would recommend Sport Clips to their friends on a scale of 1 to 5. We use the Net Promoter Score (NPS): 5s (always recommend Sport Clips to my friends); 1s and 2s (do not plan to recommend or are not likely to recommend). NPS is the acid test of how well our clients perceive our service, and if they feel strongly enough about Sport Clips to recommend us to their friends. I am happy to report that our NPS scores run in the 60 to 65 range, a very strong score compared to most excellent companies—over 50 is considered to be outstanding; 3s and 4s are not considered, since the client does not feel strongly one way or the other. This system also sends an immediate alert to the Team Leader [franchisee] for that store and to us at the Corporate Support Center when a client tells us that we are not delivering our Championship Client Service. We track these also, and have an automated system in place so we can ensure that these not-so-favorable comments are followed up on and the client is contacted when he requests a desire or willingness to be contacted."

At Sport Clips, the Area Developers are measured on how well the stores in their areas perform on these surveys. Sports Clips has found a strong correlation between high scores in general and NPS in particular to high-growth and highly profitable stores. If scores do not meet expectations, "We get with the Area Developer and/or the Team Leader to determine the cause and to develop action plans to bring these scores up," says Logan.

## Closing Ratio

Every company should know what its close rate (or conversion rate or retention rate) is. Do you know what your close rates are for each sales person? At John Robert's Spa, our retention report is our version of "close/conversion rate." We have always placed a significant focus on retention rates, from tracking them regularly, to creating companywide awareness of them, to having a system of rewards and ramifications for strong and weak retention rates.

Depending on the John Robert's Spa location, our appointment book can have anywhere from 15 to 75 service providers. Our reservationists are trained to book "no request" appointments with the first available service provider from right to left in the book. A significant number of our appointments are "no-requests," meaning the guest has no specific service provider in mind and trusts that all our service providers are well trained.

So you can see that it is extremely beneficial to be as far to the right as possible. Our service providers are positioned in our appointment book according to client retention. The higher the retention rate, the farther to the right that provider is listed; the lower the retention rate, the farther to the left the provider is listed. We call the left side of our appointment book "Siberia" because those providers don't get a "no-request" booking unless all providers to the right are unavailable. Is this fair? Absolutely! If we give a new guest to someone who retains fewer than 50 percent of her clients, then we stand a less than 50 percent chance of that new guest returning; but if we give that new guest to a provider with a higher retention rate, our chances of retaining that new guest can be 70 percent. Not only does our booking system provide a much better return on investment; it dramatically reduces the amount of advertising we have to do.

We regularly celebrate individuals' positioning on our appointment book, using companywide voice mails and posting stories like this in our team newsletters: "We congratulate Sandy Hoyt, who jumped 4 spots to the right in the appointment book lineup due to her incredible retention rate of 72 percent. For the 6th month in a row Chris Wojo maintains the coveted #1 position of experienced service providers posting 79 percent retention rate. Congratulations to these service providers, who truly provide the JR Experience. It is obvious by their retention rate. As a result, they get the most desirable position in our appointment book, get more new clients, and make more money!!"

This accomplishes several things:

1. It sheds light on the importance of your client retention rate.
2. It makes the positioning of the appointment book more prestigious.
3. It reminds the service providers of their performance each time they look at their schedule.
4. It results in high retention, more new clients, and more income!

This concept works in many different businesses, for inside and outside sales, for nearly all sales that aren't geographically based. Closing rate should drive lead distribution. For instance, in a car dealership, walk-in customers would be directed to the salesman with the highest close rate. Forget about, "It's Jim's turn." Why give Jim great potential leads if he can't convert those leads to sales? Jim isn't making cold calls. These people are walking into the dealership; they are coming to you. They should be given to someone who knows how to deliver a proper sales experience. All of a sudden, you will get your salespeople to start doing the proper techniques they were trained to do. I ask you again: Do you know your people's "close rate?"

# Can't Be All Things to All People

Companies have to avoid the danger of listening to everything a customer has to say. Companies cannot be all things to all people and trying to please everyone is a sure way to go out of business quickly. The survey sample has to be large enough to reveal what the majority of your target niche is saying and to identify the real priorities and needs. For example, Southwest Airlines would never please people who want first-class travel and VIP treatment. You could say that Southwest Airlines has lost certain customers because it is a no-frills airline; but this is not their niche. In a difficult industry over the past two decades, they have had the most profitable track record.

## Do It Yourself

Even if you are fortunate to have a partner like SMG or Direct Opinions doing your customer satisfaction measurement that still doesn't mean you should not be checking the pulse of your customers on a regular basis. Verne Harnish, the leading fast-growth consultant, author of the best-selling *Rockefeller Habits*, always emphasizes the importance of having every one of the senior leaders of a company call at least one customer per week.[14] He suggests four questions:

1. How are you doing? What's your focus, challenges, priorities? (Rather than first asking up front "How are we doing?")
2. What's going on in your industry/neighborhood?
3. What do you hear about our competitors?
4. How are we doing? (Save this for last.)

"You must make your goals measurable, meaning they are tied to a specific metric, that lets you know if you are winning or losing the fight," stressed Harnish.

Examples can be tracking the changes in any of the following key measures:

- Retention rate of new customers.
- Resign rate of customer's renewing their contracts.
- Average ticket.
- Customer satisfaction score.
- Net promoter score.
- Number of customer complaints.

- Number of unresolved customer complaints.
- Customer referrals.
- Employee turnover.
- Amount of training hours dedicated to soft skill, experiential training.

It needs to be measurable to know if you are achieving it.

## Demonstrating the Impact of Improved Customer Satisfaction

When I work with companies that are trying to improve their customer's experience, the first thing I ask them is: what are your key drivers, critical metric numbers? Typically it is things such as average ticket, number of tickets, frequency of visits, re-sign/renewal rate, average contract, retention rates, and so on. Let's look at a real life scenario; I was working with an advertising company, their top two drivers are re-sign/renewal rate currently at 65 percent and average monthly contract of $1,800. By increasing re-sign rate of their existing contracts by just 7 percent to 72 percent and their average monthly contract by 10 percent to $1,980, this demonstrated an increase in sales of more than 1.8 million dollars and an increase in profit of 27 percent.

It was clear that the level of satisfaction of their customers determined both their re-sign rate and average monthly contracts. Therefore in addition to their top two drivers, a third critical metric they measure is their customer satisfaction scores. Without demonstrating the financial benefit of improved customer satisfaction, employees will not see the value of providing a better customer experience.

## Crystal Ball

If you don't know where you are going, how will you know when you have arrived? Trying to provide a world-class customer experience without measuring is like navigating a boat blindfolded. The level of a company's satisfaction can typically be an excellent forecaster of its future success. Every company is obsessed with "comp sales"—same store sales comparing this year versus last year. Rightfully so, it is one of the most important benchmarks of a company's current success in its market. However, comp sales do not tell you where you are headed. Author Joe Calloway says it best, "If you want to see how a company is doing now, look at their current sales; if you want to know how a company will perform in the future, look at their current customer satisfaction scores."[15]

# Notes

1. Joe Calloway, author and speaker.

2. "Five Things We Learned from Talking to 100 Million People," SMG Client Education document.

3. Jeffrey Gitomer, *Customer Satisfaction Is Worthless, Customer Loyalty Is Priceless* (Austin, TX: Bard Press, 1998).

4. See note 2.

5. See note 2.

6. Eda Galeno, "Borders Uses Survey Data to Improve Service," *Chief Marketer*, September 8, 2005, http://chiefmarketer.com/crm_loop/borders-uses-090805/index.html.

7. Jennifer Korolishin, "They Care Enough to Extend the Hallmark Very Best," *Stores*, June 2005.

8. "Mercedes Benz—Poor Customer Service ROI," francois posted in Worst Practices, *Emergence Marketing*, April 9, 2006, www.emergencemarketing.com/2006/04/09/mercedes-benz-poor-customer-service-roi/.

9. *Harvard Business Review*, November 26, 2003.

10. See note 2.

11. See note 7.

12. Fred Reichheld, *The Ultimate Question: Driving Good Profits and True Growth* (Boston, MA: Harvard Business School Press, 2006).

13. See note 12.

14. Verne Harnish, *Mastering the Rockefeller Habits: What You Must Do to Increase the Value of Your Growing Firm* (New York: Select Books, 2002).

15. See note 1.

# 14

# Commandment X:
# World-Class Leadership

## *Walking the talk*

---

*Take my building, my equipment, all my money, my land,
but leave me my people and in one year I will be back on top
again.*

—Andrew Carnegie

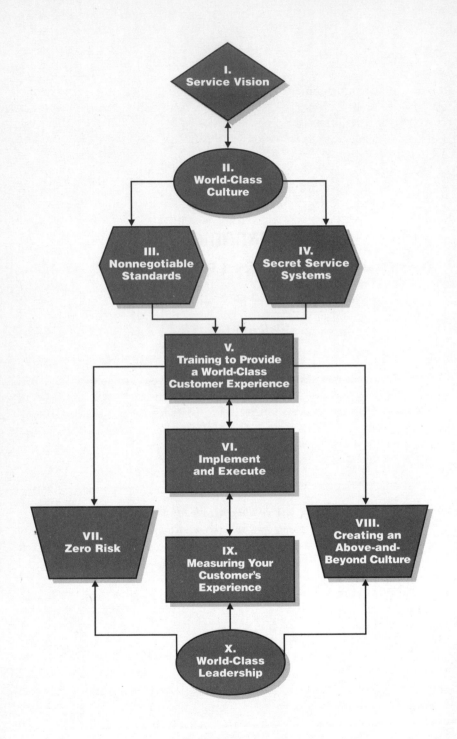

The final commandment to providing a world-class customer experience is Commandment X World-Class Leadership. Every world-class customer service organization is world-class to work for. And that takes world-class leadership to provide the passion, inspiration, and discipline to all employees.

While this book is all about world-class customer service, and certainly is not a leadership book, it would be remiss to leave out this critical element of the formula. Being a great leader is about getting the most out of your people and inspiring them every day to see how much potential they have and how important their contributions are overall to the company.

While this is the final commandment, it is the most important, having the biggest impact and responsibility for the success of all 10.

On a scale of 1 to 10, what would you rank your company's (or department, or whatever you are in charge of) culture? Is it fantastic (9 or 10)? Or does it have a lot of room for improvement (6 or 7)? Whatever score you gave your culture, understand you have just figured out your rating as a leader. No more information needed!

Have you ever heard a song on an elevator or on hold on the telephone, the song may not be one of your favorites or even one you would put on your iPod, however, since you were forced to listen to it, hours later you cannot get that song out of your head? Well, that is how I want the next phrase to impact you. I want it ringing in your head later, haunting you:

## CULTURE REFLECTS LEADERSHIP

Do you like your organization's/department's culture? Are you proud of it, or is it lacking? Do you wish you could change many of your employees attitudes? If you don't like your culture, look in the mirror, because every time, in every organization, culture reflects leadership. How good your organization's or department's culture is, is a direct result of how good you are as a leader. Great leaders create great cultures. You don't even need to take a survey, do any studies, or even see any turnover reports; a culture is something you feel when you walk into a work environment. There is either a "buzz" about the place, where everyone understands the organization's purpose and their role in achieving that purpose or you may feel a "fog," a thickness in the air, a place where people are trading hours for dollars. How strong is your culture? Remember:

CULTURE REFLECTS LEADERSHIP!

## Guess Who

Let's play some "guess who" trivia. Answers are on the following pages. See how you do. Guess who:

1. Got fired from his first job by his newspaper editor for lack of ideas, then proceeded to go bankrupt several times
2. Got cut from his high school basketball team
3. Dropped out of college, only to become one of the wealthiest persons in the world
4. Grew up in a dysfunctional, poverty-stricken home and was physically abused, yet has become one of the wealthiest and most influential women in the world
5. Was diagnosed with terminal cancer, given less than a year to live, only to have become one of the most successful athletes in sports history
6. Guess who:
   - Grew up in the projects of Brooklyn, New York
   - Quit his job over a conflict of vision with owners
   - Eventually purchased that same company
   - Today that company is one of the most recognizable brands in the world
7. Guess who:
   - Was adopted at birth
   - Dropped out of college after six months
   - Started a company in his garage that eventually became a billion dollar organization
   - Got fired from the company he started

- Created Pixar Animation Studios
- Eventually returned to run the company he started
- Created some of the hottest technology gadgets ever

8. Guess who:
   - At age 6, watched his father leave his mother and his five siblings
   - Went from upper middle class to welfare overnight
   - Was labeled ADD and LD in school
   - Was requested to repeat many grades in elementary school
   - Was suspended a few times
   - Was not accepted into the high school that his older brothers attended
   - Graduated at the bottom of his graduating class
   - Flunked out of college after a year and a half

**Answers:**

1. Walt Disney
2. Michael Jordan
3. Bill Gates
4. Oprah Winfrey
5. Lance Armstrong
6. Howard Schultz (CEO of Starbucks)
7. Steve Jobs
8. John DiJulius (author of this book)

> *Would the person who keeps saying it cannot be done*
> *please stop interrupting those of us that are doing it!*

I am a good example of someone who struggled severely growing up and any success I have had is a big surprise to many who knew me when I was young, especially my teachers. Figure 14.1 shows my grade school transcript, and you will see that my average from first grade through eighth was never higher than a D+.

| YEAR | 1970 | 19₇₁ | 19₇₂ | 19₇₃ | 19₇₄ | 19₇₅ | 1976 | 19₇₇ | 19 | 19 |
|---|---|---|---|---|---|---|---|---|---|---|
| GRADE | 1 | 2 | 3 | 4 | 5 | 6 | 7 | 8 | | 162 |
| DAYS ABSENT | 6 | 16½ | 2 | 9 | 6 | 5 | 13 | 11 | | 106 |
| TIMES TARDY | 0 | 0 | 2 | 0 | 0 | 5 | 0 | 1 | | 203 |
| RELIGION | S | S | S | C | B- | A | C | S | | 204 |
| ARITHMETIC | B- | C | A- | N⁺ | A⁺ | A⁺ | C- | C- | | 210 |
| READING | F | F | A- | N⁺ | C- | A⁺ | D | D | | 207 |
| LANGUAGE | S | S | U | N⁺ | C- | A | C- | D⁺ | | 109 |
| SPELLING | | S- | U | C⁺ | C | D | D- | C | | 111 |
| SOC. STUDIES | S | S | U | N⁺ | A⁺ | A⁺ | D- | D⁻ | | |
| SCIENCE | S | S | U | C⁻ | A | B- | D | E₊ᵣ | | |
| MUSIC | S | S | U | | | U | U | E₊ᵣ | | |
| ART | S | S | U | | | U | U | R₊ | | |
| PHYS. ED. | S | S | S | | | U | A | B | | |
| PHONICS | F | F | A- | | | | | | | |
| HOME ECONOMICS | | | | | | | | | | |
| OTHER 1) Handwriting 2) Health | | | | D⁺ | U | U | | D⁻ | | |
| GEN. AVERAGE | F | F | D- | D⁺ | A⁺ | D | D | D | | |
| EFFORT | S | S | S | S | S | U | U | U | | |
| CONDUCT | S | S | S | S | S | U | S | E₊ᵣ | | |
| CODE: | | | | | | | | | | |

1972-73 Speech Therapy

**FIGURE 14.1  John DiJulius's Grade School Transcript**

My mother and teachers didn't always agree on what was best for me. My sixth grade report card which read:

> John was **PLACED** into the seventh grade at parental insistence. His teacher strongly urged John repeat.

Obviously I did not appear to have the right formula early on in my life. However, things are not always as they appear.

I have always enjoyed studying world-class leaders, those who seem to do things very few others can even imagine, not only in business, but in all aspects of their lives, professional and personal. In doing so, I have found that all of them have very few things in common. Some came from wealthy families, others had great genetics, some had really high IQs, or graduated with high degrees from great schools. While they certainly come in all shapes and sizes, there are a few constant habits that each world-class leader does possess.

# Habits of World-Class Leaders

There are five things all great leaders have in common, which has enabled them to overachieve personally, and more importantly get their people to overachieve. They are:

1. Live Your Dream.
2. Fight for Your Dream.
3. Sell Your Dream.
4. Be a Dream Maker.
5. Believe in People.

> If you dislike your job, you have to work every day for the rest of your life; if you love what you do, you never have to work again.

## Live Your Dream

There is a high percentage of people that do not like what they do, in traditional jobs, and they dread going to work. Not enough people go after their dreams. Fear and other people's lack of vision hold them back. This is why I share the story of my childhood. I tell people all the time: You will find millions of people smarter than me, who came from more wealth, have higher degrees, or better genetics. But you won't find many people who have the passion for what they do, like I have for what I do.

In 1989, I drove a UPS truck and made really good money doing it. But every day I drove to work and thought to myself, in 29 years, five months and 4 days, I can retire. I wanted to grow old quickly. UPS was a great company to work for, but it wasn't what I wanted on my headstone. In 1993, my wife and I took a huge pay cut and a big gamble and opened up a four-chair, 900-square-foot salon. Today, I cannot believe all the great blessings in my life. I have multiple extremely successful companies, where many people are making a really good living, purchasing their first homes or their dream homes, accomplishing things they never thought possible and loving what they do. I get to travel all over the world, sharing my passion of customer service with some of the most amazing companies in the world. And I am living proof that passion will compensate for a lot of shortcomings.

## Fight for Your Dreams

I think the number one reason why I might be more successful than others is because many people give up too easily. In nearly everything I have ever attempted, I have found myself in over my head, but I always do whatever it takes to figure it out.

Too many people quit once they hit a wall. Determination is a pretty vital quality to posses. You can count on facing obstacles; it is those few, who no matter what they are faced with, remain focused and persevere. Think of how different our world would be today, if the people mentioned in the "Guess Who" trivia had given up.

## Sell Your Dreams

Name me a great leader and I will show you a person who had an incredible vision, a person who got the people around him to buy into this vision, and a person who proceeded on a mission to make it happen. The idea is to get people fired up about being a part of a great purpose, something they can have an impact on, versus punching in and out and collecting a paycheck. Great leaders make their vision their people's vision and they run with it as if it were their own.

Leaders need to wear their vision and dreams on their sleeve, so that everyone can get excited about it. This is where many leaders struggle. Not only do they stop wearing their vision on their sleeve, but they stop being inspirational leaders. Leaders need to bring their "A" game to work every day. This is difficult, especially since the higher a person gets in management, the more responsibility and pressure they get, and the more people they have to answer to: employees, bosses, stockholders, customers, spouse, kids. They tend to come to work with the weight of the world on their shoulders, yet still point at the people around them who don't have the right attitude. When they are asked, "What about you?" they say, "I am fine."

I tell my leadership team: "Do not motivate anyone other than yourself." It is a 24/7/365 job to motivate John Robert DiJulius III. I don't always do it well, but when I do, and I come to work with the passion I am capable of, I have 150+ employees ready to go to battle with me. But when I come to work with my traveling wearing me down, worried about making payroll, thinking about what my teenager got in trouble for, and I am barely present with my team, I start getting morale issues popping up.

It is difficult; some days we may have to be an Academy Award winner. We have to discover our own personal formula that keeps us motivated and inspired. Are we inspirable?

> Surround yourself with brilliant people and hopefully you will be guilty by association.

## Chief Visionary Officer

Back in the early days of John Robert's Spa, we were growing and it became evident that our growth required a management team that was beyond what my wife Stacy and I were able to provide by ourselves. We were fortunate to stumble on two candidates, Denise Thompson and Eric Hammond. At the time, they didn't have any management experience, but were clients of John Robert's Spa and really liked our concept and culture. At this time, however, we did not have a track record of success that would impress anyone. We had been open for only a few years, operating a small, 1,300-square-foot salon, doing $500,000 a year in revenue. On paper not drastically different from any other neighborhood corner salon. The only thing we had was a dream of growing this concept bigger. We had two posters in my office: on one wall was a map of Northeast Ohio, with dots all over it for where we were going to open up future salons (Figure 14.2). On the other wall was a diagram of a 8,000-square-foot dream spa we wanted to open someday with amenities not seen before in the Midwest.

I remember interviewing Eric for what was our first management position, front desk manager. I really liked Eric; even though he had no management experience, he was hungry and wanted to learn. I felt he would be a great fit for our company, until I asked Eric what he was making at his current job and he said $38,000. I said, "Interview over, this position pays $23,000." I was not going to insult him by asking him to take a $15,000 pay cut, or a 40 percent reduction in his pay. And I certainly couldn't pay more than $23,000 at that time. To my amazement, Eric said, "I really want this job and am willing to take the pay cut." I said, "Are you crazy!" Eric responded, "I know I want to be on the ground floor of this organization, otherwise I will regret it someday." And he pointed to the map of Northeast Ohio and the diagram of my dream spa. Basically Eric forced me to hire him that day and took a $15,000 pay cut. I remember thinking after he left, "Damn, now I have to actually do this stuff!" I am not sure I was that serious or if it just made my office look better, having those posters hanging on the wall. Either way, now I was forced to deliver what I was promising.

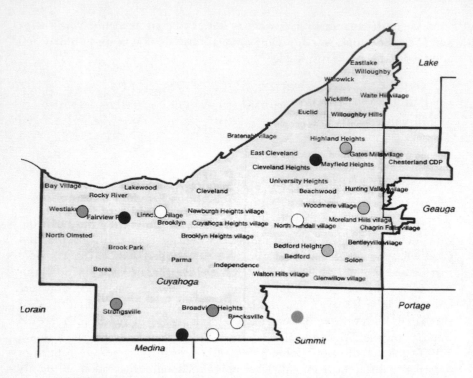

**FIGURE 14.2**   Map of Potential John Robert's Spa Locations

It was very similar with Denise Thompson. Denise also took a pay cut from her former position and both Denise and Eric made significant sacrifices, repeatedly, because our dream became theirs. They got so caught up in our vision for where we wanted John Robert's Spa to be some-day and how the purpose benefited so many others, and how important their role was for the realization of that dream, that they didn't ever think short-term or what was in it for them. They had this incredible blind faith in our vision, which made me even more focused on helping them get their dreams fulfilled.

Today, as a result of Eric and Denise, I have two successful businesses. Eric is the Vice President of Operations of John Robert's Spa and Denise is the Chief Xperience Officer of The DiJulius Group. A vast majority of my time is spent in The DiJulius Group, traveling, speaking, consulting, and writing books and articles. I probably physically didn't step foot in my salons 10 times in the past 12 months. Yet, we set records in revenue, number of employees, and turnover (low). I get to do what I love best, share my passion for service and culture, while Eric and Denise execute my vision for both organizations. This would not be possible if I hadn't found two incredible people who bought into my dreams and visions.

> The highest honor I receive is the privilege of helping others achieve their dreams.

## Be a Dream Maker

This is truly one of the best privileges we have as leaders. I have found that when leaders have the ability to help others get what they want, they end up getting what they want sooner and more often. This applies to employees, coworkers, bosses, family, friends, and neighbors. It is so easy to do. Find out what other people around you want and help them get there. Many times it doesn't even cost money. It is just knowing what it is your people truly want and connecting them with the right people. Is there any better legacy than helping people accomplish things they never thought possible? The leaders that learn this gift, are always the most successful and fulfilled.

### Director of Dream Making

When I realized it was about helping other people get what they want and not nearly as much about focusing on getting what I wanted, my success accelerated significantly. A great example of how this works is when we hire someone, we have him or her fill out a personnel sheet, which asks things such as favorite flower, restaurant, and "wild ideas." At manager meetings, we share this information to make our leaders aware of the personal goals of their team members and to be cognizant if an opportunity arises where they can assist in helping a team member accomplish a "wild idea."

I spoke for Sea World back when they were in Ohio and one of their managers told me that if my boys would like to swim with the dolphins, he would arrange for it to happen. I immediately thought of Patti Burke, one of our top hairdressers for well over 10 years at John Robert's Spa, who had listed swimming with the dolphins as one of her "wild ideas" back when she was hired. I was able to help her realize her wild idea.

Working with Nemacolin Resort, who for many years held the 84 Lumber Classic, a PGA tour, I got an invitation to play golf with Vijay Singh and John Daly, two of the top golfers in the world. While this was an honor, I am not a golfer. However, Eric Hammond, the guy that took the $15,000 pay cut to work for me years ago, is a golf fanatic and I gave my invitation to him.

In January 2008, I got to cross off an item on my "wild ideas" list and enjoy one of my proudest moments. As a result of the commitment and loyalty that Eric Hammond and Denise Thompson have made to John Robert's Spa and The DiJulius Group, and more importantly, Stacy and myself, we made Denise and Eric partners in our companies. Denise became a shareholder in The DiJulius Group and Eric became a shareholder in John Robert's Spa, thus helping make their dreams come true and hopefully making all their sacrifices they made for us worth it.

> See a man for what he is and he only gets worse, look at him as if he were what he could be and then he becomes what he should be.

## Believe in People

There is not one great world-class leader who won't tell you there are two reasons why they have accomplished so much: (1) because someone believed in them when they weren't easy to believe in and (2) they themselves believed in people around them that helped make their vision and dreams a reality. The key is: Believing in people when it isn't easy to believe in them, when they don't even believe in themselves. We have all been there. I certainly wasn't too believable growing up. The salon my wife and I opened almost went out of business within the first six weeks it was open, and my first book, *Secret Service: Hidden Systems That Deliver Unforgettable Customer Service*, got turned down by over 200 publishers before one publisher (AMACOM) wanted it.

Fortunately, I had my mother, five older brothers and sisters, and a wife who have always believed in me and supported me. As a result, today our salons have been named one of the top 20 salons in America a few times, my first book has enjoyed incredible success, I travel all over the world working with incredible world-class companies, The DiJulius Group is regarded as THE authority on world-class customer experience, but more importantly, what I am proudest of, is that I am a husband to Stacy and the father of three amazing boys, Johnni, Cal, and Bo.

Figure 14.3 is a note I received from Denise Thompson that reminds me not only how important it is to constantly practice and work on those five habits of world-class leaders, but their rewards.

12/31/2007

John,

I have difficulty finding the right words to show how I feel. You do so much for all of us. I don't even know how to begin to thank you. The trips, gifts, etc are all great, but the lessons you have taught me are beyond measure. Top of the list are 1) See people for who they can be, 2) You can always do more than you think you can and 3) Dream big!

I enjoy having the time with you, from teaching us different things to how you come in and lift everyone's mood with your presence. You really do set the tone in the office when you come in, sharing your dream and vision so that we could all help you get there. We all believe so strongly in you. There is a quality in you that few possess, that ability to paint the future so beautifully that we all want to pick up our brushes and add to it, we want to be a part of the masterpiece and sign our names below yours. It has never appeared to be a job for you. It's been something real and natural, not contrived or out of some handbook, it's what you felt and believed in and we happily 'drink the cool-aid' with you.

It's deeper than respect that I feel for you. It is knowing that you're someone I can count on, that you have my back as much as I have yours. It is knowing that I don't have to fear taking a chance on something if I believe it's the right thing to do. I think the only fear any of us have is the fear of disappointing you.

I do build you and our company up to everyone I meet. It's hard to apologize for pride. I explain that I am amazed at how fortunate I am, that so many people hate going to work, despise their bosses, don't agree with what they do; and I get to work with great people, have an owner who is bright, funny, and successful in his industry and who teaches us about business, life and dreams.

Anyhow, after all this…Just want to remind you how much you mean to all of us.

Wishing you a very Happy New Year!!

Denise

**FIGURE 14.3** Letter from Denise Thompson

The following are some of my favorite quotes for what determines "success":

- *The number of people's lives you added quality to and impacted.*
- *That you spent your life your own way.*
- *Having enough that those around you benefit from your success.*

- *Creating good, dignified jobs, providing a feeling of safety and stability for your family and employees.*
- *Knowing that you have built something substantial through completely honest and ethical efforts.*
- *The person who wakes up in the morning feeling whole, rested, and happy, conducts his day on his own terms, finding joy and peace in the moment, and then retires feeling fulfilled.*

## Secret Service at Home

The final piece to being a world-class leader is having the proper balance. Secret Service is not something you deliver; it is something you are—not only to your customers, but to your employees, coworkers, family, friends, neighbors, and community. In order to be great leaders and avoid burnout, leaders have to learn how to effectively handle the constant struggle of professional achievement and personal balance. One cannot overpower the other.

One of my biggest fears in life is that when I am gone, my legacy will be being remembered as a good businessperson. That thought truly haunts me and I work very hard at not letting that be what I am remembered for. I have a picture of my wife and kids, above my desk, that has this saying over it:

> I want to be remembered as a loving husband, father, and friend who happened to be a good businessman.

Like most entrepreneurs, I have a lot on my plate. I have six locations with over 150 employees. I am an author and have a consulting business. I spend over 150 days a year traveling doing customer service seminars. I am also a husband and father of three young boys, and a baseball and wrestling coach. When people ask me how I sleep at night, I tell them, "Like a baby, I wake up every two hours and cry my eyes out!"

I do not want to miss a thing, a day, a moment. I want to share in all their events. I cringe at every birthday and at the start of each new school year because I realize that they are another year older. Nothing is more important for me than to be a great father and husband. It can be difficult with all that I do and I have failed from time to time. That is why it was necessary for me to create habits and personal systems in order for me to be the best father I can be.

I travel around the world and teach organizations how to create world-class customer service systems. I teach people that in order to have world-class customer service, you must provide great service in four areas of your life: Secret Service to your customer, your team members, your community, and at home. I truly believe world-class starts at home. I have to walk the talk in my personal life as well. So I created some Secret Service systems at home. I do all of these on a regular basis and doing so has enriched my life and helped me to be more present with my kids.

The following are the Secret Service systems I have created to gain more personal fulfillment with my children. I hope by sharing them you can borrow and recycle some ideas that will provide you with as much joy as I get out of mine.

## Daily Journals

Working long hours and traveling a great deal, there were many days I didn't get to see my kids before they went to bed. This is when I realize that I totally missed out on those days and have no idea if something significant had occurred or if they needed me or my advice. I missed an opportunity to "high-five" them or give them needed comforting.

I created journals for each one of my children. These journals are kept on their bed stands and are filled out every night before they go to bed. We start a new journal every season: fall, winter, spring, and summer. The first page is the current data we collect the first day of the season (Figure 14.4). I fill out all the information and ask them questions like who their current teacher is, what sport they are playing, height, weight, favorite color, breakfast, lunch, dinner, movie, restaurant, activities, TV show to what do they want to be when they grow up. We only do this four times a year (start of each season) but it is funny how the answers change so drastically each time.

The rest of the journal consists of blank pages with lines on it waiting to be filled out (Figure 14.5). And every night before bed, they tell me how their day went and I write down whatever they say. They tell me what happened at school, at recess, after school, and the rest of their day. We finish with their highs and lows of the day. We have been doing this for about four years. We have boxes full of journals that have so many amazing things written in them. I cherish these and know my boys will cherish them someday when they are older. It has become such an important part of our daily routine, that when I travel, I bring the journals with me and call them from wherever I am at precisely 9 PM Cleveland time and we do their journals over the phone.

**Current**

Date _____    School _____

Teacher _____    Grade _____

Sports _____    Age _____

WT _____    Height _____

Push ups _____

**Favorites**

Color _____    Breakfast _____

Lunch _____    Dinner _____

Restaurant _____    TV Show _____

Toy _____    Activity _____    Sport _____

Movie _____    Place to go _____    Book _____

Song_____    What I want to be when I grow up_____

**FIGURE 14.4**  Daily Journal Cover Page

## Bedtime Stories

I wanted more opportunities to share my values and philosophies with my children and it was sometimes awkward to just start these conversations unprovoked. Today, after we do our nightly journals, I start reading my boys a story from a feel-good book such as *Chicken Soup for the Soul*—great short stories that have a touching message. After I read one, we all talk about what the story meant to them. We have great conversations and I am able to teach them how it ties into their lives at home, in school, and with their friends. I also bring the book with me on the road so I am able to do this when I call to do the journal.

## After School Phone Calls

I ask my boys to call me every day when they get home. I want to hear how their day went at school and help them prepare for the rest of the day. I remind them to do their homework before they play, clean up the garage or basement, and so on. I just enjoy hearing from them and seeing how their

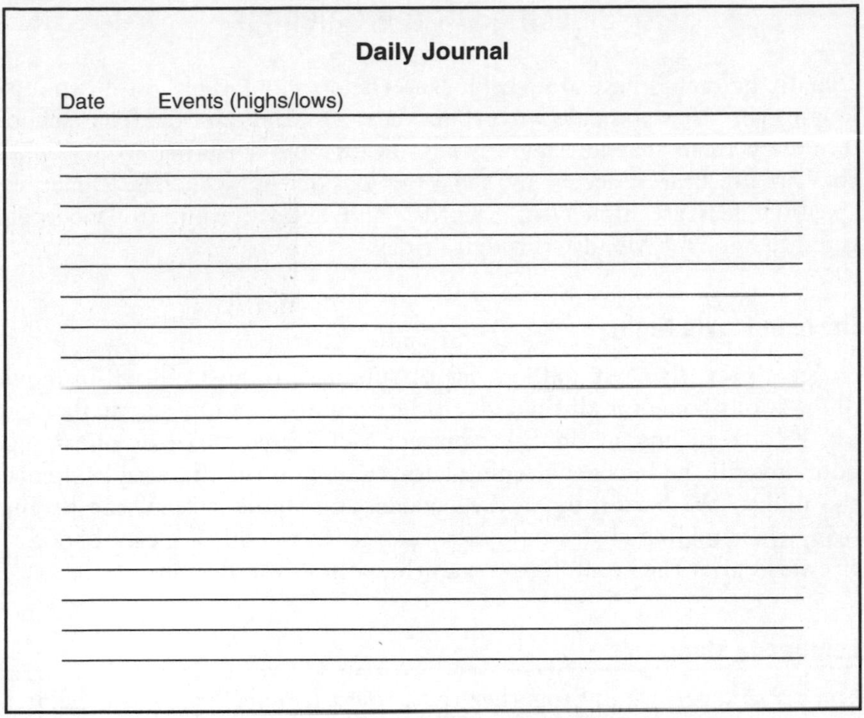

---

**Daily Journal**

Date     Events (highs/lows)

_____

_____

_____

_____

_____

_____

_____

_____

_____

_____

_____

_____

_____

_____

_____

_____

_____

---

**FIGURE 14.5**   Daily Journal Pages

day went at school. Sometimes they forget to call me, so on the computer, I have daily pop-ups at 4 PM to call them if I haven't heard from them yet.

## Surprise Day with Dad

This is one of my most favorite traditions that I started 10 years ago. Every day when I drive my boys to school, I always say, "How about we blow off school today and just go play?" And they say, "Really?" And I say, "No." Well one day a year my answer is, "Yes!" And I pull out of their school parking lot and we are off. It's typically planned ahead of time, but they don't know it. We have done things such as spend a day downtown at the Arcade, Science Center, Omni Max theatre, and Chucky Cheese. There have been other days where we have driven right to the airport and flown to Winter Haven, Florida, and spent the weekend watching the Cleveland Indians play their spring training games or we've gone to Disney World. The looks on their faces when this surprise unravels is priceless.

# Blocking Off the Calendar

Usually by June, I have already blocked the days and weeks off for the following year that coincide with their vacations and days off from school. This way I can schedule my business events and speaking around when they are off. I rarely accept any speaking jobs on the weekends. In fact, my speaking fees are higher for Saturday and Sunday events to encourage them to book me Monday through Friday.

### Drive-In Movie Night

Twice a year, the first and last day of summer, we host a drive-in movie night at our home for all the kids in the neighborhood. It's actually more like a "bike-in" movie night. We project a PG-rated movie on our garage door, and all the kids get sleeping bags and lie on the driveway and enjoy the movie. We have fully stocked concession stands and all the parents bring their folding chairs and enjoy the movie as well. We even shoot off fireworks after the event. Sometimes the police even stop by.

### Lemonade Stand

Once a summer, we put together the coolest lemonade stand in the area. We pick a hot Saturday in August and put a long table at the front of our development where the cars from all 300 houses have to enter and exit. We get five or six kids in the neighborhood to help out and position each of them at the four corners with signs. Our signs read: "Super Size Lemonade and Iced Tea to go." Our cups are 16 ounces, with lids and straws. No one has to get out of their car; they just roll down their window, pay a $1, and receive a super size drink on the run. We not only offer lemonade and iced tea, but smoothies and slushies. All the money goes toward Rainbows Babies and Children's Hospital. It is quite an event and people are extremely generous. We have raised as much as $300.

### Video a Life in Our Kids' Day

I wanted to videotape a day in my kids' life. As you can see, we have many traditions and I wanted to capture them so we can look back someday and see all the great times we shared together. However, I never seemed to be able to coordinate a day where I could videotape them waking up, going to school, coming home, and going to bed. So I finally decided I would do it in stages. One day I videotape them waking up, eating breakfast, getting ready for school, and getting on the school bus. Another day I videotape them getting ready for bed, reading their story to them, doing their journals, and going to sleep. And yet another day, I videotape them getting off the bus after school and doing their after school activities. Then I cut and put the three different tapes together as one morning, afternoon, and evening to capture a day in their life.

## E-mail Notice

Like most businesspeople, I get between 50 and 100 e-mails per day. Each time one arrived, my computer would make this sound effect that after a while would start to annoy me. I would think, "Another e-mail to read, hooray." Then one day I turned my e-mail notice into something that I wanted to hear. My wife and I grabbed our boys one night and just tickled them, all three of them at the same time for about 30 seconds. We taped them laughing while we just went crazy tickling them. The sound of my kids laughing immediately puts me in the best mood and reminds me what life is all about. I took that sound and created a Wav file on my computer. Whenever I receive an e-mail, I hear my three boys laughing hysterically. Now I welcome e-mails because they make me smile from ear to ear.

## Surprise Late-Night Movie

Once a quarter, I try to surprise each one of my boys, separately, by sneaking into his room after we have put all of them to bed and saying, "How would you like to stay up and watch a movie?" The first time we did this, they thought it was so cool, I made it appear that no one knew we were watching a movie, including my wife. She would act like she heard us and we would shut off the TV and pretend we were sleeping when she opened the door. After she left, we turned the TV back on. Very cool.

## Breakfast before School

Again once a quarter, I try to plan one day, with each of my sons, to get up early, and go to a local restaurant for breakfast—just the two of us. They love this and really look forward to their turn. Knowing you just made your kid's day is a great way to kickoff the day.

I have been very blessed with an unbelievable family. I enjoy great quality time with them, even though I lead a very busy and successful professional life. I hope some of my Secret Service at home can aid you in getting closer to that balance we all seek.

# Index